D0554021

PERGAMON INTERNATIONAL LIBRARY
of Science, Technology, Engineering and Social Studies
The 1000-volume original paperback library in aid of education, industrial training and the enjoyment of leisure
Publisher: Robert Maxwell, M.C.

EXPERIMENTING
WITH
TRUTH

Other Titles of Interest

BUNGE, M.
The Mind-Body Problem

CATTELL, R. B.
A New Morality from Science: Beyondism

DUNCAN, R. & WESTON-SMITH, M.
Lying Truths

ELTON, L. R. B. & MESSEL, H.
Time and Man

FITZGERALD, R.
What It Means To Be Human

JANTSCH, E.
The Self-Organizing Universe

JOHNSON, R. E.
Existential Man

JONES, A. A.
Illustrated Dictionary of World Religion

JOSEPHSON, B. D. & RAMACHANDRAN, V. S.
Consciousness and the Physical World

LASZLO, E.
The Inner Limits of Mankind

WENK, E.
Margins for Survival

Related Journals*

History of European Ideas Editor: **Ezra Talmor,** Haifa University, Israel
A multidisciplinary journal which studies the history of the cultural exchange between European nations and the influence of this exchange on the formation of European ideas.
Studies in the History and Philosophy of Science Editor: **Gerd Buchdahl,** Cambridge University, England
Publishes detailed philosophical analyses of material in the history of science and philosophy of science.

* *Free specimen copies of both journals available on request.*

EXPERIMENTING WITH TRUTH

The fusion of Religion with Technology, needed for Humanity's survival

RUSTUM ROY
Pennsylvania State University, USA

The Hibbert Lectures for 1979

PERGAMON PRESS
OXFORD • NEW YORK • TORONTO • SYDNEY • PARIS • FRANKFURT

UK	Pergamon Press Ltd., Headington Hill Hall, Oxford OX3 0BW, England
USA	Pergamon Press, Inc., Maxwell House, Fairview Park, Elmsford, New York 10523, USA
CANADA	Pergamon of Canada, Suite 104, 150 Consumers Road, Willowdale, Ontario M2J 1P9, Canada
AUSTRALIA	Pergamon Press (Aust.) Pty. Ltd., P.O. Box 544, Potts Point, NSW 2011, Australia
FRANCE	Pergamon Press SARL, 24 rue des Ecoles, 75240 Paris, Cedex 05, France
FEDERAL REPUBLIC OF GERMANY	Pergamon Press GmbH, 6242 Kronberg-Taunus, Hammerweg 6, Federal Republic of Germany

First edition 1981

British Library Cataloguing in Publication Data
Roy, Rustum
Experimenting with truth.
1. Religion and science—1946—
I. Title
215 BL240.2 80-40658

ISBN 0-08-025820-4 (Hardcover)
ISBN 0-08-025819-0 (Flexicover)

Printed in the United States of America

Preface

After the sense of having been honored far beyond my merits or deserts in being invited to present the Hibbert Lectures had moved to the background, my dominant feeling is one of trepidation. I have especially good cause for this. The list of Hibbert Lecturers would impress any distinguished theologian or philosopher. But for a journeyman scientist, my response is described exactly by W. H. Auden's remark on his feelings when he is in a roomful of scientists: "I feel like a country parson in the company of dukes and earls." And there is a second cause for my discomfiture. For an Indian, one has to grant that Rabindranath Tagore, India's only literary Nobel Laureate, and Sarvapalli Radhakrishnan, philosopher and the country's first President, my Indian predecessors in this series, are a formidable act to follow.

It behooves me, therefore, to play through any rather different, if modest, strengths I may have. These are of two kinds: one of form and style, the other of substance and content. As a layman with no formal training in theology or philosophy, I bring of necessity to this task the view and style of the vulgarizer. For some years I have been working hard at improving the public's understanding of science and technology. In parallel, I have tried to restate a lay-theology and Christian ethics for the ordinary person caught up "in the midst of life." I place the highest possible priority on interpreting the *basics* of both science and religion in the common tongue. Our culture is in dire peril because the seminal ideas and the cardinal rules by which it operates are unintelligible to the vast majority of the populace. In the tradition of Luther, I think it is time to provide the basics in the simple, declarative English of *our* day. I will be writing, therefore, for the educated, open-minded, and unavoidably technology-influenced person, many of whom I assume to be without religious instruction or allegiance. There is little doubt that readers with a background in science or engineering will be more at home in the idiom and the somewhat drier didactic style partly forced upon me by the attempt to be precise. In thus narrowing my audience and approach, I find a striking dearth of recent books in the field.

The first exception is the work of C. S. Lewis. The *Screwtape Letters* and *Mere Christianity* are enjoying a great revival. Yet for all the brilliant writing and sensible apologetics, they lack the contemporaneity I believe to be essential. Of a clear, contemporaneous exposition of the Christian faith there is one striking example. As I got further and further into the work it became evident that J.A.T. Robinson's *Honest to God* was nearly exactly what was needed. Moreover, it was so extremely well done, that I remained continually aware that I could complement it in some small way only by bringing my very different perspective of a working layman scientist to bear on it.

The Bifocal Perspective of a Christian Immersed in the Scientific-Technological Enterprise

What is this different viewpoint or perspective that I bring to this effort? In keeping with one of my major themes—the Dice Playing God—it was an interweaving of accident and intention, of both totally uncontrolled fate and individually willed purpose, that made this possible. Because of the role of this element of fate, "luck," chance, I feel less diffidence in claiming that there is something rather special here. What is different is binocular vision. We all know how significant the use of both our eyes is to gauging distance, getting perspective, maintaining balance. Likewise, many, especially in middle age, learn the importance of bifocal adjustment. Useful complementarities (often confused with dichotomies) abound: from the classical yin-yang, through inward–outward, to our modern, left brain-right brain; and Dionysian-Apollonian.

The special complementarity which this work brings is the coupling of the world view of the modern enterprise of science *and technology* with the world view of the "radical," "avant-garde" Christian community. For twenty-five years, my consciousness has been shaped simultaneously by these two world views, both evolving (changing rapidly in relative importance and impact on the masses). During that period, it has been my privilege (mediated partly by luck) to sit at the feet of some of the world's leaders in both fields, and over the years to come to know some of them personally. Hence, it is not as an academic observer or visiting journalist that I will be writing. My special perspective is that of the participant in the midst of the fray, learning in the school of hard knocks. My right brain was processing the signals of the emergence of structural ecumenism from 1948 onwards; of the retreat movement in Protestantism, of cell groups and Civil Rights; of the "Death of God" and the birth of the free meal ticket; of Vatican II and Exodus II (of priests and ministers from the "sinking ship"); of encounter groups and the "con" game of a generation of narcissists. At the same time, the left brain was dealing with the new solid-state physics which would bless (curse?) us with transistor radios, color TV, and the ubiquitous computer. It included the societal impacts of the misunderstood and ignored threats of nuclear weaponry, the black holes and Apollo 13, and DNA and the genetic code, and the slow recognition of the ambivalence of all technology: the SST and pollution, and nuclear waste, and MIRV's and Cruise missiles, the coming and going of the Golden Age of Science. My experience on the "science" side is rather different from that of most who have written in the field. It encompasses not only the knowledge about nature and humanity, but mission-oriented applied science, the science policy, the actions, the decisions, the choices which are all properly included by Ellul under the word "Technology." My base is, perhaps, most accurately described by the term Science-Technology, and it bears the same relation to Science as the Christian religion does to "Theology."

It is *this* integrated view—of the perspective of one immersed in the modern technological enterprise, and simultaneously in the religious avant garde—of the world and the times in which we live, and the mental notebook in which I keep my results, that I will be sharing with the readers of this volume.

Two Linguistic Crises

Our society, which uses verbal (and written) communication to a much greater extent than any before it, is much less disciplined in its use of words. We are now paying the price, in our rapidly diminishing capability for describing, debating, or transmitting the very fundamentals of our individual and collective existence. Hammarskjöld's warning: *"Respect for the word is the first commandment in the discipline by which a man can be educated to maturity—intellectual, emotional and moral"* has not been heeded; the Tower of Babel is not far away. This is the crisis which—again to use Hammarskjöld's words—*"undermines the bridges and poisons the wells. It causes man to regress down the long path of his evolution."*

There is a less well-known crisis, the crisis of monolinguality of the religious and scientific communities, each unable to understand the other's tradition. The timeless truths of spiritual insight and their translation into religious myth, parable, and practice are the results of ten thousand years of humanity's "experiments with truth." They are couched in the language of the humanists and religionists. Over the last two or three centuries, a small segment of humanity—the scientific community—has been "experimenting with truth" in a new, narrow, but extremely powerful way. Because of its successes, many of which have shaped humanity's day-to-day existence in profound ways, the practices, results, and language of this scientific community have become a—if not *the*—dominant force of twentieth century culture. But this motif is couched in a "foreign" language of science and mathematics.

One cause of the problem lies in an apparent discontinuity. It is as though scientific TRUTH had arrived full grown from another planet, and was not the result of a very human activity, embedded originally (at least in its most "successful" form) in Judeo-Christian culture. This apparent discontinuity is caused and sustained principally by a language barrier. The language barrier is maintained by both the scientists (partly by an imperial attitude and partly by sheer lack of concern for their patron society) and by the public, unwilling to learn the language and especially the dialect of quantification. Because of this monolingualism, our culture has failed to graft the powerful insights of science onto its own centuries-old traditions and, thereby, has lost the potential for growth in self-understanding and self-direction.

This book and the lectures abstracted therefrom are written by one person who, by the happenstances which form part of our lives, was born, brought up, and remains bilingual. He has tried, and continues to try, to maintain the "radical"* Christian world view and life-style. Simultaneously, he is fully immersed in the world of modern science and technology, as an active research worker, mentor of dozens of Ph.D.'s, director of a major research laboratory, and active participant in formulation and critique of national science policy.

This stance, with a "standing leg" in both worlds, required a working "bilingualism," nay, biculturality. It provided the opportunity to develop a sufficiently "broadband" understanding of both languages,** so that for the last ten or fifteen years, the real equivalence of various terms in each language has been recognized. Thus, the author is puzzled—often saddened—by the apparent inability of both parties—the worlds of science and of religion—to see beyond the verbal screens and distortions to the obvious (to one who knows both languages) agreements and synergisms bridging the two approaches.

This book is an attempt to single out the most important points on which modern science and contemporary Christian thought agree, and to synergize and provide a sure, if flexible, "Guide for the Perplexed." Such a tack, by its very terms of reference, requires the author to eschew a pedantic or scholarly approach or display of what little erudition he may have. Our willingness, if not our ability, to follow closely reasoned argu-

* "Radical" is used, of course, in its proper meaning of "rooted," or going to the "root" of the matter.

** Compare the same sentiment found in Teilhard's "Le Christique" written a month before his death in 1955. *"In me by pure chance (temperament, education, environment) the proportion of each happens to be favorable and they fuse together spontaneously. The fusion of the two . . . is enough to show that an explosion is possible and that sooner or later the chain reaction will get underway."*

ments, even in the simplest form, in a subject far from our formal training, or in which we have a deep, committed interest, seems to be extremely limited. Even with a strong interest in general science, I find myself—in common, I have observed, with most of my colleagues—unable (= unwilling) really to follow through more than a single article in the issue of *Scientific American* which appears monthly on my desk. I am very committed to the widest possible dissemination of an understanding of science and technology, and our work over several years has taught me how we must start where people are—with their concerns, their language, and their capacities. I am even more concerned that as many as possible have a chance to understand in their language, as it affects their experiences, the content of a Christian way of life and its meaning. But given the facts of our resistances noted above, and our culture's experience, with its poor understanding of technology, the task may seem hopeless. It is nearly, but not wholly, so.

Careful observations and what little "research" there is agree that there are two effective aids—one motivational and one methodological—for communication with persons in the physico-psycho-social condition of the "average middle-class" person in Western society. All persons are *motivated* at the point of need. An accident in a nuclear power plant will activate a certain percentage of the population to try to understand the rudiments of how such a plant works, the hazards of radiation, the units in which it is measured, etc. Parents learn all about drugs when their children get involved. International economics is less formidable when a foreign coroporation is negotiating to buy and "save" the *local* factory. The *methodological* aid is as old as the history of religion, and central to the Judeo-Chris-

---

Jesus transmitted his message (energy) at the voltage we use in our households (say 100 or 200 volts). His parables convey the essence of his teaching and connect directly to our existence, just like the current in the house which runs the lights, stoves, hair dryer, and washer. (Indeed, many of his parables are like portable flashlights running at a few volts on batteries, easily moved into many new situations.)

Professional theologians transmit their learnings (= energy) at 11,000 volts or higher—no individual can use them directly. *They pass overhead in the high voltage power lines we see crisscrossing our countryside. To be used by the people, they are reinterpreted (stepped down in voltage by the local transformer) by a local minister to connect with the man-in-the-street situation.*

The messages in this book are designed to be directly usable and, hence, are transmitted at household voltage.

---

tian tradition. The use of the parable—typically involving persons or situations with which one can identify—is as powerful a tool for communicating concepts as one can devise. The parabolic teachings of Jesus written in the common language of human experience can here be contrasted with the writings of Plato or Aristotle. The former are directly accessible to virtually all humankind (at least for centuries after his time). The latter are invaluable to scholars, who may then interpret them to others. The parables of the Sower, the Good Samaritan, the Prodigal Son capture the essence of Jesus' ethics *more* effectively than the systematic theology of Paul Tillich (although his work has illumined my faith greatly). There is, of course, need and room for both. But it is my personal judgment that we have an enormous oversupply of the more sophisticated versions—the high voltage but unusable energy in terms of our own parable in the insert. At the same time, we have neglected the creation of contemporary parables—stories which connect to everyday experience but have the special quality of being saturated with meaning.

A Note on "Sexist" Language

The context within which I live and work and write is acutely troubled by the realization of much in our cultural conditioning which works against the realization of a genuine equality of self-expression by women. Part of this conditioning is carried through a very strong bias in language. So strong is this bias that any effort to change it adversely affects the quality of writing. Yet I have been committed to working for such equality for some decades. Hence, I must and will make the effort to eliminate such bias as far as possible. But what to do, and how to do it, leaves room for experimentation—not all of which will sit well with all readers. I trust that such readers will forgive the infelicitous phrase as a concession to my intention.

"Experimentation" with Life and Truth as the Common Ground

My title is patterned after that of Mahatma Gandhi's autobiography, "My Experiments with Truth." The rationale for the title is developed at greater length in the epilogue. We seek to bring together the communities of religion and science. They share a common goal: to discover and proclaim what is most "real," what is true. This commonality has been obscured by procedural and linguistic screens. They arrive at their conceptions of realities by trial and error, by experimentation—though this is often totally unconscious on the part of the religious community. The latter's experiments with life take place over generations and centuries, while scientists operate within months and years. It is this long "time-constant" of the development of religious truth which has tended to give the term "revealed" truth a static, fixed quality. In fact, of course, all religious revelation comes only out of intensive "experimentation" with truth.

My goal for this volume, then, is that it be seen as a restatement in simple language of the insights of the mutually reinforcing aspects of the Christian faith and modern science. The first Hibbert Lectures were given by Max Müller, whose masterful and deeply sympathetic treatment of Hindu thought remains a landmark down to our own day. The last Hibbert Lectures were given by a distinguished scientist, Sir Alister Hardy. I found it fascinating that I agreed with so much of what both had written. In the 100 years in between, the physical, social, and political environment in which much of humanity lives has been changed beyond recognition, yet the nature of the humans embedded in it has remained fundamentally unaltered. And during this period, hundreds of brilliant and perceptive minds have shared their insights and built on their own individual backgrounds and experiences. Following standard scientific tradition I will, in Newton's words, build *"standing on the shoulders of giants."* Indeed, I find that the bulk of what I have to share is, to a large extent, my witness to the reader of the value and meaning which a particular set of books, and the persons behind them, have had for me. The style will be in the genre of a "vulgarization," and it will be my personal account, not only of my reading but of my experiences. Both scientists and Christians start with their own personal observations and end, in the last analysis, with a personal witness to the truth as they have experienced it. This is such a record of *my* Experiments with Truth.

Contents

1 Technology's Need for Religion's Hegemony

1.0 A Synoptic Introduction

I begin on a note of extreme urgency. Humanity's highest aspirations expressed in its religions and its highest creativity in shaping its own future via science and technology have lost touch with each other. Humankind must indulge in *cultural* genetic engineering or it won't survive. It must interbreed religion and technology. Genteel contact between these forces won't be enough. The prognosis for modern civilization to make it through the next century is, as I will report, according to the most thoughtful and experienced observers, very poor. The situation is so grave that it would be irresponsible of me to start a book on why and how science-based technology (SbT)* and religion mutually interact without indicating that the overriding reason is human survival. There is absolutely no reason, scientific or religious, which guarantees continuance of the species, and certainly not of contemporary civilization. The path of evolution is anything but straight. Twists and turns and unexplained breaks warn us of what has happened. Toynbee's civilizations have come and gone. The prophet's voice offers no vision of smooth sailing. "Go now to Shiloh" says the Eternal through Jeremiah, and see how I destroyed that once-famed place and people of mine.

The highest traditions of the religions of humanity embody the most precious learnings of the race. They embody at once the brightest sparks of creativity, human or "divine," and the distilled empirical experience across large numbers, time, and space. Modern science-based technology (SbT)* is clearly the contemporary era's characteristic and distinctive contribution to human culture. The absurdity of seeing the main direction of these streams of human creativity as opposed to each other is a luxury we simply cannot afford any longer. Konrad Lorenz in his recent book, relevantly titled *Civilized Man's Eight Deadly Sins,* has this to say:

* I will use this term science-based technology, and its abbreviation SbT throughout this book to refer to the complex continuum which, in the language of the public, is identified interchangeably with either science or technology. SbT does describe more precisely what is distinctive about modern science and technology. Neither is possible without the other.

The enormous underestimation of our nonrational, cultural fund of knowledge and the equal overestimation of all that man, as Homo faber, is able to produce by means of his intellect are not the only factors threatening our civilization with destruction. Being enlightened is no reason for confronting transmitted tradition with hostile arrogance. . . .

But there is no time for recrimination or allocating blame. "What the world needs now" is a guidance mechanism for its juggernaut, a system of control rods for a runaway fission reactor. Our parable of the car without a steering wheel accurately states the condition of human society. It is imperative that we bring together the knowledge, skills, and creative insights of religion and SbT. I feel rather confident in saying that no new relevant theology will ever be done again, which is not cognizant of and fully based in modern SbT. Recycling of the old formulas will, of course, continue and with some purposes. Yet, not only is Rome burning but the issues of life, love, growth, and death all demand attention to the interaction of R with SbT.

On the other side, many analysts voice only the intuitive suspicions of the millions, that it is out of human control. Silly exercises of cost-benefit analysis and technology assessments have proved their utter futility because SbT does not carry within itself any criterion by which it can judge itself.

My experience in the world of science policy at the microscopic level of choosing between alternative routes for the disposal of radioactive wastes as well as the level of greatest complexity in dealing with the use of SbT in the development of nations has driven me to an unexpected conclusion. "Science" policy, I am convinced, must be done in a framework of, or under the hegemony of, a specific "religious" world view. Since so many national policies are infused with science-policy components, this means that SbT and religion must become extremely interactive to help humankind govern itself. To be able to begin such an interaction, however, requires a degree of mutual knowledge and understanding which simply does not exist. It is to that task that I have been devoting a substantial fraction of my recent activities. This book is the first in a series which attempts to outline the issues and clarify the concepts so that the two communities of SbT and religion can begin the process of dialogue and interaction. Such a "dialogic" process and its inherent difficulties appear in the structure of the book. It is, of course, necessary to go back and forth between topics, concerns, and issues originating in one area, and the knowledge and understanding gained in another. The reader unfamiliar with one or the other area's basic linguistic framework may be less interested or less able to follow parts of the book in spite of the vulgarization attempted.

The first chapter is largely a description of the state of the SbT-dominated world. It describes the "situation" in which modern theology must be done before proceeding to the theology itself. Its principal themes are that:

a. The future of the world desperately needs the hybridization of the insights of SbT and religion.
b. Both science and religion have recently been perceived (in the West) as "lights that failed" by the leaders in the field.
c. International Technology has become the masses' chief "God,"—in any case, a superstate—with billions of followers but with no philosophy, plan, or goal.
d. The good news is that we are at the end of the scientific era. The SbT revolution is over conceptually and (except for *horizontal* proliferation) with respect to *impacting* technologies. Humanity has a chance to regroup.
e. The bad news is that no one is in charge of any attempt to regroup. A new minority from within science and religion needs to come into being to address this task.

Readers who start with a background in religion may find it easier and more interesting to read the second and third chapters before completing the first.

A Parable of Our Times

THE CAR WITH NO STEERING WHEEL

> *(Behold also the ships, which though they be so great and are driven of fierce winds, yet are they turned about with a very small helm.)*

It was at the Annual Meeting of the International Society of Conveyance Designers that the new model of the "Car of the Future" (this year's model, of course) was unveiled. This event was a veritable summit meeting of designers of cars, those vehicles designed to convey us into the future. The idea of designing a single, composite, "International Car XXI" for the twenty-first century with the best features contributed by each nation or group had emerged only recently (of course, there was resistance from the Eastern bloc who also had a "Peoples of the World Car" and there was talk of the Group of 77 designing jointly a Motorized Pedicab).

After the unveiling by the Secretary General of the United Nations, large crowds thronged around the car to comment on its wonders. Great admiration was expressed for the Franco-German team of mechanical engineers which had come up with a most fuel-efficient engine giving 80 miles to the imperial gallon. The Italian designers had lowered the wind resistance and, to show again the social conscience of the engineering community, had removed all traces of chromium plated strips. The British had contributed new materials for the fenders and exhaust system which would last twice as long, and the Scandinavians, a fine super-hydraulic braking system. The Secretary General in his speech alluded frequently to "the responsiveness of modern science and technology to the needs of the times"; he spoke of the "esthetic sensibilities of the scientists and engineers which were so finely tuned to the new decade that they had dispensed with all offensive ostentation"—now that it was clear that this no longer sold cars! And so it went, as throngs vied with speakers to comment on the wonders of science and technology—unbreakable windows, lifetime fenders, and on and on. This was truly a world car of the future.

Therefore, it caused no small stir when the French woman physicist, who was also a newly ordained priest, together with her Buddhist monk colleague from Bangkok noticed that the car had no steering wheel. At first, attendants went scurrying around to rectify this terribly embarrassing slipup. Some local engineer assembling the car had surely forgotten to fasten the steering wheel. After the normal whispered conversations followed by unobtrusive gliding in and out among the guests, it was determined by the staff that no steering wheel had even been shipped. Now the pace of unobtrusive but obvious gatherings-in-little-knots of the management picked up. Among the crowd, however, only a minority seemed concerned about the absence of a steering wheel; most kept milling about admiring the latest technological advances. With time, however, it became obvious that some comment was needed from the car designers. The one-time chief consultant to Mercedes, who was head of the planning unit, explained to the audience that the engineering team, of course, had been given a limited responsibility. This did not include, he noted, the steering of the car, nor indeed the highways over which it was to travel, nor, he added in jest, "maps for the way or advice on the best motels en route." While conceding, somewhat defensively, that the car with its low clearance was suited only for very smooth highways, he pointed out that, since it was planned that 100 million units would be built in the next few years, no doubt each society "would have to adapt its other systems to the car of the future. That's the way it has always worked."

As the reporters scattered to the phones down the long corridor of the Waldorf-Hilton, some of them passed another room in which another society was holding its meeting. Attracted by the noise and acrimonious debate, two or three reporters stopped in, only to be astounded by what they found; for in this modest room was meeting the "Society on the Origin and Nature of Guidance and Steering Mechanisms." The special topic for this year's meeting was "Steering the Car of the Future." Bearded gentlemen and serious women discussed drawings of steering wheels; some even had slides projected of their models. But the showstopper was the working model around which many had gathered. It was not a very finished or polished affair—but, as was mentioned a dozen times, that is, of course, *merely* a matter of engineering—"after all, we must leave those chaps something to do." Word had spread and a crowd had drifted over from the Grand Ballroom where the car was on exhibit, to the smaller "Steering Wheel Room." It was the same French priest who first noticed that the steering wheel model on exhibit was not attached to, nor indeed designed for, any real car. It was, in fact, only a toy wheel designed for the seats in which young children are confined in the front seats of cars. And when the woman priest-physicist questioned the Society whether or not a steering wheel had actually been designed for the "International Car XXI," they were nonplussed but no immediate uproar ensued. Instead, there were vague and diffident responses from various individuals to the effect that steering mechanism designers didn't usually work on such practical or mundane topics. A Greek noted that their society had, in earlier times, actually designed steering mechanisms for Alexander's chariots. Indeed, right down the ages, while vehicles were driven by natural forces such as animals or winds, the Society provided the guilds of vehicle-manufacturers with the specifications on vehicles to fit the roads of the day and the steering mechanism required.

It was with the coming of the locomotive that ran on rails (and the so-called Industrial Revolution) and less need for steering, that the Society had taken a position that only more theoretical and abstract studies were important. For centuries to follow, topics such as "Steering Mechanisms of Angels" or "Probable Road Maps for Heaven" became fashionable Ph.D. topics. Only in the last few decades had some younger members insisted on reexamining the steering of real cars. After much debate, the compromise had been to work on the kiddie-seats for cars since that might provide a "model" of real life. The party opposing involvement with the real car pointed out that the enormous difficulty of designing a steering wheel for a real car was in how to interact with the scientists and engineers, since "we" would have to couple "our" steering wheel to "their" column. Besides, none of the uncultured engineers had ever managed to learn Latin very well, and how could you work with someone who didn't speak Latin?

And that is how it came about that the new International Order got a most efficient and effective vehicle for going into the future, but without a steering wheel, a highway system, or a map for the roads ahead. At the same time, steering wheel designers flourished working on models totally decoupled from the needs of real people and their cars.

1.1 The Modern Context, Dominated by Science and Technology

It became acceptable in the late fifties and sixties to consider ethics, not as an immutable deductive science based on certain "revealed truths or laws," but as an interactive science relying on both deduction and induction. Right and wrong behavior were, to a substantial extent, determined by the context or situation. After a few minor skirmishes, mainly about terminology, situation ethics or contextual ethics soon established itself rather comfortably within the contemporary religious establishments.

This represented a momentous change. It has received insufficient attention from theologians and students of culture since, although many of us might wish it otherwise, for most citizens religion *is* ethics. Most American church members, when asked to describe what it means to be a Christian, would certainly include "Keeping the ten commandments" and various moral laws in the first three phrases of their response. Yet, in one of those miracles of major changes which pass unnoticed, the present *interpretation* of this statement has become totally dominated by the invasion of "situation ethics." Except for the right wing minority in both Protestant and Catholic circles, the culture's interpretation of all moral "laws" has become extremely elastic. Examples of the changes abound in every Church body. On swearing—from a culture which blanched at the use of d . . . and h . . . through the Filthy Speech Movement—it is a long way to the permissive language excesses about God, humanity, and society; from keeping the Sabbath holy by not reading the Sunday newspapers, to the biggest sales day of the week; from the unmentionable topic of s . . , to hours of debate on contraception, abortion, premarital sex, and ordination of homosexuals.

If, then, a major part of religion—ethics—was so easily adapted to its real environment, why, one may ask, is the other part—theology—still cast in the same old classical, deductive molds? The answer is not far to seek. The fact is that the people changed their behavior first, and some time later the keepers of the keys decided to modify their standards to catch up with the experimentally determined *truths*. The most dramatic example of this is the startling statistic regarding the Catholic nonobservance of the proscription against contraception found in study after study. Vatican II's more elastic "conscience" guidelines permitted Catholics to absorb this reality into the ethical canon, without even conceding to the term "situation ethics."

With respect to theology, matters are different. *People* have not been involved in doing theology so far; they do not make it, change it, and since they do not see it as all that important they are quite willing to let "the Church" take care of it. Hence, the only persons who can change the theological teachings are the theologians and clergy. This brings one up against a common stumbling block: the inability to teach faculty. Now, it is well known that in the university *new* approaches and *new* subject matter are readily absorbed by a good fraction of the *students* who are directly exposed to such. (After all, they don't know that it is new, never having had the old.) But when one has to rely on going through the faculty or teachers to the students, the task uniformly proves impossible. While rightly refusing to respond to every whim or fashion, since they are unwilling to carry out the difficult task of identifying the true and new, the faculty as a whole are virtually unteachable. They "know better"; "it was not invented here and can't be any good"; they have an obvious vested interest in not changing because it would require more effort, and so on. And so it is with the laity (teachable where you have direct access) and clergy (only a minority likely to accept change). This is why, in 1980, we already have a widespread acceptance of situation ethics, but virtually no progress on what I will call here "situation theology." The latter has had, so far, to go through the clergy.

In what way would "situation theology" be different from any classical theology? Just as situation ethics was a response to new situations which opened up new options or reexamined old options in the light of new knowledge, so situation theology must be done in the light of new gods or new knowledge about God. Now, I submit that, to an even greater extent than was true in the matter of behavior or ethics, the public has in measurable, quantifiable fact, switched allegiances to a new god. At the operational level, the attributes of the deity are: the source of truth, of power, reward, and punishment; and the source of salvation of body (short range) and soul (long range).

In an international context in which one devised a meaningful, carefully worded survey of the citizens' actual (behaviorally maintained) allegiances, it would, I believe, be foolhardy to put one's money on any "God" other than "Science and Technology" as against any traditional religion.

I submit that the new context is that there is a new boy on the block. Science and technology is the most reliable source of truth on most matters for most of the people in Christian Britain, prosperous America, or Marxist Rumania, in Hindu India or Islamic Egypt. Those same people regard SbT as having more power than any other god "in real time," to use the computer world's language. Most significantly missed, I think, is the soteriology of science. Whole cultures literally pray for the scientific salve, or the techno-fix, as fervently as women and men of all ages have prayed to other gods for rain or deliverance from locusts. Science has surely become "the Savior" and, almost as surely, the opiate of the masses.

How, then, have so many theologians—Christian, Islamic, Hindu and Zen—managed so successfully to avoid really doing theology in the new situation of the competition from SbT? The number of professional theologians who have entered into a thorough study of the works of science and technology is vanishingly small. This lack of *theological* (as distinct from ethical) interest is, I submit, a conceptual and perceptual error. The study of comparative religions has been a respectable field for decades. Indeed, in reading again the very first Hibbert Lectures by Max Müller, one is struck by the incredible scholarship and depth of penetration of Indian religious thought which is manifest there. Thus was the best of relevant other-religious thought—in this and many similar efforts—brought into the consciousness of Christian *theologians.* It had, as the record shows, but little impact. The "unteachable-faculty" syndrome was operative. The lay public, so far, has neither been absorbed nor systematically exposed to the great truths of other religions in any culture. For, in a very real sense, it was unnecessary. The contact with another whole system of behavior and way of viewing reality was so limited that only a miniscule proportion of any citizenry ever had opportunity or need to deal with other theologies.

The situation today is radically different. The contact between different parts of the world occurs on a very wide front; for, while colonial powers had exposed conquered territories to *their* whole culture (including religion), it took world wars to reverse the flow and expose any large numbers in the Christian West to direct contact with other religions. Travel and tourism have now taken over from the war, and Eastern religions are marketed vigorously in the West from airports to academe. Second, there is a new religion which has invaded all the other home territories, and it is selling well against each local product. SbT has a growing number of conscious and unconscious adherents everywhere. It would be preposterous, therefore, to attempt any kind of "theology"— to discuss the nature of God, of humankind, of sin, grace, redemption, heaven, and hell—without diligent searching for the insights we may glean from SbT. It is essential for any theology to determine and present not only the points of congruence between different theories, religions, and viewpoints, but also points where disagreements are clear and sharp. In the case of Christianity and SbT, this task is absolutely vital because on it, as I will try to show, may hinge the survival of the human species.

Recent Changes in Attitudes toward SbT and toward Religion

To begin this process of examining the context of our "theology," I first wish to comment upon a most remarkable phenomenon (occasioned by developments in the technological world).

In less than 15 years, the world has radically altered its attitude toward science and technology. From being seen as the hope of humanity, SbT is now seen as an alien force in culture, separating humans from their roots in nature, causing ecological problems, posing threats of total annihilation. What is remarkable is that very few in the Church or the sociologists of science have commented on such a significant change.

To take the measure first of the extraordinary speed with which this has occurred, let me quote Governor Adlai Stevenson, that perceptive, urbane spokesman for the best of postwar, American socio-political thought in a remarkable upbeat statement:

> *Yesterday, most of mankind could look forward only to a life that would be "nasty, brutish and short," on the verge of privation in good years, starving when the harvests failed. Now wheat pours out of our ears. We swim in milk. We are threatened with vegetable and fruit surpluses and even, in some happy years, wine gluts as well. Water, man's precious resource, will be captured from the oceans by desalinization; nuclear power promises unlimited energy; the rocket, unlimited speed; electronics, unlimited technical control. All the old locks of scarcity have been sprung, the prisons flung open. From the first stone tool to the cell which snaps a camera shutter on the far side of the moon, the stride of man's abundance is all but unimaginable—and yet it is here.*
>
> *This is the basic miracle of modern technology. This is why it is, in a real sense, a magic wand which gives us what we desire. Don't let us miss the miracle by underestimating this fabulous new tool. We can have what we want. This is the astonishing fact of the modern scientific and technological economy. This is the triumph we hail today. This is the new instrument of human betterment that is at our hand if we are ready to take it up.*

To make the comparison as close as possible, let me now juxtapose another quotation a scant 13 years later from another state official in a similar situation. Governor R. D. Lamm of Colorado (who once took a sabbatical as governor to study at Union Theological Seminary), speaking before the AAAS in 1977, said:

> *I find that one of the great challenges of the future will be to differentiate what science and tehnology can do from what it cannot do. That will be the problem. Their promise is great. They can and will continue to make dramatic breakthroughs in field after field.*[*] *They can continue to significantly improve the human condition. But I fear that people have too much faith in their miracles and that the cornucopia of the benefits of science can seriously excuse, postpone and delay some public policy considerations that we must soon institute.*

Not only is Stevenson's euphoria gone, but in its place is an attitude warning of the dangers of overreliance on a not wholly beneficial technology. In that period, the "ecology movement" followed the announcement of the environmental crisis. On its heels came the raising of the flag of the "Limits to Growth" and, before we could get our breath, "The Energy Crisis." Not only the public, but the intellectuals, who had grown used to a succession of problem—solving technological miracles, were confronted with a series of crises emanating from technology.

The nontechnically-trained, monolingual intellectuals reacted in many ways. There was, at first, the pleasure of observing the discomfiture of the dominant scientific elite. Some groups, especially within the applied social sciences, seized on the signs of change as the harbinger of the New

---

* You will find later that I disagree with Governor Lamm on that question.

Consciousness, an Age of Aquarius, and other equally puerile fantasies. But embedded within the counterculture revolt were the seeds of a substantive attack on the role of science in society. For brevity, I will cite the single example of Theodore Roszak's *Where the Wasteland Ends* as the prototypical statement of this new view of SbT, because the language he uses is very compatible with my own. Here is his summary on the danger of SbT and what society should do about it.

> *My argument has been that single vision, the ruling sensibility of the scientific world view, has become the boundary condition of human consciousness within urban-industrial culture, the reigning Reality Principle, the whole meaning of sanity. On that Reality Principle and on the artificial environment which is its social expression, the technocracy has been raised as a benevolent despotism of elitist expertise. Whatever else we must do to supplant the technocracy, we must indispensably throw off the psychic style from which it draws its strength. This is necessary not only if democracy is to be preserved, but also if we are to be healed of the death-in-life of alienation, which is the psychic of single vision.*

While my theme will, indeed, be that we need binocular or multiocular and multifocal vision, some of Roszak's prescriptions about the new consciousness appear to go too far. *"Science,"* he says, *"is not in my view merely* another *subject for discussion. It is* the *subject."* Yet he would . . . *"ground it [science] in a sensibility drawing on the occult, mysticism, the Romantic movement. . . ."* In a response typical of much of the literary world, Roszak replies to an interviewer: *"I am certainly not anti-scientific in the sense that I want to throw science out of the culture. But I am anti-science in that I want to question the cultural dominance of science. I want to put it in a somewhat more subordinate place in society."* Whatever the case, it is evident that not only the honeymoon but the love affair of Western society with science-technology is definitely over. A new marriage contract is in the process of being negotiated;* it will expect less and demand more from science-technology.

The Changing Role of Religion in Culture

The climate for religious thought has gone through a rather similar change. On the positive side, there is the most extraordinary advance, brought to a climax, almost single-handedly, by John XXIII: the healing of the Roman Catholic-Protestant split in practice even more than in principle. But theological thought, which after the war was building on solid foundations through the early sixties, was suddenly destroyed. The Barth-Niebuhr alliance of neoorthodoxy and social gospel had been

* I have developed the theme of the new contract between SbT and its patron society at some lengths elsewhere. (See R. Roy, ITEST, Nov. 1978.)

capped by the insights of the martyred Bonhoeffer. "Religionless Christianity" and a new costly concern for the world captured the imagination of the idealist young and middle-aged and old alike. Pierre Teilhard de Chardin was a name becoming increasingly well known, and his comfortable blending of science and religion in the language of the mystic struck many responsive chords. The enhanced role of the laity, the central role of persons-in-community as experienced in small groups, the focus on "others" and the "world" all made it possible for the avant-garde of the Church to take risky excursions, to experiment with both radical theology and radical Christian (sex) ethics.

It was this long, fruitful spell, I believe, which prepared the way for the enormous impact of John Robinson's book *Honest to God.* In this climate one could attend to new needs. His preface leads to the heart of the matter: *"A much more radical re-casting, I would judge, is demanded—in the process of which the most fundamental categories of our theology—of God, of the supernatural and of religion itself—must go into the melting."* Robinson put into plain English the obvious difficulties which ordinary men and women had with the very word "God," and many of the meanings attached to it. He sympathized with those who urge that "we give up using the word God for a generation." In this book he attempts, he says, *"to be honest—honest to God and about God. . . ."* Yet, nowhere in the entire book, nor in the works of Tillich, Bultmann, or Bonhoeffer was science or technology mentioned. Nevertheless, I had the occasion to introduce Bishop Robinson on one of his earliest visits to America, and I recall what I said because it is very relevant to the issues here. I compared the possible watershed effect of *Honest to God* on theology with that of Planck's 1900 paper on the quantum theory for this reason. I saw in Robinson's expression "beginning at the other end" a radical change in how theological truth was to be arrived at. For what he was affirming was that it was necessary in matters of faith to begin with experience, with empirical evidence, with scientific knowledge, if you will. He was placing the role of empirical truth on an equal footing with that of revealed religion and its system of deductive logic. The True and the Good had to be, by definition, mutually consistent.

Moreover, part of Robinson's effectiveness as a theologian in the world's eye was due to his own participation in the public life, taking positions on political and social issues from homosexuality to immigration. In America, Protestants were being introduced to retreats at centers like Kirkridge, patterned by its founder John Oliver Nelson on the Iona community in Scotland. And in Washington, D.C., its capital city, a "working model" of a faithful, small, ecumenical congregation was being hammered out by Gordon Cosby and the Church of the Saviour. The windows of the Church were wide open, the lilt of the guitar was heard in the land; Catholic nuns joined Southern Baptist ministers on marches, and situations determined Christian ethics in part. Extraordinarily fertile minds and faithful bodies had breathed new life into the faith.

I will not try to account for it historically, but today, a dozen years later, the scene has shifted so dramatically that it is hardly recognizable. Theology faltered as it atempted to connect *Honest to God* with the *Secular City* and has not recovered from its "Death of God" affair. The social gospel, riding high from its success on the racial issue and the martyrdom of Martin Luther King, appears to have bled to death over the Vietnam issue. The Church, once the avant-garde of social change in America, is nowhere to be seen. In 1960, small experimental groups were breaking away *leftward* from the mainstream churches, demanding more community and social action. In the late seventies small groups are backing away *rightward* from those same churches, which are now themselves much more conservative, to *avoid* the "abomination" of women priests, or to return to more "Bible-centered preaching." Lay leadership has vanished; the vestry and the session members have never heard of *Letters and Papers from Prison* or *Honest to God.* The vague platitudes of the human potential rhetoric linger. Everyone has been told s/he is "beautiful," is wonderful, is a born leader in this orgasmic cultural self-affirmation. But the continuing experience of most is one of anomie and lostness. Moreover, since all are lost and have been instructed not to follow anyone else, they stay lost.

As we enter the eighties, the majority of the Church is in a chastened, skeptical, mood; they are looking but not offering to lead any new ventures to heal body, mind, or spirit.

Two Lights That Failed

In the worlds of religion and of science, then, things are strangely similar. The peak of the golden age of science* (late 1960s) has passed, and most leaders accept that it will never come back. The intellectual leadership is much more humble about what science and technology can do for the nation and the world. They have been brought face to face with national and international issues and made to realize that science and technology are, after all, but a small part of the whole fabric of society. The rank and file of science and technology has plenty of work to do solving society's

---

* I use as a measure here the funding for science as a fraction of the GNP. Other qualitative measures of the excitement, rates of discovery, and technological advances (e.g., space ventures) all point to a peak near 1967–68.

many obvious problems. But the excitement of pioneering has died down, and dedication to truth and exploration is not the driving force of most young scientists. Science now looks for allies within society as it steps in as one force among many to make its place in the sun.

The "Reformation" of science is just beginning. Indeed, it has been selling technological indulgences—cheap grace—as the Church did 400 years before. The establishment is now confronted with very basic questions: What are the purposes of science? How can one honestly reply "increasing knowledge" without acknowledging that 50–75% of the U.S. R&D budget is for defense and space? No, all that propaganda is as dead as Stalinist rhetoric about democracy. The truth is that organized science and organized religion are perceived as joining Koestler's other "Light That Failed." A rebirth of either in this populist, open, worldwide culture will have to be rather directly coupled to human needs and aspirations.

If I were to summarize the situation of contemporary "Western" society to which any theology we do must be addressed, I would include the following key characteristics of our culture:

- It is profoundly ignorant of the very bases of its existence both in SbT and in religion.
- Yet it is dependent (and vulnerable because of its dependence) on SbT for its very functioning.
- Any critical appraisal of the gods that failed (SbT and Religion) is warmly received.
- There is a lack of discipline of thought, of persistence in action, and depth in attachments (fundamentally tied to the mobility in culture and overload of intellectual and emotional circuits).
- There is an unhealthy (exclusive) focus on personal experience, fulfillment, and satisfaction.

In spite of all these, indeed *because* many of the middle class are, like Siddhartha, "on the other side of physical and material desires" having experienced their hollowness, there is a new openness toward an understanding of our world and our experiences. Most significantly, there is the deep sense of lostness and of a need for a map to guide. But precisely for some of the reasons noted above, any such "guide for the perplexed" will have to be in simple, direct language. It will have to be consistent with everyday experience and the more obvious "truths" of SbT. The new theology will have to transcend these mundane, everyday facts and figures and sensual fulfillments, since all over the world the hunger is two-dimensional; one needs to feed both Body and Spirit.

Tiny signs of hope may now be seen popping up—just here and there—like the first crocuses of spring. The tortured, structured ecumenical venture has been leap-frogged by events. In the world of ideas and social action and the persons who breed them, the Catholic-Protestant division already appears archaic. Across the broader spectrum of religion, the first flush of the importation of Eastern religious "experiences" has passed, and left in its wake is a more genuine respect for the other paths to enlightenment. In these same 15 years, we have already noted that the dominant position of science in Western intellectual life has been turned upside down. Not only is it no longer the sole arbiter of truth, but technology, which had been recast from humanity's deliverer to its torturer for a while, is now being rehabilitated in a more modest role of humanity's ambivalent helper.

The Beginning of a New Synthesis

My reading of the world of (theological) ideas is that we are on the threshold of a great era of syncretism. Moreover, it is quite certain that as new syntheses occur, they cannot be confined to one dimension alone. For example, to synthesize Protestant and Catholic thought alone or even Judeo-Christian and Eastern religious thought alone is simply not good enough for humanity today. The key new element which every religious world view must learn to deal with explicitly and combine with synergistically is SbT.

There are three striking features of the emerging efforts to create a new synthesis incorporating the distinctive contributions of science and technology into a holistic religious world view. First, one is struck with enormous force at the disastrous implications of the absence of the official Christian Church—Catholic, Protestant, or Orthodox—from the engagement. Let us note how thoroughgoing is the alienation. No theologian of any stature has ventured into this area in 200 years. At the same time, hundreds have become expert in "comparative religions" studying the contributions from India, China, and Africa. Virtually no priest or minister receives in her/his seminary training *any* exposure to the dominant weltanschauung of the entire world. One can hardly find a single course listed in any U.S. seminary on the religious and philosophical impact of SbT. No church body maintains a standing committee or organizational unit to deal with theological, sociological, or political impacts of SbT. There are hardly any continuing forms* for encounter and debate. (The World Council of Churches is an exception in providing two such conferences within four years, but their impact on those in the pew is negligible.)

---

* Here and there valiant small efforts, such as ITEST (The Institute for Theological Encounter with Science and Technology) under Fr. Robert Brungs, do appear.

On the fringes of the established Church, the situation is exactly the reverse; fundamentalist sects vie with each other to latch onto the authority of science with booths at "World Fairs" or national radio programs. Most systematic and prominent of these are the efforts of the Rev. Sun Myung Moon through the annual conference on "The Unity of the Sciences" where a few hundred delegates including a smattering of Nobelists and many distinguished scientists and philosophers spend three expense-paid days every year to discuss this whole range of subject matter. Whatever else may be questioned about Moon's movement, it is beyond dispute that it takes science and technology very seriously.

The much more hospitable reception given to science by the Eastern–influenced religious movements is a general phenomenon. The Transcendental Meditation movement of the Maharishi Mahesh Yogi appears almost desperate for scientific respectability but, motives notwithstanding, there is a genuine attempt to blend the insights. At the other end of the spectrum is a work such as Fritjof Capra's *The Tao of Physics* which appears to seek long-term "public acceptability" for particle physics by linking it to Hindu, Zen, and Tao mystical thought. Capra's book is a model for finding parallels between mystical categories and those of modern physics, even though I believe that the choices of parallels betrays the irrelevance of both, since they are not the most central or helpful ones in our world.

Capra's less than world-affecting choice is symptomatic of the second feature of the religion/SbT situation: the dominance of science, as opposed to technology, and of particular sciences in the interface with religion: astronomy, subatomic physics, and the new biology. We find that most of this work is that of individual, and regrettably isolated, laity. Nevertheless, the quality of the lay-theology has improved remarkably from Eddington and Jeans a generation ago to Coulson, Alister Hardy, and Birch, and in the United States, Harold Schilling and Ian Barbour.

The third feature related to the emphasis on science as distinct from technology is the preponderance of effort in demonstrating consistency of understanding rather than generating synergistic policy. I shall cite later the closing paragraph of Capra's book. Suffice it here to point out that while Capra correctly observed the absolute necessity to bring about a "radically different social and economic structure" in order for society to survive, and while he points to the danger that "scientific [and may I add mystical] knowledge can often stay abstract and theoretical," his book advocates nothing to change that state. *He does not refer in a single paragraph to a contemporary human or societal problem.* Nuclear war does not appear in the appendix, nor the energy or resource problems of the world. In a permissive, nondemanding society there is a much larger market for helps on the "inward journey." Religious bookstores consist almost exclusively of such short reflective works to give the reader a new sense of inner connectedness, however vague, to "something," using some new angle: humanistic psychology, separate realities, Eastern mysticism, even quasars and black holes.

As far as professional theologians are concerned, my own view is that science and most definitely technology and, perhaps most centrally, science policy is the point at which the contact with our religious insights must be made. Science policy is the "outward journey" of science. The outward journey of religion—the social gospel and political activism—has been quiescent for a decade. Here is where the greatest need exists. The field is not without its pioneer lay theologians: the chemists Coulson and Conant had leanings in this direction. Two social scientists, Raymond Cattell in his work, *Beyondism, a Morality from Science,* and Jacques Ellul in his masterpiece, *The Technological Society,* have provided a secular and a Christian approach to action in our world today.

It is, however, Carl Friedrich von Weizsäcker who, in a truly unique way, has made the connections between modern science and Christian faith in both their yin-yang aspects: from understanding self and nature to carefully calculated actions in the world. His books, *The History of Nature, Relevance of Science,* (and *The Politics of Peril*), are the absolutely essential foundation works for any serious student of the synergism of SbT and contemporary *religion.*

But this book is not aimed at professionals. For the ordinary person, the relations between society and science and theology have to be very much simpler. P. W. Bridgman refers to the need to translate scientific interpretation back into everyday language:

> *Furthermore, I believe the experts would at present agree that whatever new way we devise to think about the microscopic universe, the meaning of our new concepts will have to be found back at the level of the large-scale events of daily life, because this is the scale on which we live our lives, and it is we who are formulating the new concepts.*

James Conant ends his book on *Modern Science and Modern Man* in the following words:

> *It seems to me more likely that the average citizen will come to think of science in totally different terms from those employed in explaining science to lay audiences fifty years ago. If I am right, in order to assimilate science into the culture of our twentieth-century highly industrialized society, we must regard scientific theories as guides to human action and thus an extension of common sense.*

I start this one in the same vein. It appears quite unavoidable to me that scientific findings and codifications, insofar as they are experienced as valid by the man or woman in the street, have already become "common sense." Religion's views on God, reality, and behavior, therefore, will be tested against this deeply accepted standard of the people. Given our situation in 1980, any theology that is done from now on which does not take SbT very seriously will probably be a retrogressive step and, more significantly, of little lasting value to those who will live out most of their lives in the twenty-first century.

1.2 Good News: Present Shock: Coming Relief

Comfort ye, comfort ye, my people
Saith your God.
Speak ye comfortably to Jerusalem,
And cry unto her,
That her warfare is accomplished. . . .

For all those reared in the Judeo-Christian tradition, these words have come to epitomize the signaling of relief at the end of a long siege and the harbinger of hope. In using the quotation from the prophet Isaiah to make a connection to a very "separate reality" from that with which it is usually associated, I will immediately set the tone for much of what is to follow. One of my persistent themes will be "All reality is illumined and made more real for me by different views from different perspectives." Hence, whenever we can connect two images, bringing them into stereoscopic focus, our grasp of reality is greatly enriched—literally given more body and substance. So it is with this message of hope.

The comfort which I have to announce is meant for a society buffeted by a series of tornados of change. In humanity's 100,000 year history, nothing has ever occurred remotely like what has happened to a substantial part of it during, roughly, the last 100 years. In virtually every sphere of activity, humanity has experienced what can very justifiably be called "the exponential explosion." Take a look at some of the facts once again to set it all in perspective. The series of graphs (Fig. 1.1) present more clearly than any words the message that the physico-bio-psycho-social environment within which human beings are expected to "live and move and have their being" has changed a hundred or thousand times more in the last century than all the change since the beginning of the human race.

Now we humans, even if we do not deserve fully the adjective "sapiens," surely are an adaptable and adapting species. We are elastic (stretch-recover) and plastic (assume new shapes under new forces). But

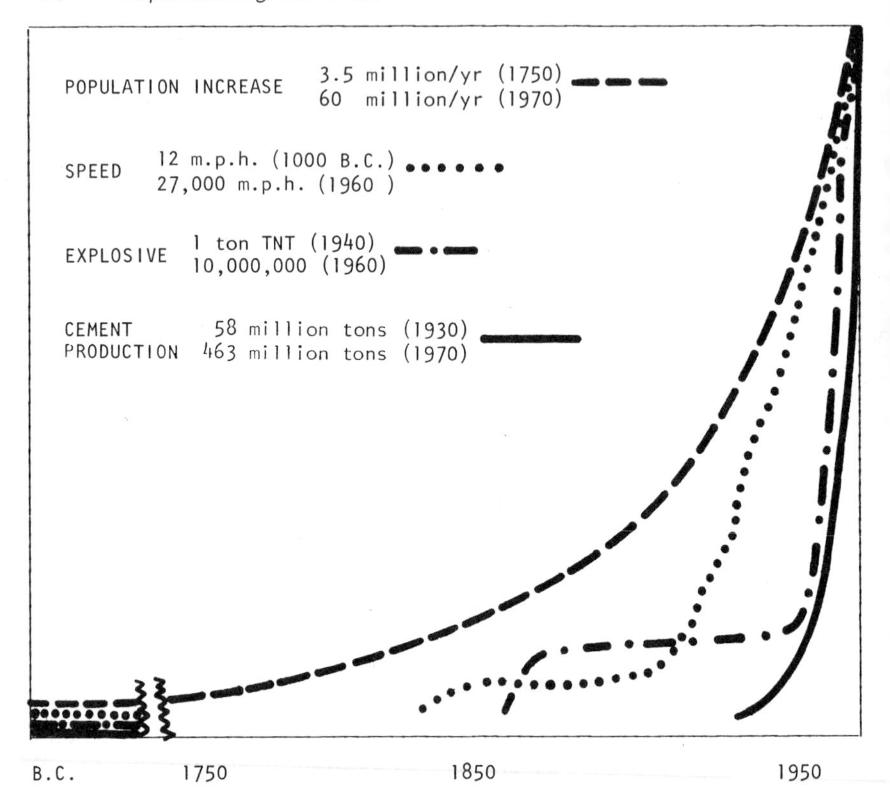

Fig. 1.1. *The "exponential explosion." This figure, which combines the data on a variety of indexes of human activities, from the population to the speeds attained by humans, to the amount of resources used and the explosive force controlled in its weapons, shows a truly fantastic increase in the last 100–150 years. On the scale of all recorded history, the curve would look like this:*

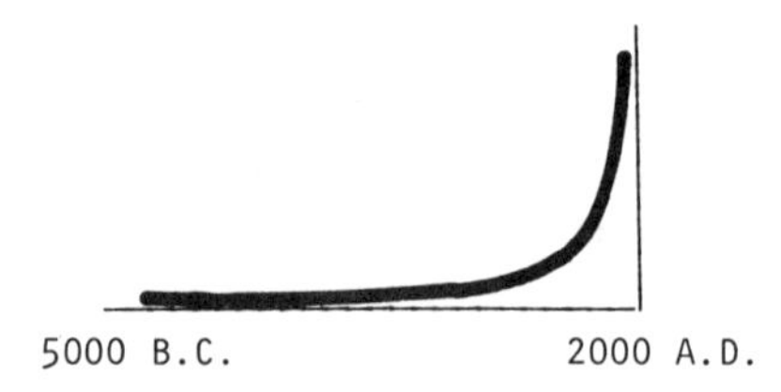

even rubber bands break, and the "silly putty" cannot be molded indefinitely. And Western society—the most stretched (strung?) out— is showing the strain, the enormous tension of being so quickly "stressed." Who will deny that it is drawn taut? Many would go further, as we will see later in this chapter, and say that it is on the verge of breakdown. Indeed, the single fact that is to me most striking and most ominous about the present situation is the unanimity of thoughtful observers of the contemporary scene. The unanimous verdict is not only that the pacesetting Western culture has brought itself (and in its wake the rest of the world) on a collision course with history, but it is also that such observers—rationally—can see no possible escape from the collision. And those tentative scenarios through which they see hope have only a low probability of occurrence. They use the following metaphor. Our society is like the passenger complement on the Titanic the night of its sinking, with a few brave souls calling attention to the fog and the probability of icebergs in the area. But what tools do we have to detect icebergs? Standing in the bow and using a long stick! This means that, in our circumstances, even our best efforts will not give us enough warning to avoid disaster.

To those outside the world of science and technology who are often critical of SbT, what I will say will sound like "good news" indeed. But "good news" of the kind that does—and should—immediately elicit the response: it is too good to be true; and is, therefore, almost certainly wrong; and, in any case, news to be very carefully examined for accuracy.

The "good news" is that, for all intents and purposes—in the time scale of even recent history—*the major changes caused by SbT are all finished.* * To avoid misunderstanding, I must restate this explicitly. The "good news" is that science has just climbed onto a new plateau, where the generation of genuinely novel information which can be translated into devices, gadgets, and technologies which will affect large numbers of humans will be much less common. Of course, there will be "horizontal proliferation," but only of technologies we already know about.** There will be many fewer new technologies discovered in the coming decades. The impact, and I repeat the word *impact,* of science and technology will now radically slow down. The scientific revolution is over!

This claim, that we are at the end of the era of rapid scientific and technological advance, appears at once to fly in the face of conventional wisdom, as well as the dreams and hopes of much of humankind. Surely, it can and will be argued that with all the enormous power, the vast re-

* I am, of course, speaking here of the SbT levels attained in the mass culture of the United States, and Western Europe, recognizing that this level has not been attained by the large majority of humankind.

** Again, this must be interpreted to include technologies and applications that the research personnel in each field are already able to conceive of, especially in the computer and bioengineering fields.

sources, the magnificent infrastructure of the modern scientific enterprise, we can only expect more knowledge, new and startling discoveries, new applications, and further impact on the human race. I believe that this is an egregious error perpetrated and perpetuated by all the normal forces of wishful thinking by the public combined with vested interests of the scientists-technologists. I am not unaware that other prophecies regarding the end or slowing down of scientific advance (including the much-quoted opinions of Lord Rutherford) have been proven to be the very opposite of the events. Most of those who argue for continued "miracles of science" express, of course, much more of a pious hope than an argument that my views will also turn out to be wrong. I do not think so, because I believe that this claim is based on a sounder "theoretical" framework for the assertion that the *impact* of SbT upon the human race is rapidly reaching an asymptotic value—a new plateau. We will also find that quite a few perceptive scientists are saying roughly the same thing.

SbT is a human activity, carried out by humans, and having its effect on humans.The simple reason why the scientific revolution is over is that we have saturated the human capacities, reached the limits of the absorption and utilization of scientific knowledge in a further meaningful way by the human race. Humanity is the predicate of the subject SbT. SbT itself, I believe, will soon be limited by the *Limits to Growth* in use of resources, albeit at levels slightly different from those suggested in the original book. The "limits to growth" of SbT *impacts* are fundamental. They are rooted first of all in the physical, biological, psychological, and sociological capacities of the human species. This theme has been developed at length by Ervin Laszlo in his book *The Inner Limits of Mankind.* He writes:

> *The critical but as yet generally unrecognized issue confronting mankind is that its truly decisive limits are inner, not outer. They are not physical limits due to the finiteness or vulnerability of this world, but psychological, cultural and, above all, political limits inner to people and societies, manifested by individual and collective mismanagement, irresponsibility and myopia.*
>
> *Many world problems involve outer limits, but most of them are due fundamentally to inner limits. There are hardly any world problems that cannot be traced to human agency and which could not be overcome by appropriate changes in human behavior. The root causes even of physical and ecological problems are the inner constraints on our vision and values. We suffer from a serious case of "culture lag." Living on the threshold of a new age, we squabble among ourselves to acquire or retain the privileges of bygone times. We cast about for innovating ways to satisfy obsolete values. We manage individual crises while heading toward collective catastrophes. We contemplate changing almost anything on this earth but ourselves.*

SbT has delivered about as much as the human system can absorb.

While the knowledge base of SbT can and will expand, such knowledge will have less and less to say to humanity. Furthermore, such knowledge will acquire the characteristics—indeed, much of everyday science has already done so—of the medieval discussion on the number of angels which could dance on the head of a pin. Finally, the pinch-off of science funding will be accelerated as the public realizes that it will not be able to realize the benefits in health, comfort, or entertainment which earlier investments in science had produced. To put it most succinctly: the growth of the power of the machine will be limited by the capacity of the individual or collective "man" on the other side of the "man-machine" interface, not by the power of the machine.

Before I proceed to give examples of the already evident limitations, let me be very clear as to what I am *not* saying. First, I do not expect any sharp, step-wise change in scientific activities. I *am* asserting that we are well past the inflection point in the S-curve and we can see and project to the plateau or asymptotic value ahead. Second, I am not saying that the "benefits" of SbT cannot be expanded and proliferated horizontally, to use current science policy language, to millions and billions of new customers. Color television sets may well "penetrate" the markets of Central Africa and Micronesia. Modern aircraft will transport villagers out of Central China. Telephones will link the highlands of Ecuador with remote mining camps in Siberia. Computers and video discs will add some useful, but mainly trivial, convenience or access to information for us in the West. To the person in Zimbabwe or the Aleutian Islands, the first arriving new miracles of SbT will carry a profound impact. But to the nontechnical power brokers in London, Munich, Novosibirsk, or Palo Alto, each new phenomenon or gadget will now be received increasingly with a yawn. So what? Unless it plays in Peoria or sells in Sydney, it is not really interesting.

Future Shock—No!

Alvin Toffler stirred the imagination of a college generation with his dramatic visions of the continuing marvels of technology and how their impact would radically affect society. As is so often the case, by the time the idea of *Future Shock* was "in," it was in fact passé. The nonscientist Toffler described very well the recent past, and we will return to the realities of "Present Shock." But, in 1966, John Platt, a physical-chemist who had turned his acute observational powers toward society, had written in his *Step to Man* about the plateaus in science and technology. The following owes much to him.

In my courses with college students, the way in which we approach the question of plateaus is to ask each student to describe quantitatively the differences in the daily lives of their great-grandparents, grandparents,

parents, and their own. What did they eat? What was the nature of their work? What tools or power did they command? With whom and how did they communicate? How fast and how far could they travel? We will use the United States and Western Europe as the models of an advanced technological culture, and consider not only what is *possible,* but also the degree to which any particular material or social device is available to a sufficient fraction of the population, to decide whether it can be considered *characteristic of the culture.* The plateau effect can be illustrated by reference to the major person-impacting technologies.

COMMUNICATION OF INFORMATION

From personal conversations with family and neighbors plus a few dozen letters per year, and a newspaper and magazine now and then, in 100 years our rural Pennsylvania resident has gone to:

a. 6–8 hours of TV signals, of voice and picture in color, at the speed of light from any part of the world (conceivably from the moon or planets!) *per day.*
b. Instant (after the 30 seconds for dialing) interactive communication with up to 100 persons among the 100–200 million telephone subscribers in the West, *every week.*
c. A veritable torrent of newspapers, magazines, letters—much of it unrequested and undesired—delivered *daily.* *

Now the question: Will the change continue at this pace? The answer is an unequivocal NO! The qualitative figure (Fig. 1.2) shows why. With respect to speed and information-density, when we can transmit 3-D and color TV signals from Nairobi to New York at the speed of light, there is nothing more we can add. The speed of light is an absolute limit. Perhaps more significant is the fact that the system is "receiver-limited." Our Pennsylvania citizen simply doesn't have any more time or interest. (Transmission of smell and taste and touch has not been found to be either effective or worthwhile; nor would it make a particularly important impact.)

Human beings receive signals by sight, sound, touch, taste and smell, with more highly differentiated information coming via the first two. Today's communication technologies already can provide total saturation of the capacity of the human system for the average citizen of the West. So neither in speed of communication nor in amount can there be

* I open my mail next to the waste basket. An increasing percentage goes unopened into the waste basket. The scientific literature has become so voluminous that we cannot even keep up with the titles and abstracts.

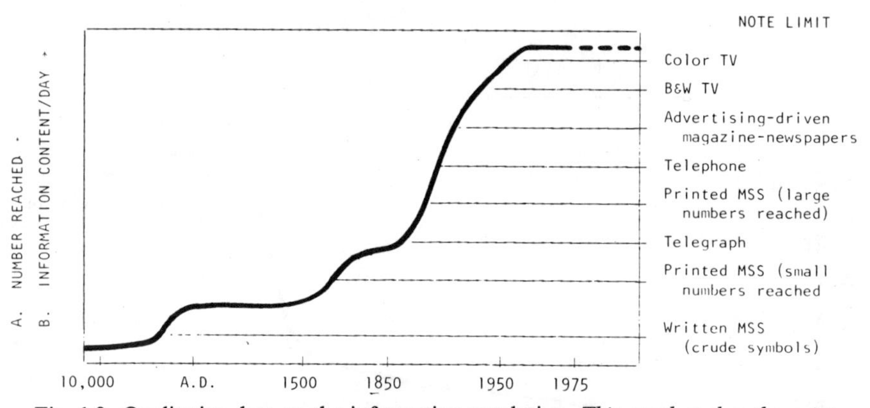

Fig. 1.2. Qualitative data on the information revolution. *This graph makes the point that each innovation's impact eventually saturates at a new plateau. The latest plateau is qualitatively different since the* receiver *is now saturated.*

any substantial change. (In all these statements, there is some exaggeration involved, since I use the approximation of "the average middle-class American or West European," knowing full well that substantial proportions of the population do not yet have the (dubious) benefit of these technologies. The point is always that *impacting* technological advance has plateaued.)

The curve for the highest speed of travel available for ordinary citizens (thus excluding the few dozen test pilots and astronauts worldwide) shows the same plateau, but a steeper rise toward it. The locomotive followed by the automobile brought in speeds of 50–100 miles an hour; the piston-engined airplane and the postwar jet brought us up to 600 miles per hour. But, one might say, we already have supersonic jets and missiles traveling at 2,000–10,000 miles an hour. Why, then, do I believe that the top speed-for-citizens will plateau? Here again, we have an example of receiver-limitation. The human recipient of this technology has rejected even the supersonic transport plane (SST) (so far) for a simple reason. The time gained by traveling at 2000 mph as compared to 600 mph is not significant for the distances usually involved, compared to the total travel time. The latter includes physical and psychological preparation for travel, getting to and from airports, checking in, delays due to air traffic congestion, and baggage handling, etc. Add to this the new energy situation, and it is highly unlikely that this plateau at 600 mph will be exceeded for a long time. To make our point about an asymptote to our achievements in a more absolute sense, instead of speed of travel one could plot speed of transmission of information. (Fig. 1.3). Here we see

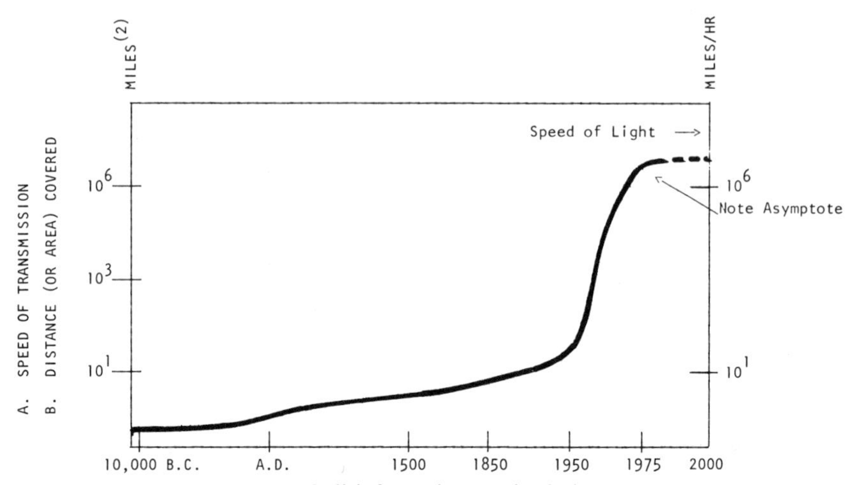

Fig. 1.3. Weighted average of all information received. *Two points should be noted: first, in the developed world, most of our information transmission is at the absolute limit of the speed of light; second, the area of news gathering covers the whole world which contains everything that most humans are interested in.*

the strong exponential increase but, also, the very sharp reaching of the asymptotic or limiting value at the unsurpassable value of the speed of light.

DESTRUCTIVE POWER

I will describe in detail only one other example of a plateau attained. I choose the technological capacity for one person or a small group of persons to destroy (kill) other persons. On the vertical axis (Fig. 1.4), I plot the number of human beings which could be killed as a result of a deliberate order, using the latest technology at hand. We have also stretched out the time-axis this time to go back to the beginning of civilization. (This measure of technological destructive power is not, of course, the same as the total number killed in a war or by pestilence.)

Until the invention of the bow and arrow, one human being could kill a handful of others. At the Battle of Hastings, a group of archers could kill in the tens. With the coming of firearms, this number rose, and by World War I bombs could kill several hundreds. The block-busters of World War II could kill thousands, and the A-bomb of Hiroshima raised this to the low hundreds of thousands. Now, consider the system which has more or less been available since the early seventies. With the megatonnage H-weapons, the MIRVed capacity of the most sophisticated missiles, and the triad of delivery systems (missiles, airplanes, and submarines), there is literally enough destructive capacity to kill every man,

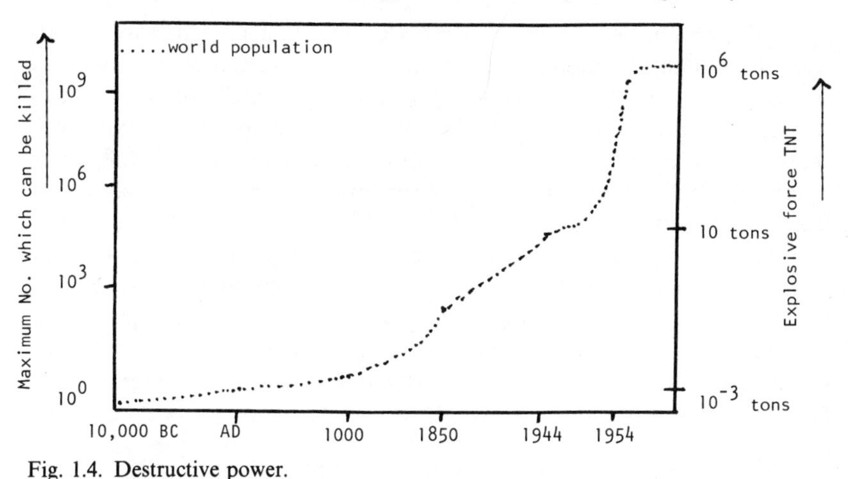

Fig. 1.4. Destructive power.

woman, and child on earth ten times over. John Platt makes the point that in 1944 the largest bombs were equal to 20 tons of TNT. The Hiroshima bomb was about 20 kilo (thousand) tons. By 1954, there were already 20-mega (million) ton H-bombs. Thus, we had a millionfold increase in destructive power in one decade. This was and is, clearly, an unsustainable growth rate. The presidents of the United States and USSR can *today* "press a button" which will decree the immediate death of hundreds of millions, and the possible extinction of most life on earth. That surely represents an ultimate sort of plateau in humanity's powers—the power to destroy most human life on earth. Fortunately, there is little room for growth in this power which has already grown over 1000 fold in 100 years and 50 fold in the last 50 years.

Many other examples may be cited of a plateau being reached in the capacity of science and technology to continue its advances whether or not such advances have major impacts on humankind. Intrinsic to science itself are examples such as:

1. Humanity's partial escape from its terrestrial birthplace is surely one of the most stunning achievements of science and technology. As an applied scientist, fully aware of everything that goes wrong in the laboratory every morning, I have nothing but awe-struck admiration for my colleagues in NASA and their Soviet counterparts who could send instruments and men to the moon, *"and bring them back alive."* From Sputnik to Vanguard and Explorer, from Kosmos to Apollo Salyut and Soyuz-Apollo, and from these to Mariner and Viking, the names of explorer ships multiply, but—and here is the point—they generate *now* only yawns as the responses of the public. The fact is that there is nothing much more

to do in space that we *can do.* In 1957, we couldn't get off the earth. With Sputnik, humanity attained "escape velocity." Ten years later (roughly) we had the power and speed and controls to get to the moon, and the planets. We have done so. Today we have the same power, but nowhere (new) to go. Remember, it takes months and years to visit the inner planets. In 1990, the distances will be the same; in 2000, the same. Maybe the velocities can be increased somewhat, but, and this is the key point, there is nowhere new to go. Why? Because once we leave the solar system, it would take tens of thousands of years to reach the *nearest* star. The next place is too far to be of interest (to this generation of taxpayers), especially since any possible benefits—mainly in a minor additon to our knowledge of astronomy—are so miniscule and of such little impact. Humanity's capabilities are bumping up against the absolute ceiling of Nature's givenness.

2. In the 1930s the resolution in the capability of our microscopes to look at smaller and smaller objects had been stable at an earlier plateau near a micron (one ten-thousandth of a centimeter) for 100 years. Analyzing the structure of matter was limited by the wavelength of light. Then, by using electrons, this barrier was penetrated, and my colleague at Penn State, Professor Erwin Muller, by the 1950s, was among the first to "see atoms." Our resolutions had reached atomic dimensions which are measured in a few angstroms (or one ten–thousandth of the previous plateau). Today, hundreds of commercial electron and ion microscopes can "see" and even analyze the same individual atoms. But this time, by the very nature of solid matter—since the constitutive and characteristic arrangements which describe and distinguish each separate kind of matter are made up of atoms—there is literally no more *distinctive* fine structure to see.

3. The increase in capacity and speed of computers, accompanied by a decrease in cost, is truly lengendary. All those fantastic-sounding facts are true. The computer which filled several rooms now sits on the top of a desk. The largest memories which were counted in "kilo (thousand) bits" hardly 30 years ago are now up to "giga (billion) bits"—a millionfold increase. We will no doubt have some more compaction in the storage systems as we go from the integrated silicon chip technology, to magnetic bubbles, and perhaps to dielectrostatic holographic methods. But the memory is already a very small part of the system. Continued reduction in size is nearing a plateau. The *speeds* in the new systems cooled in liquid helium already have reached the velocity of light: here, no further advance is possible. The results may be seen mirrored in the prices of the simplest hand calculators. In one decade, they fell from say $100 to $10, and have plateaued there for a simple reason: that is the cost of the materials and the costs of marketing and distribution. They can only go up in

cost now; technological innovation has met its twin nemeses: resource limits and human limitations.

This projection of a plateau in scientific advance appears here and there in the writing of a variety of very thoughtful scientists. It does not, therefore, represent a personal idiosyncratic bias which fits my case. Here is Victor Weisskopf, formerly head of M.I.T.'s Physics department and Director General of C.E.R.N. in Europe, speaking:

> *Very few scientists today would maintain that there are new fundamental principles to be discovered with regard to life or the other phenomena I have mentioned. . . . Nonetheless there is today a general belief that the basic principles of the atomic world are known and no additional law or principle is necessary in order to explain the phenomena of the atomic realm, including the existence and development of life.*

And even though most scientists expect the new "revolutions" to come in the field of biology, it is Gunther Stent, the molecular geneticist at the University of California, who writes in his *Paradoxes of Progress: "Scientific knowledge, like our Universe, must be finite and the most significant laws of nature will soon have been discovered"* and concludes that *progress as we have known it is nearing an end.*

I do not believe that the full force of this approaching plateau in science and technology has been even dimly perceived by either the philosophers of science or the national R&D policymakers. Although Platt's seminal book appeared in 1966, the dozens of committees setting national R&D policy in Washington, on many of which I serve, all plan within the framework of a linear growth and progression hypothesis. The public keeps expecting new "miracles" on schedule. Strangest of all, the anti-technology activists have not grasped the momentous significance of the coming SbT plateau, up the brow of which humankind appears now to be scrambling. To close this section, let me summarize:

- The scientific establishment in its very success has come very close, in the last 30 years, to a series of absolute limits: atomic dimensions in "seeing" matter; the dimensions of the solar system and its nearest neighbors for space adventure; the speed of light in the speed of communication of information.
- The technological establishment is *now* up against both these absolute limits and new limitations which, though not at all absolute in the same sense, are as real in their impact. The first of these is the "saturation effect" of the spectacular or the powerful. The public's reaction of deja vu will determine the decline in space budgets. The costs of "big science" are already starting to put the lid on further advance in certain lines. (The cost of each "modern miracle" even in medicine, where the alleged benefits are so *obvious* and *generally applicable,* are leading to the "enough is enough" reaction.) Most important, the "inner limits"

of human abilities to accept, absorb, and organize to utilize SbT will prove insuperable.

Many readers will no doubt have wondered about my exclusion of the "biological revolution" so far. The reason is not only my lack of direct expertise in the field, but also that it is the one exception to much that has been said above. But first to calibrate ourselves.* The fact is that there has been, to date, no "biological *technological* revolution." The health technologies which have impacted humanity are those of improved sanitation, availability of pure water, improved diets, better living conditions, etc. Though much ballyhooed, the wonders of "modern medicine" from the 606 of Salvarsan (to cure syphilis) through aspirin, the antibiotics, the new psychotropics, and the currently fashionable prostaglandins, to the miracles of modern surgery have not impacted anywhere near as many as the mundane preventive health measures. The net result of the impact of modern *advanced* medicine and surgery in keeping people alive at enormous cost has been to raise the life expectancy of a 60-year-old male in the United States by a couple of years since the turn of the century. Better preventive health measures have largely accounted for the increase in life expectancy among perhaps the two billion poorer citizens of this world, from say 25 years in 1950 to 45 years today.

So far, the one major impacting "biotechnology" is that of artificial contraception. This is at the heart of a sociological and psychological revolution that may dwarf all others since the dawn of history, because of what it means for the role of women in society and to the fundamental interpersonal equation which impacts 100 percent of humankind. I will return to this topic of contraception, the sexual revolution, women's liberation, and the nature of the "family" in a later chapter. Suffice it to report that here, also, there are no new *technological surprises in store.* True, we will probably soon have implantable, semipermanent (i.e., for years), reversible male and female fertility controllers. But though they will be more convenient, their effect will not be different in kind from presently available technologies for birth control.

There is only one new technology possible with awesome potential on the same scale as nuclear weaponry. That is, of course, "death control." Aging research goes on apace. A classic "breakthrough" is possible here. The desire to "live forever" has been implanted in us, I believe, by the same force, the same "Cry" of Kazantzakis, which some call Life and the others, "God." The social and psychological chaos which would result from the discovery of a "pill" that would stop or reverse aging is best left

* There is no doubt that we will learn an enormous amount about the human brain and much new understanding is sure to emerge. New technologies would mean chemical or electrical means of erasing memory or injecting information.

to science fiction writers. Yes, as I observed in a speech before the National Association of Science Fiction writers, the plateau in science and technology is most easily proved by the fact that they (the science fiction writers) have run out of scenarios which are unachievable. Achievement has surpassed even the unfettered imagination. One can also see by studying the science fiction literature that the trend is away from technological marvels to social utopias, from space travel to communal living. All this, with one glaring exception—the possible development of aging or death control, would again confirm our thesis that the SbT revolution is over.

This plateau and the limit to the impact of SbT means is so profound that one is puzzled by the little attention it has received so far. If I am right in my reading of the "cloud now no bigger than a man's hand," the psychological orientation of the world of 2000 toward SbT will be very, very different from that of today. In the next 20 years, the world will have stopped expecting and stopped receiving as many new "miracles/problems." Scientists will not be producing those unexpected "breakthroughs" which often generate as many problems as solutions. They will return to a more quiescent style, only partly because the society that pays the piper will call the tune.

The analogy of a scientific discipline to an ore body is not inappropriate. The same attractions of scientific challenge, of new principles to be discovered, of sudden advances in relevant instrumentation which draw the best minds to a field today also spell out its finite lifetime. A veritable army of talent now descends on every new strike of a mother lode. And in a decade, the race having gone to the swift, those with the biggest machines having scooped up the richest seams, the best minds move on, the R&D managers decree that there is better use for their funds, and the big machines are pulled out. The boom town is replaced by a mere ghost town. But there is always some room for smaller operators to work the lower grade ores and work over the tailings pile. It is only that kind of clean-up science which will be left in many fields.

For the spiritual journey of humanity, the plateau in SbT impact will mean a gradual return from the century-old focus on triumphant conquest of the understanding of nature and of nature itself to new foci as yet unknown.

1.3 Emergence of International Technology as The World Power and Philosophy

While modern science is rapidly nearing a period of stagnation, modern technology is just approaching maturity—and, incidentally, fulfilling the predictions of certain social prophets. For the first time in the history of the world, we have a sharp discontinuity between the economic allegiances and forces, and the political and military allegiances of hundreds of millions of citizens.

The Creator's Apprentice

It was in that masterpiece of percipience, *The Technological Society,* that Jacques Ellul first accurately took the measure of the nature of "Technique." Ellul identified technology as an autonomous force in the world, either bulldozing away the frail edifices of eroded ancient cultures or, in guerilla fashion, infiltrating the skyscrapers of the dominant Judeo-Christian Western bastion. A great deal hinges on the accuracy of this analysis. Is technology the religion of the twentieth century and science its theology? Of course it is! By any of the statistical yardsticks of the social sciences, one would have to claim more achievements for this religion of SbT than for any other. SbT now sets the standards for Truth in East and West alike: earlier that was the function of religion.

But note how in true Ellulian fashion this is achieved. First, science describes some natural phenomenon: the conduction of electrons in a semiconductor or the unexpected growths in a Petri dish. Next, applied science produces something tangible or useful from the knowledge: an integrated circuit combining rectifiers and amplifiers on a pinhead and an antibiotic compound. Then, technology delivers to the hundreds of millions of citizens a tangible product that is useful, often invaluable, or even life-saving: digital watches or hand-held computers, and an entire spectrum of miracle drugs (penicillin, streptomycin, chloromycetin), and on and on. This is "incarnated," embodied truth.

SbT *always* delivers the goods. The Biblical story of the competition between the prophets of Baal and Elijah recounts the testing of truth by its ability to deliver fire. President Kennedy promised to get to the moon in a decade. Many of us in the scientific community cringed because we thought it impossible, but technology got us there a year ahead of schedule.

Technology gets its power in the most democratic way possible. It provides the maximum number of persons with the maximum number of goods and services which they desire. A wise man wrote "Beware what you set your heart upon; it surely shall be yours." Most insidiously of all, technology plays Eve offering humankind new apples every day, *defining what we want by what it can offer.* And thereby hangs our tale—and our fate.

What is more remarkable is that 25 years after the publication of Ellul's *La Technique,* neither philosophers of science nor national planners of technological policy have fully grasped his main thesis. The case can be made that International Technology (IT) is a worldwide power slowly bringing large numbers of individuals (and through them, directly or indirectly, every nation) under its control. The nation-state is not withering, but its power is being destroyed by a new superstate. This superstate (IT) has infiltrated every government because it has fifth columnists planted not only at the highest levels but in the stomachs and hearts of the vast majority. Does the U.S. Secretary of Defense want "verification" ability to back up his case for the SALT II treaty? He does obeisance before the "God of Technology." He lays on the altar his tribute of another few billion dollars. The nation goes along with this ludicrous sacrifice, although as President Eisenhower put it: *"Every gun made, every warship launched, every rocket signifies a thieft from those who hunger and are not fed, those who are cold and are not clothed."* Who would, say that the parallel with other gods and other offerings is farfetched? The golden calves to deliver one from Egyptians, or a few virgins sacrificed before Mayan deities can, by no rational standard, be judged to be any less "sane" or "civilized" than MIRV missiles or MX tracks which deprive millions of health and education the same money could have provided.

Does the local housewife or bank president fear death? Of course! So they vote a half-million dollars for a "CAT-scanner" for the local hospital, that seductive fruit of medical technology which promises that maybe, perhaps, some day, if I were suspected of cancer, it might help the local doctors locate my tumor a tiny bit more precisely. Another sacrificial offering to the "Gods of IT."

Thus, by satisfying the most obvious and most basic *felt* needs (food, shelter, clothing, security, entertainment) of the masses, *in the most direct, and quickest manner,* with little concern for the infinitely complex impacts in space and time, technology has made slaves of humanity. The new bargain is as old as the "Old Covenant": "I shall be your God and ye shall be my people." Look at this for a "deal:"

IT (International Technology) guarantees the following:
BENEFITS:

National & Personal "Security"	*Health*	*Comfort*	and	*Riskless Adventure*
better weapons, arms; financial security, etc.	longer lives, less pain, less disease.	less work, more leisure, power at our finger tips.		Spectator activities from sports to drama to help us pump adrenalin into our systems, sitting in our armchairs.

In exchange it has demanded the following:
COSTS:

Breaking ties to all earlier authorities: God, tradition, family, which were the bases of security.	Less control of our own health and how we live and die.	Mobility for stability, conformity to mass values.	Trading action for reflection, other directedness for inner directedness.

The parallel to the God of Moses is even closer. It is technology which has "brought (many of the world's people) out of Egypt" and "delivered them from bondage." Petroleum technology has put the Middle East, Nigeria, and Venezuela into Canaan, if not Eden. It is technology that has literally elevated Hong Kong, Singapore, and Taiwan out of the depths of Asian poverty and squalor into at least the forecourts of the technological palace.

The debate on whether technology is humanity's slave or master has been inadequately formulated and addressed. Robert Sarnoff, one of the major forces in developing the Radio Corporation of America and long its chief executive officer, presents the positivist view: *"Rather than determining our destiny, technology is increasing our ability to master it. It is giving us the means to shape our future,* and the capacity—if not always the will—*to act, not merely react."* (Emphasis added) Contrast Ellul's formulation: *"In the modern world the most dangerous form of determinism is the technological phenomenon."* The truth lies somewhere "in between," but in a special sense. Sarnoff is historically right: technology *was* humanity's slave from earliest times and is still partly so. But Ellul is more relevant: technology *today* is increasingly out of control; the slave has become more powerful than its master, and there appears to be no conceivable way to bring IT under control. Moreover, as sociologist Robert Merton remarks: *"The essential point, according to Ellul, is that technique produces all this without plan; no one wills it or arranges that it be so. Our technical civilization does not result from a Machiavellian scheme. It is a response to the laws of development of technique."*

Is there a sorcerer to undo what his apprentice let loose? The concept of humanity as cocreator with God is now a commonplace, especially among process theologians. "Cocreator" is, I submit, too advanced a rank; at best we are only apprentices. The dimensions of the obvious bungles and subtle errors which the Creator's apprentices have managed would have been wonderful grist for Goethe's mill. J. D. Bernal, the British physicist spotted the danger inherent in scientific "curiosity" 50 years ago. He commented in 1929: *"The scientists are not masters of the destiny of science; the changes they bring about may, without their knowing it, force them into positions which they would never have chosen. Their curiosity and its effects may be stronger than their humanity."* (Oppenheimer and Szilard made similar statements 20 years later after the development of atomic weapons.)

But a more subtle truth would elude us if we let the debate hinge on the issue of power. In a world where struggles are termed East-West and North-South, the 'directionality' of a power seems to be critical. With which, if any, of our political vectors is technology aligned? Here again, Ellul recognized early the political neutrality of technology in the major struggles. But there is more to be said, for technology is very, very far from value-free. Is technology a blind juggernaut? Or is it a remotely guided tank clearing the underbrush for Marxism? Or a bomber fleet softening up the Third World for increased domination by the developed nations? Correct answer: None, and all, of the above. If my analysis is correct regarding the changing role of technology with time, then, of course, we can see that while it could have been considered an instrumentality of humanity in the past, IT is now in the driver's seat. The multinational corporations buy and sell the mineral resources of nations—their veritable birthrights for a mess of pottage. With little evil intent, but with much evil as an unintended byproduct, technology organizes the whole world. Developing nations starve because they have turned over food crop lands to cash crop sugarcane or garden vegetables in order to earn dollars, buy tractors, and raise more cane while they starve. The more interesting questions hinge on the intrinsic properties of this emerging world power. For it is with those properties that other *national political philosophies must align themselves* in order to gain political and power benefits.

With respect to the East-West differences, the answer is characteristically ambivalent. Technology is absolutely and inexorably collectivist. It demands and gets regimentation, standardization, planning, and order. The eastern bloc clearly has an advantage in this regard. My scientific colleagues in the Washington establishment are confronted by a paradox and a nightmare. On the one hand, they bemoan the fall from lofty places of the role of SbT in U.S. national life and political favor. They plead for increased budgets—for what purpose is never very clear. We all plead for better planning and continuity of funding of R&D. We see the sorry spectacle of the academic scientists making the annual pilgrimage to Washington to use innuendo and outright deceit to persuade Congress to allocate more money for "basic research" (a meaningless term which, in the context, means simply "money to universities"). The deceit occurs in the implication that more basic research will result in technological superiority, hence, economic health for the United States. As every college student taking a course in science policy now knows, and as increasing numbers of nonuniversity scientists are willing to testify, this claim is distilled poppycock. This is not to argue against or for a particular level of university research, but merely to support the case that such research which pours into the general literature available to the technologists of Japan, Germany, and the USSR does not guarantee improvement in the technological position of the United States.

The paradox which faces U.S. scientists is that the USSR is providing exactly the conditions for science which the former urge. Is the East's system, then, better tuned in the long run to scientific and technological advance? Is Western superiority merely a vestige of a favorable postwar economic position and favorable access to resources? My reluctant conclusion is Yes to both questions. Pure science is elitist and not inherently and directly useful. It was nurtured, in part, first by the culture of Christendom, next by a quasi-church-university system. And in the post World War II explosion of science, it was sustained by powerful leadership not having to respond to populist pressures. Building the edifice of science from quantum theory to the giant accelerators was the cathedral-building of our culture. But no one ever *voted* to build a cathedral. Today, as the populist, direct-democracy tendencies emerge in all democracies, the support for undirected, nonpurposeful atelestic* science is certain to decline there.

But one paradox only leads to another. For the same reason that totalitarian regimes can support science without the consent of their people, so also can they resist the allures of comfort, entertainment, and consumer goods, thereby *limiting international technology's* power over their people and countries. Other ironies are that, as the fruits of technology produced by planned collectivist action become more disseminated, they increase the power of the individual. This power, in turn, is a weakening of every collectivist hold. From private cars to blue jeans to rock music records, small fruits of technology become symbols of protest and freedom. The newer, smaller, transistor radios to bring in Western broadcasts are easier to conceal, undercutting the power that provided them.

Yet more ironies and paradoxes provide evidence that the control of the course of technological development evades us. In a democratic India the father of political nonviolence, Mahatma Gandhi, argued on spiritual

* I have coined the term "telestic," or purposeful, goal-driven science and its opposite "atelestic" to distinguish the only two classes of science which the public understands. Atelestic science is what many university faculty now regard as their birthright—to pursue knowledge wherever it leads. This *is* everyone's right in every field. The issue is: how much should the public pay for this? Telestic science is what the public thinks it is paying for: the science which leads to socially useful or desirable products or information.

grounds against the acceptance of the modern technological pattern for India. He alone had sensed the price that technology would demand in changes in values, in centralization of power, in the move to the cities, and so on. But in a little known watershed decision for humanity at the 1947 Working Committee meetings of the All-India Congress Committee (the soon-to-be-ruling political party), the Father of the Nation lost to his own heir-apparent—Jawaharlal Nehru. The natural scientist trained at Cambridge, responding to the will of the masses, could do no other but speak for the Western ethos and more science and technology. And who would fault Nehru's judgment given his time and place? Thus it was that the mantle of Gandhi—calling for a decentralized society built on locally appropriate technology—fell not on the local Elisha, but was wafted 5000 miles northeast to alight on Mao Tse-tung.

Under a totally authoritarian system for thirty years, from 1948–1978, the People's Republic of China stood apart from and very much outside the control of International Technology. It provided the only major alternative model for "development" of a nation outside the clutches of IT. Yet, in a recantation as dramatic as any in history, the Chinese are now scrambling for a place in line to place their gifts also on the altar of IT. Such are the quirks of history.

The New Power Struggle and the Resurgence of Religious Forces

Within the last decade we have witnessed the partial dissolving of the "East-West" Cold War syndrome. In its place, or at least alongside of it, has emerged the "North-South" tension between all developed countries (East and West) and the large mass of humanity in the developing world. But clearly visible already, I believe, are the intimations of a more fundamental division in all humanity. The image of the "global village" has been given a great deal of visibility. Let us grant the substance of the claim but look more closely at it.

Every nation on earth is fed within a few hours with the same information, via radio, TV, newspapers, and magazines. The same leaders meet at a dizzying succession of sites, the same staffs of foreign secretaries and international bodies develop data, prepare long analyses, and take positions. The question not often asked is: What will be the political party structure within the global village? Conservative-Labor-Liberal; Republican-Democrat; Right-Left; East-West, or North-South?

Let me suggest that the basic division in the global village will likely be the adherents of the IT values and solutions, and its opponents. This division cuts across all the old dividing lines. On the one side stand the forces of "Technique" offering the nearly irresistible Faustian bargain: the cornucopia of modern science and technology is spread before the voter. Only through more technology can the rich get much richer and the poor a little less poor. Who can resist that? The price tag is discreetly hidden: a bewilderingly complex society, intelligible to and increasingly managed by a small elite; a fragile structure because of its very complexity; a structure not tuned to providing the greatest good for the greatest number but the short-run good for sufficient numbers of only those who can continue the present leaders in power. Those distant in time and space and beyond the next election count for very little. IT has long since learned to optimize for the local political climate. In so doing, in Western democracies, it has totally subverted the very electoral process to its own ends. Every democratic leader must pay obeisance to the limited in scope, short-run nature of technological payoffs to get reelected. The electorates see names like Nixon, Carter, Brandt, Giscard d'Estaing, Macmillan, Thatcher, Palme, or Trudeau, but they are mere front men and women for the impersonal powers behind the throne with appropriately digitized names: GM, ICI, BASF, and IBM.

Contemporary Prophets and Prophecies of Disaster

In the global village, arrayed against these powers and their unwitting puppets, the leaders of the nation-states, is a rag-tag band of prophets. They proclaim the coming of IT, call for repentance, point inward for direction, and offer long-term benefits and modest material comfort. This group is more representative of the people of the world, but it is now quite powerless—except, of course, that it may just be right on all counts. Led by the "Naked Fakir," Mahatma Gandhi, prophets of this guild pop up everywhere: Mao Tse-tung in China, Martin Luther King in America, a Pablo Neruda or Ivan Illich south of the border; Pasternak, Solzhenitsyn, and Sakharov east of Eden; and Fritz Schumacher, Barbara Ward, and Jacques Ellul in the cradle of Christendom.

By its very nature, this party can never be tightly organized. In its very diversity is nature's own guarantee of long-term victory. Social evolution will take care of the dinosaurs of excessive complexity. But will the citizens of the global village repair to these banners of a new simplicity, modest control over nature, of new satisfaction in at-oneness with nature and fellow humans? These banners speak against neither science nor technology, but they are for putting SbT in a subservient role to humanity's larger "religious" goals. In every land, a new political alignment is emerging: those who trust IT for salvation—literally, for saving of body, mind, and soul—and those who speak of another way. The emergence of

Mao, Castro, Desai, and Ayatollah Khomeini cannot be read in any other way but as the resistance to IT on a worldwide scale by the reaffirmation of the spirit-dimension. "Man does *not* live by bread alone," even though "bread on the table is always preferred to pie in the sky."

The ultimate political division in the global village is, and is gradually being recognized as, a division along religious lines—it is the followers of science-based technology who affirm IT as the *ultimate* source of value versus those who believe that ultimate values have dimensions beyond the concrete, and that such values have been revealed over the ages and will reappear in humanity's visions and dreams, poems and prayers.

The thesis of my last section—fiercely and derisively contested as it will be by many of my colleagues—has been that our science and technology-dominated culture stands in 1980 near the brow of a plateau, that the steep ascent, the rapid changes in humanity's control of the physical environment are essentially over. We will have some decades (perhaps centuries) to regroup, to recount our spoils, lick our wounds, and turn our creative energies elsewhere. That is the "Good News."

The "Bad News" is that, whereas while humanity struggled across the plains of the Medieval period, and even the first gentle foothills of the seventeenth, eighteenth, and nineteenth centuries, it had a map—imprecise and inaccurate as all maps are, but, nevertheless, it had a religious/philosophical framework which guided its directions. During the headlong rush to the technological ascent of the twentieth century, all the maps seem to have been lost. The "advance party" of humanity stands just below the brow of (what we from our helicopter can see) is a plateau! As the scouts gather at evening to plot their strategy, there is a growing sense of being lost. All look for bearings: compasses strangely disagree, the setting sun is hidden behind clouds, and moss is on all sides of the trees. Some argue that the hill goes on forever, others that they see a plateau, a few urge retreat to get their bearings. Even though no one is certain which way to go they keep moving, hoping for signals that never come.The sense of lostness becomes pervasive. One thing is quite certain: there is no consensus among the most thoughtful leaders on which direction is North, nor which of the nearest hills, all separated by gullies, will lead upward. Meanwhile, the mass of humanity scrambles onward, consuming its way along the seductive technological ladder, but only now sensing from the confusion or silence of the leadership that maybe something is awry.

This metaphor and our more playful parable for this chapter are as good a way to describe the condition of near twenty-first century humanity as any. In this chapter I will try to detail how lost we really are. I will quote the "scouts," the leaders—who think about the present and future of our society—rather than the main body, because it is evident that we are at that stage when the scouts realize that they are lost, but are conferring among themselves. The leaders hesitate to announce the news to the main party, for besides being lost, they know neither what to do nor in which direction to proceed.

1.4 The Bad News: Probability of Calamity

In the sections above, a case has been made first that the world and the "religions of man" are in a radically new situation or context—one dominated by an all-pervading science and technology. However, it has also been claimed that a part of the scientific community now predicts a major easing in the rate of scientific discoveries and of development of new technologies which will have a major impact on large numbers of persons. This section will claim that paired with this "good news" is much "bad news." During the past century of very rapid change, technology, as it became ascendant, cut loose from its moorings within Greco-Judeo-Christian culture and so disoriented all of civilization that it destroyed or affected deleteriously the frames of reference which are the vertebrate structure of cultures.

Is this large claim the solitary opinion of a Jeremiah? No! In this section, I want to quote from a large number of the most prominent members of the guild of prophets to show that many assessments of the state of Western culture and its prognosis for the future are surprisingly similar and remarkably pessimistic.

At the end of his book *Technological Man,* Victor Ferkiss, who examines the proposition that technology was influencing and creating a new "technological man" adapted to the new environment, concludes as follows:

> *Technological man, then, does not exist. There is no new man emerging to replace the economic man of industrial society or the liberal democratic man of the bourgeois political order. The new technology has not produced a new human type, provided with a technological world view adequate to give* cultural meaning to the existential revolution. *Bourgeois man continues dominant just as his social order persists, while his political and cultural orders disintegrate.*

Donald Michael, then Director of the Center for Research on Utilization of Scientific Knowledge at the University of Michigan, in reviewing Ferkiss' book, comments: *"However, at least this reviewer heartily, if desparingly, subscribes to his conclusion."* But Michael goes further. He takes Ferkiss to task for the latter's last ditch effort to clutch at some straw:

> *If this sounds utopian . . . utopia may be the only viable social system in the world to come. . . . If this sounds as though Ferkiss finally leaves the cat unbelled,*

I would argue that the situation is even more disheartening. The author omits attention to what seems to me to be the most disturbing fact of all: we don't have a bell, much less a skilled volunteer to attach it.

Again, Michael criticizes Ferkiss for pointing out only the physical and biological resistances to change in contemporary "industrial man." Michael's own research in sociopsychological factors involved in change casts an even deeper pall of gloom:

The risks of individual, interpersonal, and organizational failure involved in deliberately accepting the uncertainty that must accompany organizational and individual change are usually too great for men to take willingly when things are going well and when men and institutions have been successful. They are so great, so threatening, that men and institutions will insist that only incremental changes are needed to keep things going well or will resort to the mythology Ferkiss debunks and insist the changes are already happening.

In Michael's view we are left with an insuperable difficulty: *"We don't now know how to become technological man,"* which is in Ferkiss' long analysis *"the race's only salvation."*

These predictions for the future of the interaction of "Technology and Man" are not atypical, but perhaps they represent only the perspective of the social scientist. Let us switch, therefore, to the views of Carl Friedrich von Weizsäcker, distinguished nuclear physicist and one of the last survivors of that small club of physicists "present at the creation" of modern physics. Von Weizsäcker, in middle life, took up philosophy professionally while retaining his interest in quantum mechanics. For the last several years, not only has he been deeply involved at the highest levels of world science policy, but has been Director of a new Max Planck Institute created for him, with the imposing title "For the Study of Living Conditions in the Scientific-Technological World."

We will quote von Weizsäcker on other matters later. Here I wish only to allude to his systematic examination of the probability of a major nuclear holocaust in the next few decades. Some of his results are presented in his book *Wege in der Gefahr.* (The English edition, which is titled *The Politics of Peril,* interestingly enough omits the chapter giving the elementary mathematical treatment of these probabilities.) In the most measured, uninflammatory, unsensational, calm language, Weizsäcker presents his five theses:

1. World War III is likely.
2. A policy which prevents war is feasible and is being attempted today.
3. This policy encounters obstacles which are rooted in social structures.

4. To overcome the obstacles confronting a war, prevention policy requires a comprehensive transformation of consciousness.
5. A war prevention policy must be conducted in such a way that it facilitates and does not impede the transformation of consciousness.

And since he agrees with all other experts such as Ferkiss, Heilbroner, and Roszak that the transformation of consciousness simply is not taking place, "war becomes likely." In a later interview at the Center for the Study of Developing Institutions, he said:

> *We are not closer to peace. I said my answer was going to be ambiguous. The awareness of people means that war is an institution which must be overcome. But a war worse than any we have ever seen will most probably come.*
>
> *I say it is absolutely natural to expect that, since there have been wars for at least six thousand years, there will continue to be wars in the future. Also, it is quite natural to expect that such wars will be more horrible than any earlier wars, because of the technical means that can now be used.*
>
> *. . . the awareness of the necessity of peace has increased. But knowledge of the ways to preserve peace has not sufficiently increased. I do not see a sufficient change in social structures and institutions to avoid the next war.*
>
> Q. No previous weapon, however horrible it might have been, has prevented war. So why should we suppose that, because new weapons will be more horrible than any previous weapons, they will not be used?
>
> Weizsäcker: *I quite agree with you. My guess is that they will be used.*
>
> Q. Then the consciousness of the horribleness of war comes to nothing in the end.
>
> Weizsäcker: *Consciousness often comes to nothing in human existence.*

Since those words were written, the Cold War has heated up, perhaps even faster than in von Weizsäcker's computer models—with Backfire bombers, cruise missiles, and MX systems being traded in a battle of "disarmament" through rearmament. A reading of the reactions to von Weizsäcker's presentation at the Center is instructive, since it illustrates so precisely what Donald Michael claimed above about resistance to change. A large number of distinguished technocrats insisted that "only incremental changes are needed to keep things going well." Very few are willing to wrestle with the *technologically defined* fact that there is a high probability (unless we make *radical* changes) that there will be a nuclear holocaust before the year 2000.

Let me give another example of the opinion of a major analyst of science–technology matters. Certainly, C. P. Snow (now Lord Snow) qualifies as one of the early analysts of the relation of SbT and culture. Some two years ago, Lord Snow spent several days at our university and, during that time, we were able to have him discuss over a two to three hour period his present views on this topic. His position was that there seemed to be no way to bring the direction of technology under human control.

Snow went on to say something I have quoted very often (*my* paraphrase): *"I am not a religious man—I wish I could be but I am not—but the only thing that could contain and direct the technological enterprise would be a framework as large as the world's great religions."* Again, Snow could see no way of getting from here to there, even if "there" were only vaguely defined.

Here is Vannevar Bush, author of *Science—the Endless Frontier,* the principal manifesto of modern American science, which formed the philosophical background for the postwar development of SbT, in an interview 30 years later:

> Q. Science should be concerned with the quality of human life as well as the quantity of it. For example, at a recent meeting in Sweden of Nobel Laureates, science was accused of leaching the meaning out of life and reducing everything to a materialistic rationale. Would you care to comment on that accusation?
>
> *A. I do regret the fact that many a young chap in science today gets carried away with it—so does the public. The young scientist is likely to turn toward a crass materialism. I do think that a very considerable part of the unrest we see about us today is because the old religions have been fading and nothing has fully taken their place.*

My last reference in this connection is to Robert Heilbroner, the author of *Inquiry into the Human Prospect.* Again, Heilbroner is basically pessimistic about the possibility of changing national societies. Remarkably enough, he also, at a later date, comes up with a statement virtually identical to that of Snow. His model for the future is that of "tightly disciplined, ascetic religious orders." He finds some of this technology under the heteronomy of religion in the Chinese model which has *"a careful control over industrialization, an economic policy calculated to untrain rather than to stimulate individual consumptive appetites, and above all* an organizing religiosity *expressed through the credos and observations of a socialist church."* (Emphasis added)

My own observations over the last 15 years run parallel to the ideas of Snow and Heilbroner. As I was writing these words, an old Latin quote—one of the targets I attacked vigorously in my youth—came to mind. *"Nulla salus extra ecclesiam."* (*"No salvation outside the Church."*) How strange to find secular humanists concluding that there is no hope for the technology-human pair outside of a religious framework—the existential meaning of Church. My evidence, which points in the same direction, comes from my experience in Eastern Europe and the USSR, which I visit frequently in connection with my research.

For over a decade, I have reported to my friends on my return from a visit that, *in many ways,* the Soviet Union is surfacing again as a deeply "Christian culture," just as the West is losing every vestige of the hold of Christendom. The fact of centralized control in the USSR and China has enabled these countries to introduce technological innovation at a rate compatible with their system's own values—i.e., under the heteronomy of religion! Here, again, the paradox. Just as the scientific community may find many of their R&D "plans" for science best carried out in the USSR, so the right wing religious community would find decency, order, hard work, no pornography, respect for tradition and culture, not to mention the expensive restoration of churches (only as museums, of course!) in the very country they set up as the model of the anathema. In 1961, in his parable *The Voice of the Dolphins,* Leo Szilard, that Renaissance man *par excellence,* physicist-idealist-activist, had a fanciful scenario in which Russia made a decision to forego war, abolishing its Navy, Air Force, and much of its Army. The savings brought her economy up to U.S. standards. In addition, it made much of the propaganda advantage gained. *"They said over and over again, that Russia was the only truly Christian nation, since she alone, among the great powers, was upholding the Sixth Commandment."*

We all know that the day-to-day political and social realities in the USSR are very far from a "Helsinki Declaration" let alone a "truly Christian nation." But for all of Alexander Solzhenitsyn's devastating critique of his motherland's government, he above all longs for religious hegemony over technological culture. This is unacceptable to the vast majority in the West; even though in principle it is not different, I believe, from what would be advocated by Snow and Heilbroner. The plebs, the hoi-polloi, in our global village have voted with feet and pocketbook to become total slaves of International Technology. Solzhenitsyn, Snow, and Heilbroner all see the present course of the world—a rampant, uncontrolled IT—as leading to disaster. They all know that only a globally acceptable, religious world view is a big and (possibly) a strong enough net to contain and manage IT.

Marxism-Leninism officially espouses a touchingly naive faith in the power of science and technology, albeit only within its own "religious" framework. So far, as we have noted above, the slowly weakening power of such state religion has not been crossed by the individual's rising demands for the fruits of IT and, hence, allegiance to it. But every day brings that crossover closer. The following comparison of the typical response of Soviet academician Markov to an interviewer, with the more contemporary reaction of Jermen Gvishiani, son-in-law of Khrushchev, and among the most powerful of Soviet technocrats today, will illustrate this change.

Q. One conclusion I drew from my seventy interviews with Western scientists was that they almost all seemed pessimistic about the future. In socialist countries my experience is different. When I related to Prof. Moisey A. Markov that Toynbee had expressed grave concern to me about the future of his grandchildren, Markov replied, "I, too, have grandchildren, but I am sure they will have a great future."

A. (Gvishiani). *Looking after the destiny of future generations is our prime and honorable task. But at the same time it is a difficult task. Here, I do not share the views of some Western scientists who do not believe in the ultimate victory of human wisdom or in the happy future of our children and grandchildren. On the other hand, though opposed to pessimistic viewpoints, I should like to caution against unwarranted optimism.*

As the Russians and Chinese vie to acquire more and more Western technology, they become victims of the same illusions of the Western captains of industry of 50 years ago. Thus is the Christian heresy, Marxism, in Eastern Europe cast in the role of Western culture's last defense against IT. G. K. Chesterton's lines:

Where risen from a doubtful seat and half attained stall
The last knight of Europe takes weapons from the wall.

written about the battle of Lepanto when the enemy was Islam sound strangely apposite. But any victories for the Eastern Crypto-Christian Marxism are likely to be as short-lived as the victory at Lepanto. If the forces of International Technology are to be overcome, it will not be by frontal attack from the left or by the right wing forces of a faded nineteenth century Christendom attempting to mend a tattered old fundamentalism with a patch of ultra-modern nylon. Jesus explicitly forecast the chances of success of such patchwork in his parable of the new wineskins.

How other religious cultures can control, confront, or adapt to IT is far less clear. Up to now, the depredations of the invading force and the taking control by the forces of IT in Asia and Africa seem complete. The traditional religions of the region as experienced and practiced by the masses are being swept aside with hardly a battle. Islam will be a particularly interesting case. Because of the cosmic fluke of the location of much of the earth's oil, the change from one culture to another will be sharpest in some of the Middle Eastern countries. The 1979 response in Iran is a major battle in the war just beginning. The evaluation from within Islam is summarized by F. Zakaria as follows:

In Western Christian circles, ultra-modern currents in science are completely assimilated, their implications objectively discussed. By contrast, Islamic religious circles restrict themselves to generalities; their knowledge is, for the most part, outdated, their analyses superficial. Thus their treatment of the problems raised by the progress of science and technology is far from being up-to-date. As a matter of fact, a great deal of the discussions that take place about the science-faith issue, in the

> *Islamic world, are still related to the very basic principles of scientific thinking, e.g., whether to accept or to reject the rational explanation of the Universe, whether there are natural causes, what role the Supernatural plays in determining the cause of events . . .*

Turning further east, although we may with some hope speak of the tradition of assimilation and adaptation which characterizes both India-based and China–based religion, it would be naive to expect any SbT *controlling* forces from these religious traditions to emerge with sufficient relevance or power to provide Lord Snow's plea for a religious framework to contain and direct technology.

At the same meeting at which F. Zakaria spoke, M. Palihawadana was unequivocal about the present status of Buddhist leaders' response to science and technology in the following terms:

> *From the Buddhist point of view, the scientific enlargement of the understanding of man and the world is quite welcome* only if it is conducted within the framework of the value system of Buddhism. *While this may be inimical to science that is linked to power and violence, it does not at all affect the vast potentialities before science to aid the development of mankind materially and even to a considerable extent otherwise.* (Emphasis added)

While the position that I will develop will be completely consonant with the emphasis in the above, the tenor of this passage is much closer to that of Newton in the seventeenth century or of Church leaders in the nineteenth century before the impact of developed science and technology was really appreciated. Another speaker from Islam, Dr. O. El-Kholy spoke in nearly identical words of the *past* attitude within Islam:

> *This Islamic epistemology enabled Muslim scholars to discover and apply what we now call the scientific method. Inductive methods and sources of knowledge were separated from the deductive, physics from metaphysics, chemistry from alchemy, astronomy from astrology and facts from values,* while maintaining the supremacy of divine values. (Emphasis added)

But are these religious frameworks of the past of any value in confronting modern international science and technology within their respective cultures? Hardly. There is no special theoretical affinity between these frameworks—indeed, much less so than in Christianity—and SbT. The human desires for the fruits of IT are already universally visible if not available to all. We cannot look to any presently constituted world religion for the slightest help in containing or taming the activities of SbT.

On the world scale, we are confronted by technologically created problems of a variety, scope, and character that are truly mindboggling. Neither Christian theologians nor any others have been able to even weigh and size up these problems and construct some hierarchy within which to study and attack them. Consider, for example, the following current problems all caused by, and potentially controllable by, directing our science and technology: making food available to all world citizens; the availability of kidney machines to the poor; the safety of coal or nuclear power plants; the availability of genetic counseling; the control of nuclear weapons; the thousands killed by drunken drivers. By what procedure would one decide which of these problems is more urgent or important than another? Even the rare lay or clerical theologian dealing with SbT matters prefers to start with the deductive theological issues, rather than the real world where humans first feel the impacts of reality, theological or technological. This was dramatically illustrated by the 1979 World Council of Churches meeting at M.I.T. where no effort was made to produce such a "BIG PICTURE," which presumably is the forte of the Churches. In order to identify those opportunities or problems that are really the most significant, with the greatest potential impact on humanity, one must think systematically about the numbers involved, the intensity of the impact, and its duration. This is a task for which there is the greatest distaste among all non-technically trained humans. Yet as William Blake wrote: *"He who would do good to another must do it in Minute Particulars. General Good is the plea of the scoundrel hypocrite and flatterer, for Art and Science cannot exist but in minutely organized Particulars."*

One such analysis of the "minutely organized particulars" shows, for instance, a list of the technologies and their relative impacts on human society (see Table 1.1). It can be seen that within this or any other set, the ethics and actualities of the preparations for nuclear war occupies a unique position. It is not one issue among many, it is the final problem, it demands an *absolute priority*. Yet, it has received until very recently what can at best be described as passing mention, and virtually zero action from the entire religious community in the West. The fight against weapons testing above ground was led by scientists—Einstein, Russell, and Pauling—who were joined by multitudes motivated partly by a selfish concern for their *own* health as well as for the millions of *others'* lives at stake. Andrei Sakharov, Nobel laureate, father of the Russian's own bombs, and courageous Soviet dissident, put it this way: *"I believe that the problem of lessening the danger of annihilating humanity in a nuclear war carries an ABSOLUTE PRIORITY over all other considerations."*

Such analyses—and it is not, I have found, difficult to get qualitative agreement on the general results of such—are the starting point for the expression of concern or love for one's fellow human beings and society. It shows, contrary to much emotional reaction, that, for example, the banking technologies which keep wealth badly distributed are much

Table 1.1. *HIERARCHY OF RELATIVE IMPORTANCE OF PROBLEMS*

A beginning on the task of carrying out the "agapeic calculus"—a semiquantitative assessment of the interacting influence which determines the relative impacts of various human actions—here limited to technologies—on human society. These very approximate *numbers—which, nevertheless, allow us* order of magnitude *comparisons—are obtained using the following relationships:*

$$\textit{Impact} = \underset{\textit{potentially affected}}{\textit{Number}} \times \textit{Probability} \times \underset{\textit{of effect}}{\textit{Intensity*}} \times \underset{\textit{of effect}}{\textit{Duration*}}$$

(**Both calculated as person years of life lost via % disability*)

Technology	*Impact**	*Comments*
Nuclear War	1,000,000	
Population/Consumption Explosion	10,000	
Appropriate (meaningful) Employment	1,000	
Resources & Wealth; *Distribution*	500	Technologies which preserve inequities among and within nations.
Resource Availability & Usage (total)	300	
a) Food	(100)	
b) Energy (total)	(100)	
Choices among sources	(10)	= The relative difference between use of one source or another (e.g., nuclear vs. coal) is minor.
c) Minerals (total)	(80)	
Choices	(10)	
Environmental Impact of Human Activity (total)	100	
Choices among options	(20)	Relative differences between alternative paths of amelioration is small.

more "impacting" than, say, the differences between two forms of energy supply or health effects of cyclamates.

But what can you or I *do* about nuclear war or world famine or the just use of international resources? The task of stopping the juggernaut appears hopeless, if not downright disheartening. What I, who study and teach this kind of material continuously, am struck by is the fact that the idea of the *probability of calamity is almost universally shared by all who have thought and written about the issues.* This list includes the rare person like von Weizsäcker with a deeply philosophical and religious bias, but also dozens of other scholars who have addressed the issue. No reader should proceed further without asking herself/himself on what basis s/he thinks otherwise. Before we turn to a (Christian) situation theology and a situation ethic we will examine the actual spectrum of responses which are being made within our culture to this bleak human prospect.

1.5 Differing Public Responses to the Present Situation

If there is such unanimity on the part of the experts, how does the general public, or even that fraction of it which makes up the readers of this book, respond to these gloomy forecasts? We can recognize three or four different groups or types of responses. By and large, it would not be unfair to say that most persons simply ignore or avoid the issue altogether. Here are six groups:

1. *"Eat, drink and be merry . . ."* The present situation is perceived by the thoughtful leadership as an impending crisis of survival. Yet, if one were to conduct a statistical survey of the response of the general population in the developed West, it would show that the vast majority of the population had no *conscious* awareness of it. The simple reality that much of contemporary American society was built on the premise of cheap inexhaustible energy, which was swept away by OPEC in 1974, has never been understood by the general U.S. populace in 1979. In five years, the main "penetration" of the fact of the disappearance of one major prop of the economy is the vague "metafact" of "something wrong in the energy supply." Although the first and continuing effect to be felt by the population was in the resulting inflation, no connection was made between the two. Even long lines at gasoline stations have only a temporary effect. The response to the "metafact" and especially to the most prominent tangible effect, inflation, has been *to enjoy it while it lasts.* The Biblical view of human nature is again and again proved to be accurate. The sales of motor homes which plumetted in 1974 were at record levels by 1978; second houses and pleasure boat sales pushed upward. For those who can, "eat, drink and be merry" is definitely the response of the majority.

2. *"Business as usual . . ."* While the general public has only dealt with the "metafact" of "something slightly wrong," the mainstream of Western technological life has simply continued doing "business as usual." Technology in this view is infinitely adjustable. The "market forces"—that other major deity—will soon right the ships of state, the winds of endless consumerism will fill the sails, and it will be smooth sailing again. If energy becomes expensive, technology will help us adjust. IT will provide smaller cars, build more energy—efficient refrigerators, and invent solar panels or breeder reactors. If Zaire won't sell the United States cobalt or Rhodesia its chromium, then the research laboratories of M.I.T. or Cambridge or Grenoble will come up with substitutes which use manganese or rare earths instead. If one polymer (plastic) does not biodegrade, we'll make another that does. More technology is the answer to the problems created by technology.

Thus, by avoiding all social and political problems which constrain technology, the technological empires continue to function day-to-day, even as their leaders sense trouble ahead.

3. *The new narcissism.* For a short decade, a vigorous hedonism—pursuit of every pleasure and comfort—gripped America. The pursuit of comfort in home and car, the pleasures of travel, new experiences in food and sex were national preoccupations. These were slowly replaced by a less active narcissism. This held sway over the psyche of the American upper middle class, but it also is now moderated and is, perhaps, in retreat. As with so much else, the "hedonist-narcissist movement" was a creation of the media. The drug era was ushered in not by street pushers alone, but by the pseudo-psychology and seductive-sell of LIFE and LOOK. "Psychedelic" was an "in" word. While anti-Vietnam war protests provided a bedrock of legitimacy, many new trends came together to create a dramatic new climate for the affirmation of Self (as against Other).

Later, I will treat this new narcissism as an expression of the new Religion of Self with its roots deep in Western—perhaps only American—middle class psychology. For our purposes here, suffice it to note that the new narcissism provided the legitimization for millions to enter new levels of consumption and spending of time, energy, and money on the attainment of pleasure and the fulfillment of every personal desire or wish. The world, for a few short decades, was literally the prosperous Westerner's oyster. For a substantial part of the population, the problems of impacting technology do not exist.

4. *Disengaging; dropping out.* The direct opposite of the business-as-usual syndrome is the modern dropout from the fray, not from life. Many dropouts are tired activists, others confirmed narcissists. There is an element of both "eat, drink, and be merry" and "of business-as-usual" in this syndrome. But its characteristic feature is *less* striving, *less* action, *less* engagement with the world. It is manifest in the retreat from city to suburbs, from suburbs to exurbia, and on to a little farm twenty miles from work. It is all old tweeds and pipes, woodburning stoves, and natural foods. Some even want most of the comforts of technology, but in a setting "close to nature." And no more causes, please! All political and social action is futile—as proved by the days of Camelot and the Great Society—so count me out. In the meantime, I shall be gentler with the people around me and with nature. My aspiration—to use today's satirical expression—is to be "well tanned and mellow." My pleasures are simple: avocados and bean sprouts, hot tubs, a good hi-fi set up with quadrophonic sound, lots of hugging, much nudity, and a little extra sex.

5. *Turning East.* Let me consider another response by reverting to the first person of a WASP college student in a Western center of learning.

> *Since the activism of my parents' western liberal tradition has obviously not produced a society which I can approve, and since I am repelled by the materialism of the narcissist middle class, I must search for a new identity in which I can feel worthy and justified. Instead of material goods I shall seek spiritual values; I will seek Eastern quietism to substitute for Western triumphalism; instead of social activism outward I will seek the Divine within in a long journey inward.*

Out of such personal rejections of the melange of the Christian faith, Western capitalism, and American consumerism came the extraordinary birth of Eastern cults in the United States and, soon crossing the Atlantic firebreak, in Europe. The Maharishi Mahesh Yogi was able to bottle the virtues of prayer and quiet and sell it to millions under the imposing title of "Transcendental Meditation." The Hare Krishna sect or the claims of a 15-year-old boy who hinted at divinity of some kind were taken seriously enough by thousands to propel the latter into the millionaire class in a year or two. The Rev. Sun Myung Moon rode the Eastern wave and the yearning for discipline of ANY kind. Supported partly by political connections to the U.S. right wing; he, nevertheless, went to extraordinary lengths—as I have noted earlier—to purchase intellectual respectability by hitching his wagon to the SbT star.

Yet we find that these Eastern cults share some features:

a. An identity-creating set-apartness including some visible mark of distinctiveness. At the least, this consisted of an Eastern mystique of books, incense, and diet; for some, the distinctive dress, and, in the most extreme case, the shaved heads and dress and public demonstrations of the Hare Krishna sect.
b. A concentration on inward journeys—abjuring political and social action.
c. Some positive *demands* on the individual, and a tightly disciplined structure of comradeship to support her/him in it.
d. A positive effort to find an ally in, and legitimation from, modern science and technology.

The very special significance of this East-looking response is that, for good or ill, it channeled the vital fluids of the traditional Christian idealism of American youth away from society's needs for at least a decade. The secularization of the "missionary concern" which began with the Peace Corps had led to its gradual withering away. The Eastward-inward drift was on.

6. *Counting on the structure, even if it is rudderless and adrift.* This is the description of an emerging minority, especially prevalent in the conservative Protestant and Catholic churches. It is a return to the old and fa-

miliar structures of faith. Back to church and Sunday school: the old form, old hymns, old piety, old Biblical literalism, old morality. The enemies are easily identified: modernism, including science and technology; the obsession with sexual "sins"—from sex education in public schools to gay liberation—to the total exclusion of all others, especially avarice and pride. Here we have a warmed-over limp anticommunism. In the most systematic effort ever made to force new wine into very old wineskins, it has all the earmarks of Custer's last stand; it is probably the last gasp of Western Christendom in the old style.

This response, in my view, is a tragic error for people still strongly drawn to the institutional church, especially the large numbers in the United States. The failure of many of the mindless excesses of the late sixties was preordained since they were undertaken in the spirit of a release from the prison of religious bondage. What a ghastly parody on the Christian faith, that instead of inviting the newly freed prisoners to join a happy, disciplined band of scouts journeying together to shape the future of the world, this alternative invites them back into the prison within a new fortress America, secure against the invasion by the world.

1.6 A Christian Way: A Strong Hand on the Tiller and a Good Compass

These different responses to the present represent a spectrum of options which, taken together, are being chosen by the large majority.

In singling out this last response, I am stepping aside from the main line of my argument and placing myself into the position of the active religious person in the West. Most such are lay or clerical Christians who use a common value framework, myth structure, and language. Is there yet one other way which such Christians, and others, may choose? What is the most creative response in the face of extreme danger, of a bleak outlook, and of seemingly hopeless odds? First, reinforcement of hope is, indeed, needed, and many eminent theologians, notably Jürgen Moltmann, have made this their special focus. Jacques Ellul has also addressed this problem explicitly in his recent book, *Hope in a Time of Abandonment.* I fully believe that a very different response to those described above can be made on the grounds of the most concrete SbT realism and consistent with religious and Christian insight.

I start with an aphorism of Norman Cousins, former editor of the *Saturday Review* and tireless champion of innumerable worthy causes. "I do not know enough to act like a pessimist," says Cousins. His point, which is literally true, is that no one knows what the future holds. We are in for surprise after surprise—the more the change, the more the surprise. The most amazing events or results of events sometimes radically transform the situation.

Let me start with one example to show how badly the very best of our technological forecasts can be in error. After the OPEC tripling of oil prices in 1974, it was concluded on the basis of dozens of national and international studies that this would mean total disaster for the economies of the Third World. The case of India was especially poignant, since India's meager reserves of foreign exchange, built up as she recovered from the costs of many famines, would now be totally depleted in paying for oil. There seemed to be absolutely no way out: the oil was essential, there was no conceivable way in which any additional export commodities could be brought into production for years or decades. Yet, instead of disaster, the oil crisis provided the most significant major *infusion* of hard currency in the nation's entire history. How? With the oil money flowing into the Middle East, an unexpected, unforeseen need developed. The Middle East needed trained workers. India has always had a surplus of such labor. Trained personnel became the immediately available export; and these citizens became a conduit for the flow of hard currency back to the mother country so that, in three years, India's reserves of hard currency had risen to the highest point ever. So much for our ability to predict the economic future.

The openness of the future is the bedrock of honest Christian hope. *"The unexpected is the gift of God,"* as Dumitriu put it. I do not need to invoke anything other than simple observational, empirical, scientifically verifiable facts. In the statistics of historical events we have absolutely no way by which we can predict local or individual happenings. The Christian continues her/his journey through life guided by distant fixed stars, long-range goals, ready to use any new event as the opportunity for serving. When Revelation affirms *"Behold I make all things new,"* it reminds us that the open future is where our faithfulness will be tested. *"The unexpected is the gift of God, and the basis for human hope."*

But let us look at a more common human response to a new situation full of threat or to obvious danger ahead: i.e., to try to take shelter in the past. We have seen this as the chracteristic response of a substantial fraction of the body religious of America in the late seventies. It is attempting to move the clock back, toward simpler times when there were no drugs or crime or birth control pills. It urges its followers to act as if the secularization of the Church had not occurred, as though the repetition of Bible verses will ward off the devil. Pierre Teilhard de Chardin, speaking out of his experience of arduous paleontological exploration all over the world, urges a very different course of action:

> *I am as conscious as anyone of the gravity of the present situation for mankind. . . . And yet some instinct, developed in contact with life's long past, tells me that for us salvation lies in the direction of the very danger that so terrifies us. . . . We are like travellers caught up in a current, trying to make our way back: an impossible and a fatal course. Salvation for us lies ahead, beyond the rapids. We must not turn back—we need a strong hand on the tiller, and a good compass* ["Esquisse d'un univers personnel," May 4, 1953].

In a time of rapid change and shifting landmarks amidst the seductive appeals to narrower and narrower self-interest, these two insights suffice. We need a reasonably accurate map, a good compass (*an understanding of our complex culture, a knowledge of the laws of reality—both of science and religion*), and a firm hand on the tiller (*avoiding turns in response to short-range trends*). In a time when victories will be rare, we will be sustained by the conviction that our calling is to faithfulness to our best insights irrespective of the probability of successes.

But what of the really desperate situations where the forces of injustice and exploitation and coercion exercise their power over us, as is so routine in so many everyday situations in the structures of the world, where the unexpected is circumscribed by the certain? Here I can only bear witness to the powerful effect which a single book has had on me. Petru Dumitriu's *Incognito* describes both the outward circumstances and the inward responses of a crypto– or incognito Christian in communist Rumania. We have become all too familiar with such situations and the realities of life in Gulags or Dachaus. What is novel and moving and gripping is Dumitriu's mystical, yet utterly practical, response to the situation of despair. Two passages give the flavor of his inward-reinforced stance:

> *What is difficult is to love the world as it is now, while it is doing what it is doing to me, and causing those nearest to me to suffer, and so many others. What is difficult is to bless the material world which contains the Central Committee and the Securisti; to love and pardon them. Even to bless them, for they are one of the faces of God, terrifying and sad.*
>
> *What is difficult is that, if I am arrested and tortured again, love must not for an instant be extinguished in my heart. If I fling myself under a train I must do it, not that I myself may escape but to save others, and I must love the world, every being, every object, every fact that it contains, more than ever at the last moment.*

> *. . . . for if I love the world as it is, I am already changing it: a first fragment of the world has been changed, and that is my own heart. Through this first fragment the light of God, His goodness and His love penetrate into the midst of His anger and sorrow and darkness, dispelling them as the smile on a human face dispels the lowered brows and the frowning gaze.*
>
> *What is most difficult of all? It is not to desire the world and my own situation to change, but to bring about this change without desiring it by sincerely and from the depths of my heart entrusting to the hands of God the fate of those dearest to me, my own fate and the fate of the whole world: for these are God's own fate. I will compel God by acquiescing in His will.*

What I found to be of great meaning, and why I give this book (never published in the United States) as my gift to any friends who dare to step onto the platform of holy worldliness, is the self-consistent naturalness with which Dumitriu's intense inward life and extreme circumstances are held together.

No one can be without hope who believes what is so obviously true. "If I love the world as it is, then I am changing it." Dumitriu is the quintessentially contemporary human—the Christian incognito—precisely because he can confront the worldly situation in which one is genuinely impotent, as most of us are realizing we are most of the time, without despair or anger or overly grandiose plans.

The New Lifestyle—Incognito

Ten years after the appearance of *Incognito* in French, Ellul's *L'Esperance oubliée* (*Hope in an Age of Abandonment*) picked up the theme of the *Incognito.* Let it be noted that both Dumitriu and Ellul are laymen deeply immersed in the objects of their observation—the technology of politics and the politics of technology. They start with their feet firmly planted in the realism of experience of our world of East and West, when political maneuvering is the staff of life and media illusion its wine. But their attitude to participation in the world's activities, even its social "gospel," is unique. One can distinguish such a Christian response to the context in which we *do* theology today by three new marks formulated by Ellul:

1. It is "present in the world" and actively participating in movements for justice and peace. Yet the nature of this "presence" has undergone some revision. *"I was, I think one of the first, if not the first, to spread the slogan: 'Presence to the modern world.' Am I taking it all back by announcing the incognito? I do not think so. . . . It is the manner of the presence to the modern world which has changed for me, and not its importance nor its necessity."*

2. It recognizes that "good works" *may* not bear witness to the Truth. *"Likewise the incognito does not consist in 'bearing witness by our works, by service, by our presence,' with no mention of witness. There is no witness through works. There is no witness unless there is union, agreement, and interaction between work and word. The incognito goes much deeper than those little ways of accommodation and adaptation to our society, much deeper than living easily in this world."*

3. It is a style of life characterized by the integrity of a person, supported by a community of other incogniti, but which appears to be totally elided into worldly actions. *"It is a matter of reminding the firm and constant bearer of a truth which is no longer uttered. There is incognito when*

behind a mask or a pseudonym there is a person, who is a person because he has chosen to be buried in this incognito, has chosen to hide the serious and the decisive.

"It is a matter of not for one moment changing this truth because others no longer believe it, or because it is incapable of being shared with others. There is incognito only in the unflagging perserverance behind these masks. Hence it is the creation of a seeming accommodation, of an acceptance of everything done in this world. It is a seeming accommodation only. . . ."

Meaningful Hope: Keeping Going Under Adverse Circumstances

Hope is based on a paradoxical mixture of certainties of the past, coupled with the uncertainties of the future. Now, is this the usual theological double-talk or simply nostalgia, with the Church as usual marching backward into the nineteenth century? Let me explain why this is a cold, sober, scientific basis for hope. We have seen in the preceding paragraphs that there is always a genuine openness in the future. We cannot predict either an individual's or society's future in detail, although we can do rather well with the *broad* outlines of *large* areas in the *short* run.* The future will throw up unexpected new options among which humanity will have to choose. Christian hope is based on the absolute ground of experience. As we look backward carefully and selectively and affirm those of the Gospel's guidelines which have made for the most creative behavior of humankind as judged in the light of history, we provide the surest set of selection criteria to choose among the future's options. The grounds for Christian hope: the future is absolutely certain to provide unexpected options. The past provides the absolutely reliable criterion of our policy for action (= faith), ex-selfish** caring, to help us select among these options.

The hope for any of us is not for any immediate success of a project or a plan, but the transcendent hope of the Resurrection. Translated into

* An analog is to be found in weather forecasting. It is quite remarkable how utterly insignificant has been the progress of this science—in either prediction or control of the weather on a local scale (tens of miles) or for a long period (months). I live in a city which houses one of the largest weather predicting industries in the country, yet I am no more certain in being able to plan a picnic a week ahead, nor in predicting whether this winter will be unusually severe, than I would have been fifty years ago. Yet with this fantastic array of satellites and computers, we can *describe* the weather in broad terms anywhere in the world, and give general forecasts of conditions in broad areas for some days ahead.

** I coin the term "ex-selfish" in response to the extensive criticism by many in my generation of excessive emphasis on "unselfishness" to the point of self-hatred. "Ex-selfish" suggests a concern for other persons and structures, based upon an established selfhood.

English and into our daily plans, this means that in the long run if I add my best intentioned, carefully planned act in support of love or justice to the sum total of all such human acts, then somewhere, someplace more justice will emerge, more love will be made real. It is like diverting a rivulet into a stream trusting that it will feed a reservoir miles away and more power will result therefrom.

There is a much more succinct summary of the proper Christian response to an apparently despairing situation. It is reported that in the late autumn of 1956, in the presidential election campaign which pitted Adlai Stevenson against Dwight Eisenhower, the theologian Reinhold Niebuhr was asked by a reporter how he could be working so hard for Stevenson who, according to the polls, had no chance at all. Niebuhr's reply says it all: *"The Christian is called to be faithful, not necessarily to be successful."* The absolutely demanded response of the Christian, irrespective of the prognostications of success or failure, is to be faithful, to live incognito in the world, striving after justice and mercy, waiting with hope for the Kairos of the gift of the unexpected event, accepting the reality that it may not come even in her/his lifetime, or even within the visible horizon of human history.

Bibliography

The following list includes the books from which some major theme or insight has been taken. It is not meant to be a traditional set of references in a scholarly article since, in this context, an author takes responsibility for the viewpoint expressed, although the viewpoint may have been shaped by dozens of sources (and factors), many of which may not have been explicitly quoted. The list is presented approximately in the order in which corresponding themes appeared in the chapter.

Konrad Lorenz, *Civilized Man's Eight Deadly Sins,* Harcourt Brace Jovanovich, New York, 1974.

Adlai Stevenson, in *Science and Society—A Symposium,* Xerox Corporation, Rochester, New York, 1965.

Fritjof Capra, *The Tao of Physics,* Bantam Edition, New York, 1977.

Raymond B. Cattell, *Beyondism, A New Morality from Science,* Pergamon Press, New York, 1972.

Jacques Ellul, *The Technological Society,* Knopf, New York, 1966.

John R. Platt, *The Step to Man,* Wiley, New York, 1966.

C. F. von Weizsäcker, *The Relevance of Science,* The Gifford Lectures, Collins, London, 1964.

D. H. Meadows, et al., *The Limits to Growth,* New American Library, New York, 1972.

Ervin Laszlo, *The Inner Limits of Mankind,* Pergamon Press, Oxford, 1978.

Victor Ferkiss, *Technological Man, The Myth and the Reality,* Braziller, New York, 1969.

Donald Michael, *Science,* pp. 165, 165 ff. (1969).

C. F. von Weizsäcker, *The Politics of Peril,* Seabury, New York, 1978.

C. A. Coulson, *Science and Christian Belief,* Fontana, London, 1960.

R. L. Heilbroner, *An Inquiry into the Human Prospect,* W. W. Norton, New York, 1974.

L. Szilard, *The Voice of the Dolphins,* Simon and Schuster, New York, 1961.

World Council of Churches: Papers presented at the Conference on "Faith, Science and the Future," M.I.T., July 1979. W.C.C. Press, Geneva, 1980.

Petru Dumitriu, *Incognito,* Collins, London, 1964.

Jacques Ellul, *Hope in a Time of Abandonment,* Seabury, New York, 1977.

D. Brown et al., editor, *Process Philosophy and Christian Thought,* Bobbs-Merrill, New York, 1971. (Especially sec. 2, "God," pp. 173ff. and chapters by Schubert Ogden, Charles Hartshorne, and John Cobb.)

Rustum Roy, "Interdisciplinary Science on Campus—The Elusive Dream," in *Interdisciplinarity and Higher Education.* J. J. Kockelmans, editor. pp. 161–96. The Pennsylvania State University Press, 1979. See also *Chemical and Engineering News* 55 (35) (1977):28–30.

J. Lukasiewicz, "The Ignorance Explosion," *Trans. N.Y. Acad. Science,* May 1972, p. 375.

A. Buzzali-Traverso, *The Scientific Enterprise, Today and Tomorrow,* UNESCO, Paris 1978.

2 Reality: Where Religion and Science Meet as Equals

2.0 Synopsis

It is certain that all religions, on the one hand, and science and technology on the other, both claim to describe what is most real in the universe. Both religion and technology (as distinct here from science) start with the individual, and the perception and impact of reality upon her or him. It is, therefore, self-evident that the perceptions of the one and the same reality from the viewpoints of SbT and religion must not only be complementary but, indeed, mutually supportive and synergistic. What has rendered such fruitful interplay less and less active over the last few centuries is the growing linguistic gulf between the two communities. Mathematics, on the one hand, and the stylized "God-talk" on the other have rendered communication well-nigh impossible.

In order to emphasize the point repeatedly, albeit somewhat awkwardly, throughout the rest of the book the use of the word God is consciously avoided and a symbol substituted to call attention to the acute linguistic problem. This chapter is an attempt to show that SbT and religion share a common belief in the nature of the most fundamental reality. Starting with the panentheist position, one elaborates on the concept of the reification of the meaning of the Beyond present in every midst (which some call) into what we call Reality. Reality is the shape which ultimate content, , assumes. The characteristic of *all* approaches to reality is that they reveal levels of meaning and, hence, deeper realities beyond the one studied or recorded. The record of scientific endeavor is one of proceeding from one level of "beyond" to the next.

How the individual forms her or his picture of Reality is systematically examined. Humans need to create a three-dimensional Reality image based on information which is obtained from many directions (viewpoints), across a whole spectrum of human sensors and their responses, and from very different focal lengths (telescopic to microscopic). But the human self is often fragmented into several functional selves, which one can group into the observing (scientific) self, the experiencing self, and the reflecting (or religious) self. The key to the present condition of humanity is the fragmentation or disintegration of the coherent three-dimensional image into separate images, or bits of information.

The road to personal health and societal salvation begins with the construction of an accurately integrated image of Reality. This action develops a distinctive position on the nature of the complementarity between "science" and "religion." They are presented not as dealing with different realms of Reality, e.g., nature and the person, but rather as differences in focus. Religion deals with the big picture, setting a context, interrelating smaller units of reality; science deals, by definition, in a reductionist mode by isolating a small area for detailed study without reference to its context.

The effectiveness of integration in revealing the hidden meanings, the Beyond, is illustrated by contemporary research on "cyclopean" vision and stereopsis. Monocular images, which are genuinely random, when fused binocularly reveal symbols which "are the unique fruits of" integration.

The absolute mandate of the new aproach is to abandon "single vision" or reductionism in religion and SbT, and to adopt a Brahma posture, integrating into a single reality even the many apparent "opposites." This calls for a new attitude to reality—scientific and religious—an ability and willingness to alter focus quickly from the focal length of the one to the other.

2.1 A New Approach to the Problem of "God Language"

The very idea of using a single word for "God" is a characteristically human error! To capture the infinite in one short word, what absurdity!! To name the unnameable; "eternity shut in a span." To break the very laws of "god" which forbid it; *"You shall not make a 'graven' image." "You must not take my name lightly (in vain)."* Why, then, do humans return time and again to this egregious error? Because we must! How shall we speak to each other of the deepest and the highest and the best? Dumitriu states our dilemma:

> *What name was I to use? "God," I murmured, "God." How else should I address Him. O Universe? O Heap? O Whole? as "Father" or "Mother"? I might as well call him "Uncle." As "Lord"? I might as well say, "Dear Sir," or "Dear Comrade." How could I say "Lord" to the air I breathed and my own lungs which breathed the air? "My child"? But He contained me, preceded me, created me. "Thou" is His name, to which "God" may be added. For "I" and "me" are no more than a pause between the immensity of the universe which is Him and the very depth of our self, which is also Him.*

Yet, if humanity is to merge into a new synthesis, the best from East and West and North and South, most especially if it will synthesize its deepest religious insights matured in the flesh and bone of millenia, with the new powerful intellectual insight into the nature of Reality, of its own modern science and technology, I believe we must be willing to pay the price of abandoning the simplistic use of the word "God." Why? Because it totally confuses the process of communication since the same word means so many different things to different people, and to the same person at different times. Each individual's personal history, family, and community and national ties give the word a specificity we seek here to overcome or avoid. A printed word (much more so even than a spoken word) provides the appearance of finitude and limitation, of definition and specificity. The power of "naming" the beasts of creation (Gen. 2:19) is a symbol of humanity's power over nature. But how can the *creature* claim the same power over the *Creator*. Dumitriu's dilemma in using any name may still be resolved as he himself does it. While we may not speak to others *of* God (since there is no shared meaning to the word), we may, of course, speak *to* God ourselves for that only involves our personal reality. But even if we begin there, we must end with a hesitation, a no, and in silence, when asked to name the unnameable among ourselves. Dag Hammarskjöld fit so well Dumitriu's model of the "Incogniti," those persons whose life policy (= faith) and observable actions are so wholly consistent that they appear simultaneously as the fully dedicated, very effective worldly functionary (in his case, as Secretary General of the United Nations) and to others as the shining witness to the integrated mystical Christian life in the world. In a most significant passage, Hammarskjöld stresses what our culture irresponsibly and universally ignores. In its more complete form the quotation, already mentioned on p. vii runs:

> Respect for the word *is the first commandment in the discipline by which a man can be educated to maturity—intellectual, emotional, and moral.*
>
> *Respect for the word—to employ it with scrupulous care and an incorruptible heartfelt love of truth—is essential if there is to be any growth in a society or in the human race.*
>
> *To misuse the word is to show contempt for man. It undermines the bridges and poisons the wells. It causes Man to regress down the long path of his evolution.*
>
> *"But I say unto you, that every idle word that men speak. . . ."*

As we begin to construct a "theology" based on our observations of reality and of each others' life-policies, we will naturally run into the word "God." In this book, we cannot defer further this most difficult question—the matter of naming the Infinite, the problem of "God-language." To share about the most important issues of existence we must use—even if *in part only*—words; and that, we will show, is the cause of much of our inability to communicate effectively.

How, then, shall we be careful about this unformed word which is literally the densest-in-meaning symbol in the universe? Shall we paste a warning label on it? "FRAGILE, handle with care." "This side up." Shall we find another word? Use one that is less tainted by familiarity? I decided part way through preparing for this book to try an experiment. Could it be done? Could a book be written on theology without using the word "God"?

I propose to follow both an ancient Hebrew tradition and modern theories of learning, and use an *unfamiliar* symbol to represent "God." In the following pages therefore, I will use , a truly random pattern of black dots on a white space as the symbol for the full meaning of "Ultimate Reality," the "I am," the "Ground of Being," the "God above gods," the "Creator of the Universe," the "Infinite concentration of Being and Meaning." I chose this symbol after much wrestling with a half-dozen options. Among the first options considered was a white space or blank. This would make the reader repeatedly aware of the undefined, the necessity continually to enlarge one's own ideas of "God," and to write in, so to speak, his or her own present understanding of . Another alternative considered very strongly was to use the Hebrew word YHWH from which is derived Yahweh and Jehovah. This would be an effective symbol for most readers who are unfamiliar with Hebrew, and it would provide a link with the Judaic tradition. For those with some theological training, it would immediately provide the connection to exactly the same problem which the Jewish tradition has struggled with for millenia, from the time of 's response to Moses: "I am that I am." The choice of a black block as a symbol had a strong appeal. For me, one most attractive connotation was that it was dense with meaning; there was enough ink there to make up many sentences. It had, moreover, scientific affinity to the recently discovered black-holes, with their strangeness and extreme denseness. The black symbol was also more attention-getting; it was sharply defined and stood out from the rest.

But it was this last property and the suggestion of a close friend which ultimately led me to the present choice. A pattern of dots, with no sharp boundaries from its background, has great synergism with many of the concepts introduced herein. Our concept of cannot have sharp boundaries for it seeps out to pervade every thing and every being. It is not made up of familiar patterns, but has the substance (dots) which could be rearranged to many patterns. Its authentic randomness reflects the nature of Reality and is tied to one of the major themes of this series. Such an open network cannot hold in its light but positively radiates it outward. It is an appropriate symbol for evolving Reality. If Shakespeare can ask his reader to exercise imagination to supplement *his* words, may I be forgiven if I also seek to enlist the reader's heart and mind in our common task of describing the indescribable. Every time you see that unfamiliar pattern, , hesitate. Let the unformed pattern remind you of our human inadequacy before such a concept. Wherever it is suitable, rearrange the dots in your mind to spell out LOVE, or YHWH, or an image of the Christ on the Cross, the serene Buddha, or the four-faced Brahma. Let the symbol speak of the vastness of creation with each dot an entire solar system, or let it represent our own very tolerable sun, unobtrusively radiant, beneficent, life–sustaining, shining even when eclipsed or clouded over. So shape the symbol to give it most meaning for you. And if is an unsatisfactory image, it will perhaps remind you to write your own enlarged consciousness in the space.

Most "Gods" Have Been (Much) Too Small

J. B. Phillips went only part way in his book titled *Your God Is Too Small.* The most significant theological impact that modern science and technology has had on Judaism and Christianity is on the concept of . The profoundly anthropomorphic limitations placed on a concept suppos-edly with the characteristics of omnipotence and omniscience were exposed first by Galileo and Newton with their discoveries of the nature of the solar system and its possible place in the larger universe. Michelangelo's symbol of the creating finger of was perfectly in keeping with the contemporary understanding of creation and the linguistic framework used by the Church to express its great truths. This framework rests directly on the Old and the New Testaments, with their rich development of the "Father" and "Son" imagery. Jesus refers on several occasions—though hardly in a definitional tone—to "my father." And it is easy enough for persons to forget the analogical nature of the parables and substitute the analogy for the reality. Since Jesus says the "Kingdom of heaven is *like unto* . . . 'the Good Shepherd'; 'the Mustard Seed'; 'the Woman with the Lost Coin,' " it is not difficult to find equated with (and limited to) the Good Shepherd, the Kingdom to a successful enterprise, and so on.

The problem of "God-language" is absolutely central not only to our writing and discussing the nature of , but to our understanding of ourselves, of the whole of reality which surrounds us, and the ordering of our experiences. In order to start afresh, imagine yourself asked to answer the following questions put by a small group of concerned, open, and sympathetic, but totally "unchurched" social workers from the USSR:

- What in the world do you mean by the word "God?"
- How in the world, if you are trying to encompass a concept of the infinite, can you expect to manage with one finite word, and one that has

had attached to it innumerable narrowing qualifications (e.g., He not she; Loving Father instead of Stern Judge; All Goodness, but not Evil, etc.) depending on each individual's personal and cultural history.

- Is not any word certain to be both inaccurate and blasphemous in its partialness?
- Do not the previous connotations of the reader with any name or word effectively filter out the possibility of new learnings about the nature of such?
- Is it not true that if [illegible] is all power and all knowledge, then that which all human learning, all culture says about the truth of science, and all my daily experience of the validity and power of technology MUST surely be wholly and easily consistent with my knowledge of and experience of [illegible]?

It is the last criterion which is the stumbling block on which religion will founder unless it makes substantial changes in its conceptualization and presentation of [illegible]. Each human being's experiences of the everyday world of reality are the most powerful witnesses to the truth that s/he can grasp. In twenty-first century culture, the accuracy and power (together with many negative impacts) of science and technology will increasingly become the single most commonly shared heritage of humankind. Religions will be of two kinds: those which are an alternative to, or escape from, the major realities of life; and those which provide a framework for, and give meaning to, *all* of life including humanity's science and technology. If contemporary religion is to continue in the latter way, it must replace "God" with some new symbol, to shake off the shackles of its own history. The stereotypes now tied to the word "God" are so firmly entrenched that it must be avoided to the extent possible.

2.2 The Goal: A Credible Science-Reinforced Theology

To start as bluntly as possible, I repeat that no significant advance in theology will ever be made again by any religious tradition in any part of the world unless the basic insights of science and technology are fully integrated into it. As the first step, not only the language but the fundamental narrowness of our concepts about "God" must go, to be replaced by reality revealed by both science and religion and moving *through* reality to the beyond.

The central argument of this section and these lectures is that insights from modern science and technology will be the source of a major revitalization toward a new and more "appropriate theology" for the twenty-first century. And that together, SbT and contemporary religion can create a "composite," life-policy* (= faith) which can be crucial to the survival of our world. If one is to attain such a practical end, a day-to-day policy, it is certain that one cannot restrict one's analysis or thought to the fringes or the subtleties of either religion or science. Unfortunately, it is on these fringes where much of the cross talk has taken place so far and why so much of it has been irrelevant to most members of both communities. If we are to help today's citizens develop a working life–policy, the mutual strengthening must be in the central concerns of both. It won't do any more to discuss theories or practices of science or religion which have no observable impacts on the daily lives of the majority. We will deal with the ideas and examples of a different set of scientists who have concerned themselves with the mainstream of human existence. Through my research interests in the high pressure field, I had the privilege of coming to know, professionally, Professor P. W. Bridgman during the last several years of his life. Bridgman won the Nobel Prize for physics for his work in the high pressure properties of materials. His research contribution was made possible by his seemingly mundane advances in the design of instrumentation. His were characteristically "practical" innovations (almost exactly what the Nobel prizes were originally designed to honor). But Bridgman holds another distinction. He is one of the very few major American scientists to have attempted a contribution to philosophy. His books, *Reflections of a Physicist* and *A Philosophy of Physics,* laid the basis for the "operational" school of philosophy. Its major feature was its stress on the centrality of *observable impacts as the only test of reality* in human affairs. This finds a striking parallel with what John Platt, the physical chemist, identifies in *A Step to Man* as the distinctive contribution of Jesus: *Change your life: start here; do it now. Reality-theology,* therefore, has some of its roots in operationalism.

My goal is to find observable, tangible structures of mutual support between SbT and contemporary religion. Science and technology *start,* for the most part, with observable realities. They study these in the minutest detail and with utmost care, and thereby learn to control and manipulate nature present in these realities. Religion, on the other hand, starts with abstract, transcendent axioms (= hypotheses), and from them derives, in part, a finer and finer set of ethical guidelines for observable behavior. And for most ordinary folk, religion is equated to these "observable behaviors." However, SbT also teaches that behind the observ-

* I introduce here the term "life-policy" as a substitute for *one* of the major ways in which the word "faith" is used. As used here, "life-policy" is the analogue for a person, of "foreign policy" or domestic policy for a nation. "Life–policy" defines the principles which guide my life, and in a continuously iterative process is manifest in my actions.

able and tangible realities are deeper levels of reality, and many a scientific construct or image or idea about reality is abstract in the extreme. What is significant for us here is that the starting point and the payoff, when we think of religion or science and technology as a whole, is *a concrete observable behavior.* A science-reinforced theology must start with, not end with, the observable realities.

New Areas of Interaction between SbT and Religion: The Observable Realities

During the last 100 years, science and technology have stolen the basic allegiance—body, mind, and heart—of the world's peoples. Large numbers—as well in the Eastern bloc as in secular Western Europe—have made the switch to SbT as life's policy guide both in principle and in fact. Even larger numbers throughout the world—the entire West, the upper crust of the developing countries—while vague on the principles, are even more loyal to SbT in practice and are fitfully trying to work out some kind of dual loyalty. Only a minority, led by luminaries such as Lewis Mumford and Jacques Ellul, actively resist the science and technology invasion in the area of meaning and purpose, and report on what has been lost by humanity in making accommodations to SbT in matters of everyday life. The vanquished parties which have gradually lost their hegemony over humanity during this century are the high religions of the world.

In the early part of this turnover century, religions fought openly and visibly against this marauding force. All the battles were lost because they were fought on the invader's turf; i.e., over the new discoveries which were the very ground most recently captured by SbT. Since the 1950s religion, in retreat from the fray, has simply and wrongly conceded much of the territory. The new attitude is: "Science knows best about nature, technology, and perhaps even societal problems." Hence, it is best for religion to ignore those older territories and, in a kind of epistemological Monroe doctrine, concentrate on personal morality, the inward journey, or mysticism, where religion appeared to remain unchallenged. It was only here in the heartland of theology—at its most abstract—that religion has felt it is strong enough to meet SbT on its own terms and try to extract from the latter ideas and insights which could strengthen its own basic assertions. This fits the caricature of the "God of the Gaps" strategy often attributed to the religious establishment.

But even here, it has been the scientists that have been doing the innovating in theology. Two examples will do. For decades much has been made by some writers of Heisenberg indeterminacy and the ages-old theological issue of free will. Though I am sure that not one nonscientist in a thousand has any idea what indeterminacy is about, and many fewer have in any sense been helped by these ideas, these are genuine theological struggles.

More recently, along come Fritjof Capra with his *Tao of Physics* and Gary Zukav with his *Dancing Wu Li Masters* to show the parallels of *present* conceptions of theoretical modern physics with selected parts of Chinese and Indian mysticism. While their parallels may or may not have much substance, and while I note that very few will understand them, and even fewer relate them to their lives, it is, nevertheless, pure theology. Observing the *typical purchasers* of the *Tao of Physics* in a university town, I wondered what they made of all the leptons, hadrons, and equations. What I found was: very little. Indeed, physics being seen as an ally of mysticism was about the amount of the learning of physics which actually occurred. In that sense, these books serve to improve the public's effective relation to science. One finds that the typical reader starts with sympathy for the mystical religious concepts, and the diagrams, terminology, and even the equations help make certain intuitive connections *that science somehow reinforces these views.* They do not, in my opinion (as I show in detail later), help form any kind of joint life-policy based on physics and Tao. But it shows clearly the opportunity of our present situation in this area of overlap of two disciplines: "What is there within SbT which can help my religious convictions, which can help shape a personal working faith (= life-policy)?"

With the rapid change in the public's earlier unquestioning stance toward SbT, the overall question of which has the most powerful paradigm for life, the most effective description of all of reality, now means that many scientists will turn (indeed, already are turning) to find support in religion. This mutual leaning on each other by SbT and religion presents an ideal opportunity to undo the sidetracking of the science-religion interaction from the esoteric, by demonstrating their value in the exoteric, the common everyday stuff of life-policy. Neither Judeo-Christian nor any other mainstream religions have, so far, examined the possibility of making common cause with SbT, not only in the area of social action, but in their own "main frame business" of interpreting and dealing with all of Existence or Reality. So far, most of the religious efforts at relating to SbT, for example those just cited, have been gnostic exercises about esoterica, not, perhaps, more positively useful than the negative impacts of the older style quarrels of the Darwin-Wilberforce debates. The enormously desirable interaction which is now possible, indeed essential for the survival of the human species, must occur at much more incarnational levels of religion (directions for the human species; guidance to individuals, communities, and nations about life styles; translation of love into new "laws") and of properly utilizing technology with all its ambivalent impact on every facet of individual daily lives and its overall domination of humanity.

This is where the real opportunity lies. Human beings live in a world of their five senses, perceiving the world, people, and ideas all around. This is the domain of the reality they can see, touch, hear, smell, and taste. There is no doubt in anyone's mind that in this kingdom of the senses, science and technology appear to rule unchallenged. What has religion or theology to say about this "real world," about Damocles' new nuclear sword, the shrinking oil resources, the maldistribution of food, the coexistence of wastage and want, instant communications in color from any point of the globe to another, the catapulting of entire cultures three millennia into the future, the sexual cornucopia and women's liberation, brand new phenomena in the billion years of biological evolution? Is this real world to be conceded to dominion by SbT with nothing but a whimper of plaintive protest?

Surely not. Yet with a very few notable exceptions, this focus on reality has not been where theological battles have been joined, books written, or peace treaties signed. Unless religion were to choose the path of confrontation on behalf of the past, instead of partnership on designing the future, all these must now be done. Not only or primarily because it is the point of opportunity, but because this Reality is the fulcrum for theology as much as it is for SbT. Here is how James Conant, chemist and President Emeritus of Harvard University, put it:

> *The parallel with the common-sense belief that other people exist and with the geologists' belief in a geologic past can hardly be denied. Therefore, I am not inclined to quarrel with those who say that a faith in the reality of the God of Calvin or the God of Catholicism or the Jehovah of Orthodox Judaism is the same sort of faith as faith in a real external world. But I would question the correctness of considering a belief in God which carries no consequences for the believer. . . .*

If theology cannot make sense of what I and every other human perceive as real, as making sense, in 90 percent of my day-to-day existence, then theology will ultimately acquire the character of a hobby or magic parlor tricks. In the first section of this book I have discussed the parlous situation in which the whole world finds itself. In this section I will use everything we call reality as the vehicle of my approach to the "logos" about "theos."

Beginning at the Other End: With the Human Subject

On the face of it, it would appear that any theology, situational or not, should start with the basics—certainly with its affirmation about "God," the object of its study. I will show that this traditional and quite natural approach would be and has been a grave epistemological error. If "God" is the object of the theology's study, humanity is its subject. Before we try to wrestle with the results of the collective human perceptions of "God" we must focus on who is doing the perceiving.

The classical positions* about starting with the affirmations about the givenness and preexistence of God have a semblance of authority. After all, we must start with the preexisting reality. We mortals must start with the immortal. We finite creatures must look to the infinite. We must not try to squeeze the wholly other God into our mold. What these positions have neglected is the subject "we" in each of those statements. Even Karl Barth's "wholly other" is circumscribed by other than whom or what. The starting and reference point of all knowledge is its subject. Our understanding of the limitations of the receiver of information or perceiver of reality will give us an absolutely essential perspective on the total possible interactions of subject and object. Especially as we remind ourselves of the enormous asymmetry—one small-brained human being addressing its own postulate of the infinite, all of reality, manifest as Creator, Sustainer, Ground of Being, Personal Savior—we must take, as St. Paul says, "a sane view of ourselves." We must agree at the start that any human theology is certain to be like sizing up the universe through the small safety peephole in our apartment door. Yet that is all *we* can do. We are humans in our own particular historical situation.

We have discussed the immediate constraints introduced by the historical situation in the last chapter. We now turn to the most fundamental limitations and opportunities which our humanity imposes. And strangely enough, it is scientists who are so sure of human limitations. Bridgman summarizes them as follows, even for the simplest case of narrowly isolated parts of nature which science studies:

> *Finally, I come to what it seems to me may well be from the long range point of view the most revolutionary of the insights to be derived from our recent experiences in physics, more revolutionary than the insights afforded by the discoveries of Galileo and Newton, or of Darwin.* This is the insight that it is impossible to transcend the human reference point.... *The new insight comes from a realization that the structure of nature may eventually be such that our processes of thought do not correspond to it sufficiently to permit us to think about it all. We have already had an intimation of this in the behavior of very small things in the quantum domain . . . there can be no difference of opinion with regard to the dilemma that now confronts us in the direction of the very small. We are now approaching a bound beyond which we are forever estopped from pushing our inquiries, not by the construction of the world,* but by the construction of ourselves. *The world fades out and eludes us because it becomes meaningless. We cannot even express this in the way we would like. We*

* Yet John Calvin already has intimations of the importance of the "receiver–center" approach. He writes in the Institutes, I, 48 *"The knowledge of ourselves is not only an incitement to seek after God, but likewise a considerable assistance towards finding him."*

> *cannot say that there exists a world beyond any knowledge possible to us because of the nature of knowledge. The very concept of existence becomes meaningless. It is literally true that the only way of reacting to this is to shut up. We are now confronted with something truly ineffable. We hae reached the limit of the vision of the great pioneers of science, the vision, namely that we live in a sympathetic world, in that it is comprehensible by our minds.* (Emphasis added)

To this let me add but one more quotation from Max Born to enable me to establish my position that to do theology today we must start with the human subject of this enterprise.

> *I had an elder cousin who was a University student while I was still at school. Apart from lectures on chemistry he attended also a course on philosophy which impressed him. Once he asked me suddenly; "What exactly do you mean when you call this leaf green or the sky blue?" I regarded this question as rather superfluous and answered: "I just mean green and blue because I see these colours like that, exactly as you see them." But this did not satisfy him. "How do you know that I see green exactly as you see it?" My answer, "because all people see it in the same way, of course," still did not satisfy him: "There exist colour-blind people who see the colours differently; some of them, for instance, cannot distinguish red and green." Thus he drove me into a corner and made it plain to me that there is no way to ascertain what another person perceives and that even the statement "he perceives the same as I" has no clear meaning.*
>
> So it dawned upon me that fundamentally everything is subjective—everything without exception. This was a shock.
>
> *The problem was not to distinguish the subjective from the objective, but to understand how to free oneself from the subjective and to arrive at objective statements. I want to say right from the beginning that I have found no satisfactory answer to this in any philosophical treatise. But through my occupation with physics and its neighbour sciences I have arrived, near the end of my life, at a solution which appears to me to some extent acceptable.* (Emphasis added)

From What Kind of SbT Can Theology Benefit?

Every branch of human activity can benefit from the lessons learned in all other areas. But just how much there is to be gained from interaction between any two specific fields is not at all obvious. There is a natural tendency to turn to neighboring fields for interaction. In cases involving mature fields, this is probably a mistake, since such mutual benefit has probably occurred naturally over the years. Thus, theologians considered for some time that an effective contact with the domain of science was being made at the theology-psychology interface. More recently, the shift has been toward sociology. Actually, that record shows that these contacts, while absolutely necessary, have not in fact provided fruitful new conceptualizations. No "paradigm shifts" have resulted from their mutual impact. If one considers the interaction with the physical sciences and the biological sciences, it is clear that the Copernican and Darwinian revolutions caused major shifts in theological paradigms. I believe that it is certain that the most useful mutual learning will continue to come in the same area. The fundamental questions of the meaning of "life," on the one side, and of genetic engineering or a good death on the other, are issues where fundamental biochemistry and biophysics meet fundamental theology. I call this the principle of the "protrusion of the fundament." It is taken from the geological analogy that the hardest and most chemically stable rocks always come to the surface eventually as the softer ones get weathered away. It suggests that theologians would do well to skip over the neighboring fields of the social sciences and examine the natural sciences, the "harder" the better. The principle is merely a recognition of the hierarchical nature of the "laws" describing reality. Thus, the second law of thermodynamics will certainly be obeyed by all matter, inorganic and living. It will be obeyed in any issue of social justice or situation ethics. Its very universality means, of course, that it may not be useful in deciding between two relatively similar options. On the other hand, it will certainly be useful to eliminate impossible options.

Tucked away in these "fundamentals" of physical sciences and engineering are many descriptions of reality which are both universal and "right." In the new increase in interaction between SbT and theology-religion, I believe that we may well encounter useful analogies, models, etc., from this other world, which, although apparently far removed, may, indeed must, share these fundaments. Let me jump ahead of myself for a minute to illustrate. Is there any guidance from the science fundamentals on the question of the most fruitful structure of human community? Well, we do know a great deal about how "societies" of atoms are built into solid matter. We know, for instance, that virtually all of the earth is made up of much matter which has building blocks of polyhedra illustrated below (see Fig. 2.1). Many nonscientific friends find it remarkable that such a very few forms with 4, 6, 8 and 12 sides should be so universal in structuring atomic society. They are surprised that 12 is the maximum coordination number, i.e., the maximum number of atoms which we can pack around a central atom (to touch it). There is at least a sermon topic if not a more fruitful analogy here to guide further reflection, on the structure of interpersonal society. Is the tremendous power of a small group in human affairs a "protrusion of this fundament," this law of physical chemistry? Or, we may phrase it differently and ask if these fundamentals of physical science can hint at the relative importance to our psychological well-being of the immediate small set of significant others, as compared to the interaction with the general public or larger sets of acquaintances. Here again, solid state science tells us that in stable crystals about 90 percent of the stabilizing energy holding the crystal together is in the forces binding a central atom to the 3, 4, 6, 8 or 12 *nearest* neighbors.

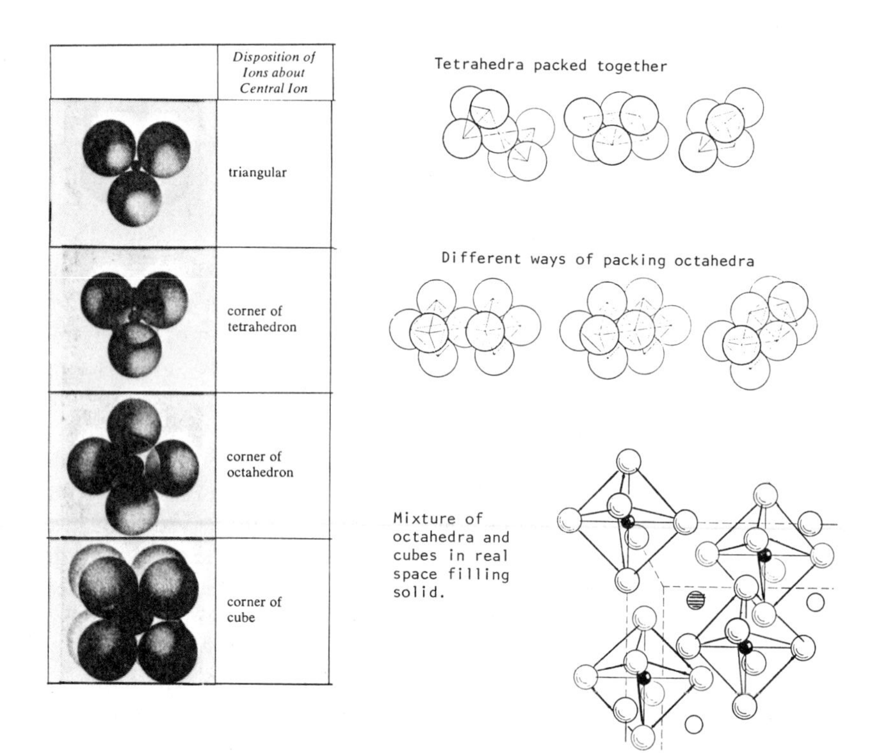

Fig. 2.1. All solid inorganic matter—that is, essentially all the earth, moon, and planets, except for the tiny skin of plant and animal life—is constructed from the mixture of these few (and one or two other) extremely simple forms: polyhedra. Even in the most complex structures, only these forms exist and interpenetrate in a myriad different ways. But no other structural units are created to accommodate the ninety or so different elements. Is there a lesson for society to be drawn from the stability of small symmetrical units? Does this basic scientific "fundament" protrude into human existence?

Perhaps the best recent example of the application of concepts from the "fundament," from physics and chemistry into societal problems, is the recent work of two Nobel laureate physical chemists—Ilya Prigogine and Manfred Eigen. The former has been developing models of urban growth and transportation which start from his insights into the "fluctuations" in systems far from equilibrium. Eigen and his collaborators, in a beautiful book entitled *Das Spiel,* have tried again to draw parallels or connections between statistical thermodynamics, patterned sequences, and relationships, with day-to-day experiences. I refer to this kind of work in passing, only to indicate that I regard it as prototypic of the fruitful interaction between hard science and human affairs which skips the whole region of social sciences, while possibly being directly applicable to society.

We are searching for guidance as to *where* and *how* Sbt and religion and theology can fruitfully interact. I have suggested herein as a new possibility that it would be most profitable to begin with the most basic questions in the field of religion and theology—i.e., those being asked by most people—and see if there are any relevant insights from the most fundamental (if general) principles of science and engineering. As evidence of the possible fruitfulness of this approach, one could note that, in a very well-known paper by Platt and Deutch describing the most impacting discoveries of social sciences, it was found that most were originated by the instruments or work of hard scientists and engineers. One can also cite examples of the counterflow of insight from religion to the basic sciences. In technical terms, one could quite properly assert that Jesus was a most original social scientist. His theory of "unselfish love" (even to turning the other cheek and giving up one's life for one's friend) could be called the First Law of optimal societal functioning. A modern sociobiologist, in the tradition of Konrad Lorenz, looking for the evidence of biological coding of such a character trait called "altruism," is addressing the right question, i.e., one of fundamental importance. Obviously, what can be found, at best, is that, without any knowledge of biology or genetics, the great religious leaders had intuitively or empirically discovered this law—that other-centered love is the most effective guideline in life. These preliminary illustrations are designed to demonstrate that cross-fertilization across the wide chasm separating SbT from religion is a hopeful new approach to potential mutual strengthening.

On What Theology Can One Build?

We start with the question: Is there a theological tradition that can be made intelligible, intellectually and emotionally acceptable and, most importantly and distinctively, synergistic with the insights of SbT?

The unequivocal answer is that a scientifically elaborated panentheism fits all our needs well. Panentheism is the view that [illegible] is known or expressed *through* all Reality. "The key *preposition* is through," as John Robinson put it. Panentheism is the "enthusiastic" affirmation of [illegible], present and manifest to us *through everything*. Every*thing*—that's one point; and the other is that there is no way to [illegible] except *through*—through the world, nature, spring flowers, fall leaves, friends, mother, prayer, Jesus, π-mesons, cups of cold water, and nuclear fireballs. Pantheism is a very different matter. Pantheism *equates* everything with [illegible]. Our parable illuminates the difference. To a pantheist strawberries, sugarcane, beets, and sugar are all "theos." To a pan-en-theist the theos is sweetness, which may be experienced through strawberries, sugarcane, beets, or sugar.

Panentheism has a respectable if relatively short pedigree. Before 1900 the names of F. Socinus and F. H. C. Krause figured prominently in its history. In recent times, however, although most have not used the term extensively, the majority of the "Process" school of theology should be called panentheists. Already, the compatibility of *this* approach with scientific world views becomes clearer. A. N. Whitehead and the school which followed him, notably Hartshorne, John Cobb, and Schubert Ogden have contributed to these positions. Nicholas Berdyaev and, most significantly, Pierre Teilhard de Chardin—again, without using the label or being as clear as we shall attempt to be—have espoused a panentheist stance. Two quotations will suffice to show both the similarity with the process school and also the distinctive parts of what is to follow. Schubert Ogden puts the case for the process school:

> *Among the most significant intellectual achievements of the 20th century has been the creation at last of a neoclassical alternative to the metaphysics and philosophical theology of our classical tradition. Especially through the work of Alfred North Whitehead and . . . Charles Hartshorne, the ancient problems of philosophy have received a new, thoroughly modern treatment, which in its scope and depth easily rivals the so-called* philosophia perennis.

He also includes the idea of "self" as reference point, as we shall note from a different base. *I know myself most immediately only as an ever-changing sequence of occasions of experience, each of which is the present integration of remembered past and anticipated future into a new whole of significance.*

However, Hartshorne, in his summary entitled "Whiteheadian Doctrine of God," deals with successive "objections to identifying God as a living person," and comes to a remarkable conclusion which cannot, I believe, be reconciled with any kind of panentheist position, nor be intelligible to humanity under the sway of SbT.

My conclusion then is that the chief reasons for insisting that God is an actual entity can be satisfied by the view that he is a living person, that this view makes the doctrine of God more coherent, and that no serious new difficulties are raised.

The panentheist position is *in general* the position espoused by Teilhard, especially in *The Divine Milieu.* John Robinson has developed what I regard as a definitive case for the recasting of the Judeo-Christian view of [illegible] into this panentheist mold. However, in his book titled, appropriately, *Exploration into God,* I do not think he pressed the case hard enough for the absolute necessity of such recasting of Christian theology toward this concept of [illegible] which he "re"-discovered so successfully as a result of his own explorations. He notes that panentheism "has never quite succeeded in establishing itself in orthodox Christian circles." But this is surely much too central and serious a defect in theology to be allowed to continue unattended. As Robinson does so deftly, it is easy to show that there is simply no more room for a "God the Father, up there," or "out there." The fact remains that the "God" as proclaimed in most of our churches and understood by most of our laity is not much better than a local Baal. It is *much* too small. A relevant faith for the twenty-first century cannot exist in persons who cannot integrate into their [illegible] much of their knowledge of the universe, the experience of the concrete realities of food, shelter, clothing, and transportation with which technology surrounds them. The creative and sustaining force of the universe is unlikely to be caught in some theological butterfly net to be examined under glass at leisure and with due decorum on Sundays at 11 a.m.

The challenge to the Church, as to all other religions, is to grow up; to give up childish things, especially "baby-talk." It is a call to the radical abandoning of one hopelessly inadequate formulation for a different one which has a very respectable tradition within the Church and which is, at once, more compatible with its own tradition, other world religions, and the major religion of the modern world—science and technology. Surely, it is time to move beyond Reformation formulations; one may start with Thomas Aquinas, Luther, and Calvin, and Barth, Bultmann, and Küng—but we cannot end there anymore. The new bricks and panels of bricks which a very different group of interpreters have brought must now be articulated into a new porch to the edifice of theology through which citizens of the twenty-first century can enter. Whitehead, Berdyaev, and, more recently, Cobb and Hartshorne, have, indeed, provided the theological-philosophical warp. It is now high time for the woof supplied by scientists typified by Teilhard, Michael Polanyi, Charles Coulson, and Alister Hardy, and that remarkable East European bureaucrat-mystic, Petru Dumitriu, to be woven in.

We shall now follow a very different approach in trying to weave a new theological fabric. Instead of trying to define what is or is not, we will start with human observation and experience *alone.* We will find that, in human attempts to describe all the reality that can be experienced, there are areas or categories to which we can affix the nameless . Moreover, we will show that the properties of this are the same as those ascribed to a panentheist .

2.3 How Humans Learn about Reality

I am addressing this book to human beings. It is virtually certain that it will be read and understood only by human beings. It is, therefore, absolutely essential that we first understand how humans learn, understand, appreciate, internalize, experience, and act on their perceptions.

The human brain receives and processes a large number of signals just as computers do, although its capacities are in some ways far beyond any present-day computer. The brain processes the signals and, through its control of the body, transforms them into several different realities observable by others. These realities—words, writings, actions—*are the only means* human beings have of communicating with each other. *Everything* I know has been communicated to me directly from the world around in its smallest part or the integrated universal wholes, or communicated to me by the ideas and actions of my fellow human beings. The sketch below (Fig. 2.2) shows, at the right, such observable results of actions by any person. To the left of the person we show the features of the total signal emitting and receiving system. If by analogy to a hot body emitting radiation, we think of every source of knowledge or every event as emit-

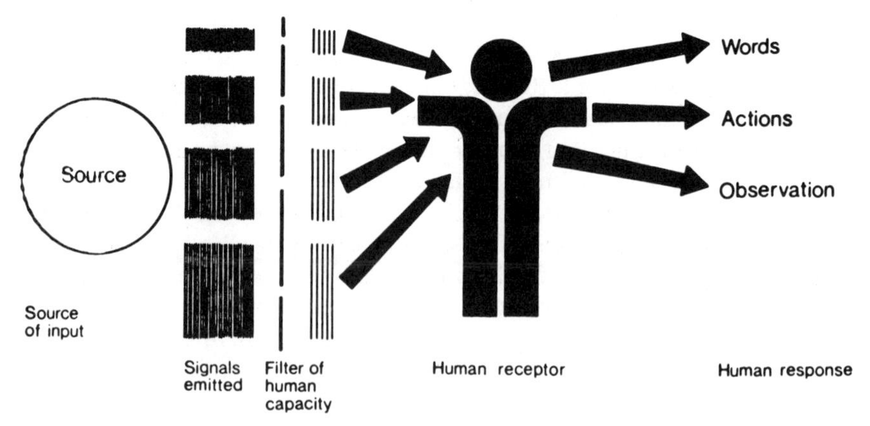

Fig. 2.2

ting information, we will recognize that such information is of many kinds (in our analogy: emitted at many different wavelengths). But between this emitted information and the receiving human being is a most important feature. This is the screen of human capabilities. Just as we cannot hear sounds with frequencies above, say, 20,000 cycles per second, nor below 30, so also, in every human capacity there is a finite "window" through which information can actually reach us. There are, of course, many holes in our filter, many finite windows into our five senses. But just as science has shown us how small a part of the electromagnetic spectrum is detected by our eyes, it is obvious that the human filter gives us a very specialized picture of the source.

This sketch, while grossly oversimplified and imprecise, is, nevertheless, an undeniably accurate analog of human learning and responses. We must take full account of the existence of the filter and its windows for all humans. We must also accept the differences in the individual filters (i.e., the limitations) of *different* human beings. The most important evidence for such *differences* is the fact of the wide variation in all human capacities: whether of intelligence, athletic prowess, or empathetic listening. Our epistemological model states, then, that finite human beings have slightly different filters, but all filters transmit, through characteristically human windows, only a small part of all the signals being received from the real world of persons and objects. Hence, in a wholly objective manner, we may say that all human knowledge is limited and, hence, distorted by the unavoidable partiality of the human factor (= anthropomorphic) filter. As we start to describe an Infinite Reality (or "God"), we can see that such views can, at the very best, be a very partial projection or section or selection of the full information emitted by the source itself.

We are confronted at the start with two choices. Either we must affirm that Reality is equal to the combination of signals received through our filters, or we must hypothesize, invent, and affirm a Reality (or a God) much more comprehensive, multidimensional and accept the fact that we humans can only perceive a very small or "one-sided" view. Yet, as we emphasized, as humans, the center of our receiving universe is ourselves. All *human* theology must, therefore, start *there,* understanding how *humans* perceive reality. When we do that systematically, i.e., when we ask ourselves how do I know what you (think you) know, we may be in for some surprises. If we introduced a second human being into our sketch, then s/he would receive the signals from the same original source with roughly the same filters. But, in addition, s/he would receive other signals at more or less full volume from other humans (see Fig. 2.3). These signals are of two kinds:

First, we learn from each other through the spoken and the written

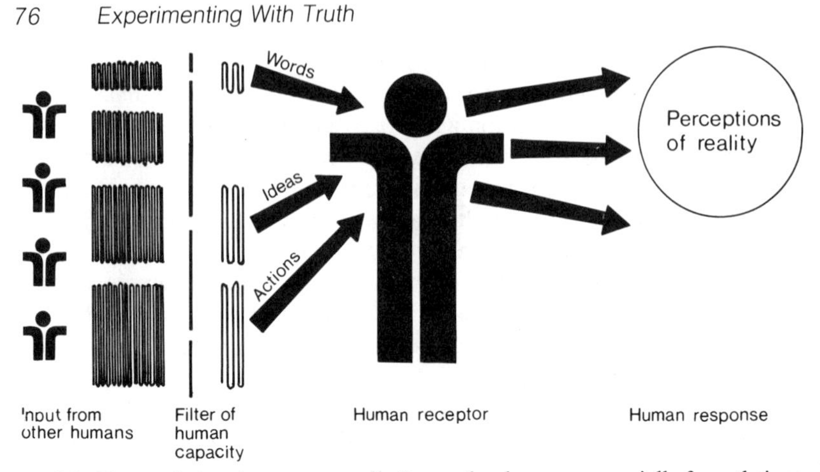

Fig. 2.3. Human beings learn most easily from other humans, especially from their actions. Their perception of Reality is a complex mixture of learning from parents, teachers, friends, superimposed on direct inputs from Reality. Or as Teilhard put it:

> *With the support of what religion and science have been teaching me for the last fifty years, I have tried in this to make my way out into the open. I wanted to get clear of the fog and see things as they really are. . . . And the first thing I saw was that only man can be of any use to man in reading the secret of the world.* ["L'Esprit de la Terre," March 9, 1931]

word. That is, of course, what separates the truly human species from all others—the capacity to learn instantly from others (far) removed in time and space.

Second, we learn directly by our own observation of nature, society and other persons.

We must insert here parenthetically that nowhere is the human limitation and the saturation effect of technological advance referred to in the last chapter more evident than in our ability to learn from others. J. Lukasiewicz has provided a detailed analysis of what he calls "The Ignorance Explosion." For all of human history until about 50 years ago, one human being could absorb more and more information from other humans and all of recorded history. Now, while the human brain's capacity is fixed (in a short time scale), the available information is increasing in volume and complexity so fast that not only is any individual's capacity exceeded a thousandfold, but every year each individual knows a smaller and smaller portion or percentage of the total of what is known (see Fig. 2.4). Even more significant, due to the strong interlinking of information, Lukasiewicz shows that the individual understands even a smaller fraction of the information he receives each year. I have described elsewhere exactly the same phenomenon in university education.

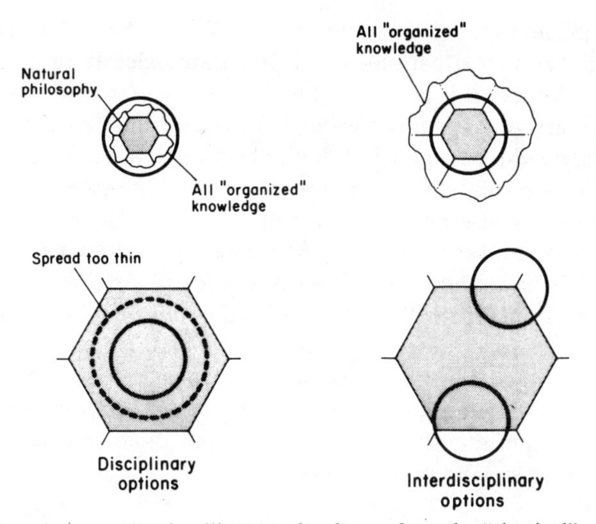

Fig. 2.4. The two upper sketches illustrate the change from the "classical" world to the modern world. The heavy circle includes the capacity of the human brain to store and organize information. It has not changed measurably in the span of recorded history. The watershed difference between the "classical" and "modern" eras is that in the former the human capacity was greater than all *organized* knowledge.

The irregular boundary lies inside the circumference of the brain capacity in the diagram on the upper left. In the "modern era" (top right and both bottom sketches), organized knowledge is much larger in volume than the brain capacity. That requires every individual to make the choice between focusing all one's professional training within one discipline (shown throughout as a hexagon), or including parts of two or more disciplines. The utter futility of the discipline-limited approach is shown in the bottom left figure. With the ignorance explosion (see Lukasiewicz), the fixed circle of human capacity becomes a smaller and smaller fraction of even a single discipline. By straddling the boundaries between disciplines (see bottom right figure), the individual learns the fundamental paradigm of synthesis and a holistic view across the linguistic and related barriers separating disciplines.

This is the basis and theoretical significance of "interdisciplinarity" or holistic approaches as the new, absolutely necessary, general education. It is the only tool for preserving the essential perspective of the whole, rather than only studying the individual parts.

But there is another kind of knowledge from other humans which we gain from observing their actions. "What you *do* shouts louder than what you say." As cognitive verbal knowledge becomes more problematical and we enter the more diffuse and deeper forms of knowledge, we turn increasingly to manifest action rather than words to learn from others. The action is a very complex synthesis of a great deal of information. More significantly, it is action which is coupled to another much misused term: faith. By far, the best definition I know of faith is: "A policy for, and only evident in, one's actions in life." What I believe most surely, I act on. In everyday situations, this is illustrated clearly in the following examples. I believe it is going to rain; I carry my umbrella. I believe that friends are arriving for this weekend; I prepare the bedroom. I believe that honesty is the best policy; I don't cheat on my income tax. I believe that love is the single absolute ethical guide. Not only do I share my worldly goods with others, but I act on carefully calculated love rather than any commandments or laws. As we start to share what we know of reality, or "believe about God," we must keep reminding ourselves how partial our best claims will be, how limited by our narrow human filters. D. T. Niles, the Ceylonese theologian, described this sharing (he called it Christian evangelism) most succinctly as "one beggar telling another beggar where he found food." This sharing of our experiences, of the results of our experiments with truth, has a profound impact on shaping human knowledge about all Reality.

Lay Approaches to Reality

Granted that we learn from each other and from reality directly by means of observations, words, and actions, what constitutes reality for the ordinary person? Surely, if one were asked such a question, a major portion of the answer would be: those objects or events which I can perceive with my senses of sight, hearing, touch, and smell in that order. In the room in which I sit, the chair, table, and lamp are real. Outside, the grass and trees and roads and hillside are the bedrock of reality, and the sun and moon and stars fit in comfortably. About these physical objects there are no disagreements by different people: this is a *shared* reality about the natural world, cross-checkable by ordinary people. It is what Born has called naive realism. But most ordinary folk would share other conceptions of reality about which they have learned through words and actions. Take for example the idea of one's community or nation. Almost everyone would agree that it is "real" to state that one is an Indian, or Englishman, or American. The reality of the Soviet communist state or Nazi Germany, although rather abstract ideas, are very real to most people because their very existence has had or has a measurable sense-detectable impact. At the "society" level, therefore, the shared naive realism persists. When one moves to the interpersonal level, this reality is less easily shared. Few would deny that maternal love is very real, as is the overpowering emotional and physical attraction of two young persons in love. These general realities we validate because we have experienced them or observed them, even though we cannot share the *specific* event or feeling. In other words, the very powerful, sexual feelings of John, aged 23, for Mary, aged

22, sharing a ski lodge room after a honeymoon-like adventure, cannot be perceived by the five senses of John's younger sister, aged 11, or his aunt, aged 65, or the hall porter. The same, of course, is true of religious experience. Here, one can include not only the kinds of specific experiences, such as those carefully recorded and studied by Alister Hardy and Edward Robinson in the Religious Experience Research Unit at Oxford (see bibliography), but the experience of Baron von Hugel's French peasant woman in her daily attendance at mass, or of the dedicated activist sharing the life of the poor in the Washington ghetto. The only reason most people can agree that sexual experience and feelings are "real," while a substantial portion cannot vouch for religious experience, is that more have shared the former experience. One characteristic that is negatively correlated with reality is volatility, evanescence, or lack of reproducibility.

The sexual experience is both more easily programmable for repitition and replication, and the physiological responses of the senses of everyone are more or less similar. Yet, we note that the differences between sexual and religious experiences are clearly only of a quantitative and not of a qualitative nature.

Thus, the lay person's approaches to discovering reality—the common-sense or naive realism level—are characterized by the tests of:

a. Direct observation by human senses.
b. Common, shareable experience by a good fraction of the human community.
c. Replicability, transferability and/or unchangeability.

Scientific Approaches to Reality and "Beyond"

The scientist-engineer builds on the lay approach, but goes well beyond it. So much so, that the scientist can call into question much that is called "real" by the lay person at another level.

Indeed, one of the most important contributions that modern science has made to the human search for wisdom is to confirm what most religious leaders have proclaimed as revealed truth, *that at the deeper levels things are not at all what they appear to be to our unaided senses.* Moreover, even the initial scientific concepts based on the latest so-called breakthrough often turn out to be just another layer of onion skin. Thus, the model of the structure of matter based on the research instruments of the turn of the century in the heyday of scientific triumphalism have already proved to have been misleadingly simple. The demise of "scientism" was sealed with the disappearance of the world of billiard–ball

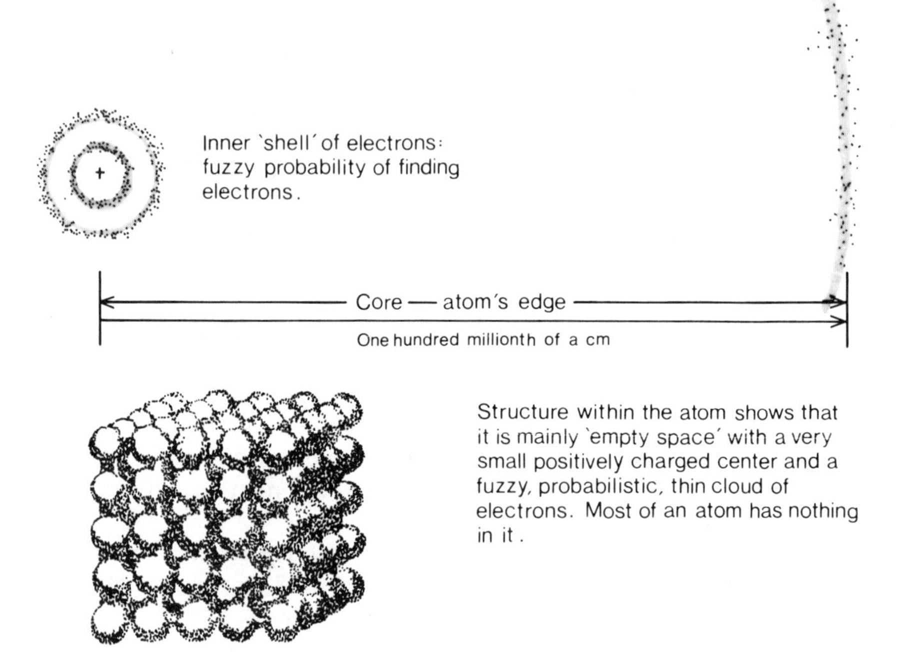

Fig. 2.5

atoms (see Fig 2.5) and Newtonian mechanics. Let us start with something as positive as our sense-proved measure of solidity or hardness. While a rock or a mineral, common salt or diamond, was thought to be simply an ordered array of solid atomic spheres, there was a congruence between the physical feel of "solidness" and the concept of reality being affirmed in the concept.

But as soon as the capability for analysis and the resulting concept of real matter moved to the subatomic level, our picture became, and has remained for fifty years, every different. Now peering into the "solid" atom we find it most ephemeral. Each atom consists of a "pin-point" of a "solid" nucleus of protons and neutrons occupying (10^{-30} or $^{-40}$ cubic centimeters) virtually no space at all, surrounded by a very thin "smoke" of electrons arranged in concentric shells. Even these outer shells seem to occupy only, say, a hundredth or thousandth of the volume of what we choose to call an atom. An atom is as empty as the universe. In 99/100th of the volume of what we call an atom, there is nothing; electrostatic fields hold the center at appointed distances, not unlike the way planets are held in orbits. And like a planet or moon, even the occasional electron particle of smoke is a rare visitor in most of this space. The only things which even suggest "solidity" are the so-called particles. But look a little closer, and even these "fundamental particles," the leptons (of which electrons are an example) or the hadrons (protons are one kind of hadron) seem to disappear. They all become concentrations of "fields," as matter is seen to be translatable into energy. Or one can say that, at macroscopic levels, energy becomes "manifest" as matter. A "solid," then, is all a matter of forces and fields, balancing acts between repulsive and attractive forces, and the binding of one lightly populated domain we name an atom to another by more rigid (covalent) or more slippery (ionic) bonds. The billiard-ball atom and the densely packed solid have completely vanished. If palpable atoms make for substance or solidity, there's no substance there; matter has dissolved before our knowing. The only reason we experience something solid to the touch is because our fingers or other probes are so gross or blunt. Take a rapier-like probe (an X-ray beam would do) and you find that matter is very insubstantial indeed.

If " [illegible] is that which Reality betrays but does not parade," then what modern physics has taught us is that matter itself betrays the presence of deeper realities but certainly does not parade them to our senses aided or unaided. In the last few years, it has become popular to try to "explain" the onion-like structure of our understanding of real matter, peeling off layer by layer of concepts increasingly "unreal" to our senses. The motivation for some of these approaches is similar to my own. They are attempts to seek points of contact between religious world views and modern science, and they all point to the same conclusion: *"Science establishes beyond any doubt that all Reality is 'apparent'."* The experiences of our single senses are misleading as naive guides, for when put together to make a pattern or examined by instruments alone, they indicate a very different kind of reality.

I wish at this point to note that I will exclude from consideration in this connection the entire submicroscopic world of quantum mechanics. The controversy between the classicists typified by Einstein and the quantum mechanicians under Born and Heisenberg is of no relevance at this level of discussion. In my treatment of this subject in "The Dice-Playing God," I use the term "Integrated Reality" and "Differentiated Reality" to separate the two worlds. The world of technology, and the entire world of the lay person's response to technology occurs within the domain of integrated reality—where we deal with relatively large objects (atomic dimensions and above), relatively large numbers, and causality. In this world, the scientists, who have shown how easily our senses may be fooled (see above), pronounce very clearly that an objective reality exists. Indeed, they are at pains to start with such an axiom, or "statement of faith." Let me use a quotation from a letter of Albert Einstein to his younger colleague Erwin Schrodinger in which Einstein is arguing the case for the existence of an objective Reality against the view that *our perception* of reality is all the reality there is:

> *One cannot get around the assumption of reality—if only one is honest. Most of them simply do not see what sort of risky game they are playing with reality—reality as something independent of what is experimentally established. . . .*

This "assumption" of a reality is a fundamental dogma of science. But it is a most fruitful one in that on it—at the integrated level—rests the entire edifice of SbT.

When the student-faculty revolts of the sixties led to an upsurge in the attacks upon the many negative effects of technology, some persons were carried away into flights of fancy. They thought that the entire SbT view of reality was crumbling. Harold Cassidy, Professor of Chemistry at Yale, comments on this theme in 1970, when discussing this alienation among college youth, and in words almost identical with Einstein's, he restates the dogma:

> *I emphasize that there is a real, objective world outside of me because in my contacts with students I sense in a disquieting way that some of them do not believe in a "nature of things." The existence of an objective reality, the behavior of which is not subject to their whim, seems to be excluded from their minds, in some cases; in others such reality as they recognize is treated as a function of "power" and "interpersonal relations." Strange echoes of discredited theories haunt their talk.*

We can summarize the scientists' approach to describing this objective reality in parallel fashion to the laity's, they add the following:

a. Use of instruments minimizes human bias and error, and increases reproducibility and precision.
b. Development of generalizations or principles which go beyond observations.
c. Verifiable and reproducible observations and principles by (essentially) all others all over the world.
d. A system for continuing experimentation, testing, and, as needed, changing views of reality.

Religion's Approach to Reality

The next few sections will develop this in detail; hence, my purpose here is only to show by comparison the differences between the approaches of the laity, the scientists, and the classical theologians. The last-named approach can be characterized as follows:

a. Partial distrust of human senses; superiority of codified principles.
b. Codification of human experience (at a certain point in time) into "principles" or "laws."
c. Experimentation to change the image of Reality (actively) *discouraged.*

THE PARABLE OF SWEET, SUGAR, AND SWEETNESS

All over the world the concept of "Sweetness" made itself known to humanity. It happened independently in a hundred different cultures. And it always happened through *experience.* Anthropologists the world over have recorded how, as humanity moved from its nomadic existence into settled agriculture, one of its greatest sensual pleasures was that of tongue or palate touched by something sweet. The first experience of sweetness in the temperate zones came from eating certain berries. Ever afterward, ripe berries became very desirable because they were sweet—that is, they embodied or provided a vehicle for experiencing sweetness. But imagine the problem of that first hunter who, on a hunt far away from home base, first ran into a particularly lush, ripe, wild strawberry which didn't grow near his village. How would he describe the sensation of "sweetness" to his tribe. No doubt he described the berry, and told them that they would have to *experience* the taste to believe it. From then on, in that tribe strawberries would be cultivated with care in special set-apart plots. There would be weekly strawberry-tasting ceremonies. Images of strawberries would be venerated. The tribe would soon change its name to "Strawberrians." Only occasionally would a radical young prophet remind the tribe that it was the essential experience of *sweetness* which was precious, not the particular form in which it was experienced.

Soon reports would filter in of another discovery by a neighboring tribe, they too have found the highest gastronomic good—but they claim that sweetness is embodied in raspberries—and the Raspberrian tribe is very zealous in proclaiming that only raspberries convey sweetness. Raspberrians battle Strawberrians in the cause of the perfect embodiment of sweetness. They fight to a draw and slowly realize that there may be some common essence behind both their forms.

But trouble still looms ahead. Word comes from distant shores that another tribe claims that sweetness is found, not in a berry, not in something red, but in the awkward looking stalk of a cane. Raspberrians and Strawberrians unite to stamp out this obviously absurd claim by uncultured foreign natives. They send armies to cut down the canes and plant strawberries in the alien climate. But some of their scientists who go there to live report that the cane does, indeed, embody the same sweetness as the local strawberries, albeit tinged with a different flavor. Bees and their honey are discovered. Ages pass and it slowly becomes evident that all over the world wo/mankind has discovered "sweetness," and each culture has its own local vehicle for the experiencing of "sweetness" by its population. Not many of the vehicles are alike, but they really are all sweet: the head of pineapple, a thousand different berries, the sap of maple trees, the root of beets, and the stalks of canes.

But that is not the end of the story. New reports originating from the shores of the eastern Mediterranean report that a Semitic sect had found the common denominator of all these forms. They had succeeded in crystallizing out a single substance: sugar. And there, in these shiny clear crystals, was the pure stuff, refined out of and present in each of those myriad forms in which sweetness had previously been experienced. Now wo/mankind could taste sweetness pure and it was utterly marvelous. Sugar could sweeten any food. But the man who had crystallized out the sugar insisted that sugar was still only an "Incarnation," that sweetness was the only reality. Sweetness was infinitely more satisfying than sugar or any of the local berries or canes. He and his disciples preached that what was important was to search for the essence of "sweetness" in all foods, in all cultures and circumstances. They urged all to pursue the *essence* and the *idea,* and not a particular form, not even sugar itself. But the seduction of the immediate taste sensations caused people to get sweet foods, sugar, and sweetness all mixed up. Then, as fast as it came, the secret of making pure sugar was lost, and never again was that tribe able to make it pure. But the story of how this pure incarnate form of all that is sweet, which was the sure doorway for sweetness to be experienced, was passed down from generation to generation. The tribe in which sugar was first found soon grew to an "empire." The concept of sweetness was too abstract, the story of sugar itself was wonderful for activists or school children, but the masses needed something concrete. So the tribe—which was a beet-root tribe—went back to the honoring—indeed the worship—of beetroots. It was, after all, the right and proper—if not the only—way to experience sweetness. But small groups of the sugar-inventor's followers sometimes, by carefully following his recipe, succeed in making microscopic amounts of sugar. They remind their fellow beet-rooters that it is sweetness which is ultimate in value; they remind them that sugar really can be extracted from beet roots. And they affirm that sugar can *never* be mass produced. Surprisingly enough, a large number of those who so managed to make the tiniest thimbleful of sugar seemed to lose their lives to a jealous multitude for so succeeding.

The world shrinks and new claims are posted about the experience of sweetness from other sources. Now the Raspberry and Strawberry tribes and the Cane tribe and the Beet-root tribe are somewhat more willing to acknowledge that there is, perhaps, a common essence which is the real object of desire. Each, however, holds more or less firmly to the idea that their local vehicle gives the least distorted experience of sweetness. But slowly, as the oneness of the entire human tribe becomes more and more real in the technologically unified global village, new similarities emerge. The Beet-root sugar followers learn that perhaps somewhere else sugar had also been crystallized out. Some reports had it yellow, others red, but the similarities appeared unmistakable.

But there is a last paragraph to this parable. It is the sudden appearance of a new intertribal conspiratorial band. By deep and searching study of the nature of human sense experience they have learned to analyze and recreate and reconfigure human desires. And the final confusion arose when this scientific tribe from another planet claimed that one could even experience sweetness through totally artificial chemicals. Every local natural product manufacturer filed suit under the truth-in-advertising act to prevent this tribe from claiming sweetness for its artificial product, but to no avail. It sweetened the junk food for the masses, and was, in fact, the principal experience of sweetness for billions. Although everyone seemed to recognize that these saccharines and cyclamates were not nutritious, they had their place.

And then, at the World Congress of Sweetness Lovers, it was agreed that it was really the experience, the sensation of Sweetness (also called God) which was the highest goal. All agreed that sweetness can be experienced only by consuming some real substance; and that many such substances exist, each called a religion, each adapted more or less to its environment. Most agreed that even artificial sweeteners contribute to our experience and understanding of sweetness, though there is for the human (= natural) condition a rather pure form of realized sweetness: sugar. Sugar was seen as the molecular embodiment (incarnation?) of sweetness, and the agent of sweetness camouflaged in the entire range of berries, roots, and canes.

All delegates to the convention took a pledge to separate in their minds, and their speech, the experience of sweetness, sugar, and specific sweet foods.

2.4 Finding Through Reality

What has all this description of reality and how theologians and scientists approach it got to do with theology? What we are leading up to, of course, is that we can learn about by learning about reality. Indeed, we will contend that *only* via that route can we learn about . The immediately preceding parable of the relation of the sensation of sweetness to sugar and, thence, to a variety of fruits is an introduction to the topic of "embodiment" or incarnation of "ideas," or principles of any abstract concept. The connection between and reality is mirrored in the relationship of sweetness to sugarcane. To get to one must *go through reality.* As we have noted, this is the basic position of the panentheists.

The pioneer of scientific panentheism was Pierre Teilhard de Chardin. His writing reached millions because of the poetry of his language. All the greater, then, the pity that he was prevented by conservatism in the Vatican from making this basic contribution to doctrine. Every scientist would naturally start with real "things." Teilhard's happy truncation of the passage in St. Paul's letter to the Hebrews (11:1) was: *"Fides Substantia Res."** It starts us on a most fruitful examination of the relationship of *"God"* to *things.* This message affirms that may be encountered

* The passage in the King James version reads: *"Faith is the substance of things hoped for."*

through all of the real world of things, experiences, and ideas. In short, that [symbol] *is the essence of all Reality.*

It is this relationship we must develop in detail. We find that scientists stoutly defend a very independent reality. The religious affirm a preexisting [symbol] and the creation. What, then, is the relation of [symbol] to Reality? Are they identical? Which came first? Is Reality only another word for the creation? No! The Teilhard quote can be transposed to read " [symbol] is the essence of things (reality)."

What am I saying then? That all reality, every bird, blade of grass, DNA molecule, skyscraper, space-shuttle, neutron-star, or infrared photon is infused with and can "reveal" [symbol] to any particular human percipient. Yes! and more, that [symbol] is also revealed through every human activity, especially its adventure—Tenzing Norkay and Edmund Hillary's climbing of Everest, the people of Israel escaping from the Pharoahs, or the reformation of Ikhnaton and Nefertiti, the transformation of Siddhartha to Buddha, and the crucifixion of Jesus. And most directly, for individuals in every age, [symbol] becomes known through the reality of deeply personal *experiences* of intense suffering, mutual in-loveness of two persons, or sharing the "cup of cold water."

Note, of course, what I have *not* said. A bird is not [symbol]; [symbol] is not a star; an unselfish act is not [symbol]. That is pantheism and it is wrong on two counts. Such a [symbol] would be much too limited by the receiver or perceiver, we human beings. More importantly, pantheism would confuse two terms, reality and [symbol], form and content. Pantheism would say (in the language of our parable) that sweetness *is* the beet root or the sugar cane. But ordinary experience tells us that the tough fiber of the cane is never sweet, and far from sweetness. Sweetness is reified, given substance, made accessible to human beings via the sugar cane or beet. Sweetness is not a private or personal reality. The experience of sweetness is available to all humanity. But the vehicles for the reification, embodiment of sweetness are many and varied: berries, cane, sugar itself, saccharin and so on. Sweetness is *in some way* connected to sugar cane. What is needed is a much deeper understanding of the connection of Reality to [symbol]. That tunnel connecting the two is *meaning.* Meaning connects [symbol] to Reality; meaning distills Reality to concentrate [symbol]. Trying to extract meaning from Reality starts me into the continuum Reality-meaning-essence.

Artists Witness to the "Beyond": The Reification of [symbol]

While we are concentrating in this book on the interface between SbT and religion, one could introduce evidence from different communities which support the same thesis.

That most articulate American artist, Ben Shahn, has made almost exactly the same case in the world of art, in discussing "The Shape of Content." Reality, in our case, would become "the shape of [symbol]." All real objects, beings, or acts bring form and reality to clothe or reify the content of [symbol]. [symbol] is the invisible, ineffable substance of things. Shahn writes and, by changing only a few words, I paraphrase as follows:

> *Reality is reification—the turning of [symbol] into a material entity, rendering [symbol] accessible to others, giving it permanence, willing it to the race. The reality is as varied as are the accidental meetings of nature. Reality in religion is as varied as idea itself.*
>
> *It is the visible shape of all man's growth; it is the living picture of his tribe at its most primitive, and of his civilization at its more sophisticated state. Religious reality is the many faces of the legend; it includes the infinite images of art; it is the expression and remanant of self. Reality is the very shape of [symbol].*

Shahn quotes the art historian Erwin Panofsky in a poetic phrase: "Content is that which art betrays but does not parade" and, as Shahn continues (with my transpositions throughout):

> *Reality arises in many ways. Reality in Nature emerges from the impact of order upon order, of element upon element, as the forms of lightning or of ocean waves. Or reality may emerge from the impact of elements on materials as of wind carved rocks and dunes. Reality in living things too is the impinging of order upon order, the slow evolving of shapes according to function and need. The reality of artifacts grows out of use too, and out of the accidental meeting of materials. Who would dream of or devise a form so elegant as that of a chemical retort* [or an Apollo spaceship] *except the need and use and glass all met to create this reality.*
>
> *For Reality is not just the intentions of [symbol], it is the embodiment of [symbol]. All reality is based first on some aspect, some theme of [symbol]. Reality is, second, a marshalling of materials, the inert matter in which the theme is to be cast. Reality is, third, a setting of boundaries or limits, the whole extent or a part of [symbol]* but no more, *the outer shape of [symbol]. All reality is thus a disciplining, a limitation, an ordering of [symbol] to be manifest in one place at one time to a particular person. It can be said with certainty that any reality that emerges cannot be greater than the [symbol] which "went into it." For reality is only the manifestation, the shape of [symbol].*

What a beautiful and beautifully accurate expression we make by transposing Panofsky's phrase into: " [symbol] is that which Reality betrays but does not parade."

But have not poets been saying this all along? Indeed, a long list of poets and visionaries have used the very same image, in describing Nature. Thus:

> *Earth's crammed with heaven*
> *And every common bush afire with God.* (Elizabeth Barrett Browning)*
>
> *The world is charged with the grandeur of God,*
> *It will flame out like shining from shook foil.* (Gerard Manley Hopkins)

---

* Indeed Browning added the other important theme, just like Panofsky, that this luminosity, this radiation, is only sensed or picked up by a very few; as the quotation concludes:

> *And only he who sees takes off his shoes,*
> *The rest sit round it, and pluck blackberries.*

Similar wording was used by Teilhard to formulate one of his central contributions. It was first formulated in 1927 and reaffirmed as late as 1955. Teilhard, in these statements, resorted essentially to poetry. His analogies were not precise. But who would be so foolish as to sacrifice the beauty of "the diaphaneity of the Divine" for the precision of "the diaphaneity of the world, letting the Divine shine through." Here is Teilhard's definitive ontology in which he reports—in our language—his gradual awareness or detection of the information or meaning radiated by Reality.

Throughout my life, by means of my life, the world has little by little caught fire in my sight until, aflame all around me, it has become almost completely luminous from within. . . . Such has been my experience in contact with the earth—the diaphaneity of the Divine at the heart of the universe on fire . . . Christ; his heart; a fire; capable of penetrating everywhere and, gradually, spreading everywhere.

The witnesses to these deeper levels of Reality are legion. And it is not surprising that it is the poets who always communicate such profound and general truths more effectively than didactic prose. Fra Angelico in the thirteenth century stated the case for looking through, and beyond, the "apparent reality" in the well-known verses:

The Gloom of the world is but a shadow behind it
Yet within reach is joy. There is radiance and glory
In the darkness could we but see. And to see
We have only to look. I beseech you to look.
Life is so generous a giver,
Welcome it, grasp it, and you touch the angel's hand
That brings it to you. Everything we call a trial
A sorrow or a duty, the angel's hand is there, the gift is
There, and the wonder of an overshadowing presence,
Our joys too, be not content with them as joys.
They too conceal diviner gifts.

Looking beyond Scientific Realities

There is something beyond. Fritjof Capra's work, *The Tao of Physics* (already referred to), attempts to trace the similarity of some of the concepts of today's modern particle and subnuclear physics and those of Eastern religions. It deals largely with the esoterica of both science and religion. Its appeal is to those mystically inclined, seeking support from other quarters. But what it certainly does is to destroy the idea that modern physics supports any single mechanical and mechanistic picture of the world. *The Silent Pulse* by George Leonard sets about popularizing the very existence of one chapter of physics—the electromagnetic spectrum and the wave side of particle-wave duality. Leonard weaves an intriguing fabric out of intersecting waves—meeting in "the perfect rhythm"—to describe much of nature and construct both a highly seductive and highly selective "religion" of partial "science." Leonard, one of the most articulate exponents of the upbeat human potential movement, has here produced a kind of "pop" and "mod" version of the "Hymn of the Universe" (without once mentioning the name Teilhard!). It is perhaps worth quoting here his "nine central ideas," especially since the first one or two again pointedly allude to the slipperiness of our concept of "solid" matter.

1. *That we are composed of waves no less than of the stuff we call "solid."*
2. *That what we call objects and events are primarily the precipitates from the relationship of these waves.*
3. *That each of us has an identity that is unique in all the universe, and that this identity is expressed as a distinctive wave function.*
4. *That each of us is also, paradoxically, a holoid of the universe, containing universal information—past, present, and some of the future.*
5. *That knowledge of the future fades away from us simply because the universe, by its very nature, is constantly creating unforeseeable new information, genuine novelty, and that the destiny of the new information is the evolution of higher forms.*
6. *That each of us is, in essence, a context, a weaving together of universal information from a particular point of view.*
7. *That what can be called "perfect rhythm" exists at all times in the paradoxical interplay, the silent pulse, between identity and holonomy within the context of each of us, and that, beyond custom, language, and ego, we can directly experience this perfect rhythm.*
8. *That intentionality, the vector of identity, is an essential element in the universe that is each of us; and that it is possible, through intentionality, to influence this universe in extraordinary ways.*
9. *That, in potentia, we know everything.*

Leonard appeals to the personal (indeed, self-centered) and religious dimension in each of us, as well as to those seeking the "mysterious" cloaked in new scientific jargon. Capra, it will be noted, likewise appeals to the "homo religiosus" whether among physicists or among devotees of Eastern religions. I am attempting to address a different audience—the one that Bonhoeffer was beginning to focus on—"man come of age," without the *need* for "God." In our contemporary context, most persons do not belong to the "religiosus" category, at least for most of their lives. While humankind may not have fully "come of age" as Bonhoeffer anticipated, it is surely well into adolescence. The connections between the essence and the reality, between our experiences and their meanings, will have to be made in terms of ordinary things and everyday life, not in terms of quarks and leptons, nor in terms of such out of context truths as each of us "knowing everything."

Thus, art, poetry, modern physics, and high religion seem to agree that there is some reality, we here call [illegible], beyond the realities of even our instrument-aided sense which may be discovered by a variety of approaches.

In trying to summarize this first part of a scientific panentheism, one is tempted to put it, as it were, in terms of a revised article of a contemporary Westminster Confession:

> *Reality exists separate from and independent of humans' views of, or relationship to, it. All things, objects, persons, ideas, relationships perceived by our separate senses or any combination thereof, known or experienced personally or collectively, constitute this reality and embody, give substance to, reify an essence. This essence, this meaning, this "Beyond in the Midst of all Reality," the religious call* [illegible].

Such an "article of faith" is consistent with, and does no violence to, any truth perceived by or hinted at by ancient religion or modern science. It can be subscribed to, I believe, without blocking out part of one's life or learning, by contemporary Christians, Jews, Hindus, Buddhists, Muslims, and so on, as well as by a large fraction of the interested science community.

The Self-Revealing Reality

So far, we have taken up the substance behind this first article of the "new Westminster Confession." Instead of "I believe in God," it affirms "Reality exists, and it is the embodiment of [illegible]."

Now, as we go on to the next articles, we begin again with another Einstein quote: *"The eternal mystery of the world is its comprehensibility."* The same idea has been stated by Christians the world over. *"The greatest mystery of all is why God chooses to reveal himself."* In place of science's passive voice, the idiom of tradition with its anthropomorphic version of [illegible] uses the third person singular and the active voice. The scientist is more modest and would formulate Article II of the new Confession thus: *"The Reality which exists is knowable and understandable and of basic significance to humanity, but it reveals increasingly deep levels beyond the immediate sense experiences or simple formulations."*

Again, those in the religious tradition can benefit from their technical colleagues. The idea of a revealing [illegible] actively seeking to communicate with this particular human creature can be distorted by the former appearing too anxious to become the latter's lackey. The danger of this anthropo-conditioning is that we end with a Freudian "projection-God" or a "God of the Gaps" to fill in for ignorance; a God to receive foxhole petitions, a God to be coerced by prayers. Nevertheless, it is the scientists who have come rather late to this kind of newfound humility at the mystery of Reality's comprehensibility. For 300 years, their dominant motif had human beings as independent forces extracting secrets from nature and reality. But for all the scientists' descriptions of reality, seemingly validated by their power over nature and society through the devices, hardware, and systems they produced, their *ideas* seemed to be totally unable to command the deeper acceptance and *emotional* allegiance of large numbers of citizens. Yet, while these developments of new views of Reality were emerging, often displacing parts of the traditional religious world view (a geocentric universe and a literal interpretation of a creation myth) other elements of the religious description of reality, about human nature, about other-centered love as the first law of society, seem to survive well. Indeed—and this is a significant part of the science-religion debate—the evidence of history is that up to the mid-twentieth century these "religious" world views (often formed through the most distorted perspective of a narrow cultural and even personal slit) proved to be the powerful and productive forces commanding the allegiance of hundreds of millions of believers and shaping the future. Reality, perceived through the lens of human experience (with all its many aberrations, to say nothing of downright chips and cracks), has been observed, recorded—and integrated—into the world's great religions. Put in that religious language: *"God has revealed her/himself, and has demanded obedience along specific life-policy lines."* This formulation connecting the understanding of reality to demanding, specific, observable behaviors has had great power among human beings.

What, then, is the relation between these different perceptions—these images—of reality described by science and that described by religion, one seeming to prove itself clearly the more accurate in describing nature, the other seeming to have more power over persons. Are the latter not merely the fumbling searchings of primitive humans, which had been overtaken and leapfrogged by the precision and power of the scientific method and its technological result? At the very heart of the systemic confusion of modern culture is this unresolved issue. It is demonstrable beyond any shadow of doubt, and to hundreds of millions of persons, that the description of reality, especially of the natural world provided by SbT, is both accurate and useful. Yet we must note that, for the vast majority (99.9 percent?), the accuracy of most scientific ideas or descriptions *is taken on "faith."* Let us take one simple example. The heliocentric solar system is a concept taken "on faith." Moreover, it is contradicted by our daily sense experience. After all, the sun does rise in the East and go around the Earth. Only by a convoluted series of mental gymnastics—not understood or remembered by most—can we "prove" that the earth goes around the sun, certainly not by the sense experience of *this* concept. In other words, the person-in-the street accepts on pure faith a scientific claim contradicting daily experience, only because science has been found to be reliable *elsewhere*—in providing electric lights, and inside toilets, better soap and whitener, or penicillin to save a child's life. The bonafides of the scientific Establishment is "guaranteed" and proved by the fact that, on the basis of its heliocentric model, it has put hundreds of satellites in orbit and managed to circumnavigate the planets. And then, again, the sense experiences of comfortable cars, working telephones, and talking calculators confirm for the public that most of the views of reality of the SbT faction are indisputably correct.

If the SbT views of reality are on this daily basis in everyone's experience being proved to be correct, where does that leave the religious views of reality? For four centuries, the tendency has been to assume a kind of zero-sum game of truth or reality description. If one statement about "God" is right, the other must be wrong. If with Laplace one understands the laws of mechanics, then one has no need for the hypothesis of God. This "competition" between the two views of reality—emerging scientific and traditional religious—I believe accurately describes the perception of the masses right down to our day. Khrushchev's crude version that the Soviet astronauts had not met God in their orbits round the earth is but the obverse of that of millions of "creationists" in the United States trying to have the book of Genesis used as a geology text.

While this "competitiveness" among various views of reality has dominated and still dominates popular culture, there has been a noble army of visionaries, prophets, and "martyrs" who have seen *a certain kind* of complementarity between these two views. They run from Newton who saw his science as detailing the handiwork of God, to Teilhard's panentheist "hymn of the universe." What I believe has not been sufficiently treated and clarified is the question: *What is the nature of the alleged complementarity between the scientific and religious views?*

Is the former gradually evolving from and displacing the latter, albeit in a continuously compatible mode? If they are in conflict, which one is right? Or—as perhaps most readers of this volume might quickly respond—do the two views simply refer to different Realities: matter and spirit? Should the reality pictures of science fit into those of religion like parts of a jigsaw puzzle? This most basic issue of the nature of the complementarity of science and religion has so far been lost in the debate as to whether they are competitive.

In the following sections I shall treat in detail the nature of the relationship between religious truth and scientific truth. It begins and ends with an axiomatic ontological certainty: Reality exists independent of any views of it. Reality may be perceived by human beings in a variety of ways. If any views of Reality appear mutually inconsistent, it may be that one of the views is incorrect. However, it may also be that what is really incorrect is our human understanding of the relationship between the information (affective and cognitive) content of the two views. What at first appears contradictory, as in Viktor Frankl's classical example of viewing

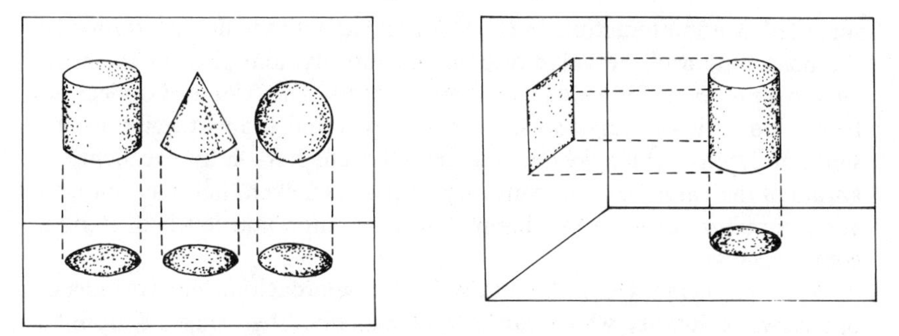

Fig. 2.6. *The reality perceived is drastically affected by the direction from which it is viewed. Viewing from more than one direction may give an unexpected addition (in this case the 3-dimensional nature) to our model of reality.* (After V. Frankl.)

the same object from different directions, which is sketched above (Fig. 2.6), can often be reconciled. Indeed, the apparently contradictory views can then often be synthesized into a much "fuller," more accurate view of Reality. It is to the relationships between scientific and religious epistemologies that we must now turn.

The most important corollary of Frankl's article is the absolute need carefully to integrate different and often apparently conflicting views of reality. This may be illustrated even in the allusions to the different perceptions of reality in many of the foregoing quotations. But, with Einstein, our axiom is that reality is a self-consistent, continuous whole. Yet, human receivers will and do perceive reality from many different angles and distances and with or without aids for their senses. It is to be expected, therefore, that any individual perspective or image will differ—often radically—from another. Only after trial and error, the synthesis and resynthesis of many images, and their testing against the memory of the race or culture can the accuracy of the resulting composite three (really multi-) dimensional image be judged. It is to this we now turn, even as we remember that in attempting to describe the abstract concept we are forced to use both language and imagery which we have just criticized. Moreover, we must remain constantly vigilant to remind ourselves not to confuse even the best model with the reality itself.

2.5 Forming our Image of Reality: Multidirectional, Multispectral, Multifocal

As we embark on an attempt to understand or relate to [illegible], the first step is to form an accurate picture of Reality through which lies the only road. We recognize a new task previously neglected: the need to synthesize or mix signals or prepare a composite out of separate elements heretofore regarded as noninteracting. We will search for both the demonstration of the possibility and the value of complementarity, and also for the most effective processes by which "synthesis" occurs. The fusion of optical information which occurs so easily in our eyes and brains to give us the sense of depth—which we detail later in this chapter—is an excellent example of the value of such fruitful synthesis. Yet, even that may not be a good paradigm of what can happen at more important levels of human consciousness.

In the following, I develop a thesis on an approach to the synthesis of our views of Reality which can best be explained by using a simplified model exercise in studying part of Reality. Let us start with the question: How does contemporary science study any new object, from a new planet to a strange pebble or seashell picked up on the beach?

First, we examine it from many directions because we know full well about optical illusions and the terrible limitations of two-dimensional projections of three dimensional objects and so on (see Frankl's simple yet profound examples).

Second, we examine it over the whole spectrum of human sense,

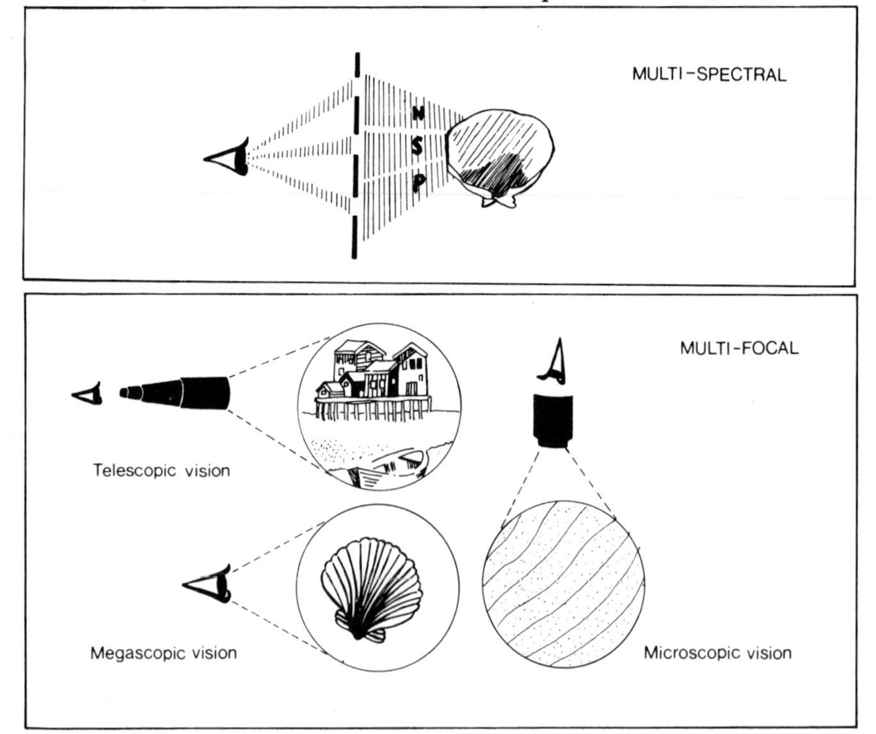

Fig. 2.7 How humans approach the examination of reality. (P = Person, S = Society, N = Nature) see p. 122.

knowledge, and experience. Just as every modern remote sensing satellite carries with it detectors for radiation in different parts of the spectrum, so anyone seriously wanting to learn the full truth about this new object must superimpose the images obtained at different "wavelengths"—cognitive, affective, meditative. (Fig. 2.7)

Third, to appreciate this object fully, we need to view it from afar in all its wholeness and relations to other bodies; but we need also to focus down to microscopic detail (Fig. 2.7) to see what really makes it tick. These are the different *perspectives* we can have of reality.

To continue to develop this model, let us now picture our body, representing reality, to be incandescent with information, that is radiating "information" at many wavelengths, i.e., of many kinds. The analogy is scientifically exact: all bodies at temperatures above absolute zero are continuously emitting radiant energy over a spectrum of wavelengths depending on their composition and structure. Reality is radiating not only energy but information and meaning. This image of a radiant reality sounds very much like the poets in the last section (though it is more precise in the form given here).

Scientists describe the electromagnetic spectrum of radiation of *energy* in some detail, as in the diagram:

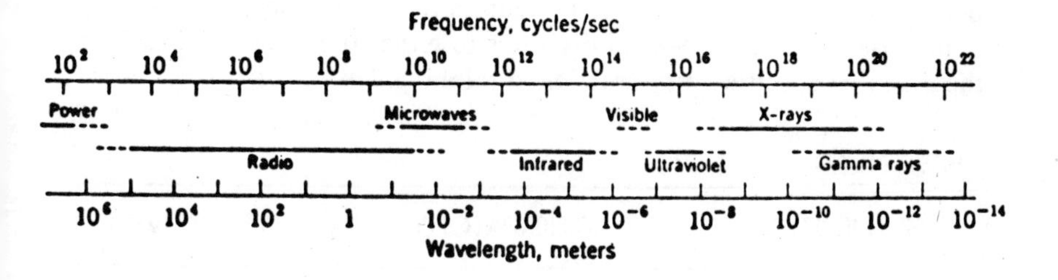

Fig. 2.8. The electromagnetic spectrum. Note that the wavelength and frequency scales are logarithmic.

On it we find familiar terms which range from the high energy cosmic rays, X–rays of medicine, and nuclear power, through the ultraviolet and visible blues and greens into the (long wavelength) red, infrared, and low energy radio waves. Just as there is this "electromagnetic spectrum" of energy/wavelength, so also one can easily postulate a "meaning spectrum." Our experience plainly tells us that. We talk of "cognitive" and "affective" learning. We speak of "scientific truths" and "spiritual truths." Our task is to try to find a *useful* scale with which to describe meanings—not, of course, a precise quantitative scale, but one that will help us sort out, order, and usefully integrate them into an accurate picture or image of Reality and, thence, the "content" it is radiating.

Because human receivers are involved, it would perhaps not be inappropriate to follow a convenient anthropomorphic simplification in science which divides the electromagnetic spectrum into *ultraviolet* (and higher energies), *visible,* and *infrared* (and lower energies) (Fig. 2.9). These are wholly arbitrary divisions represented below (compare the more general scale above) based on the human eye as the reference point. We can justify such a simplification on the grounds—as Bridgman and Born pointed out—that we cannot transcend this reference.

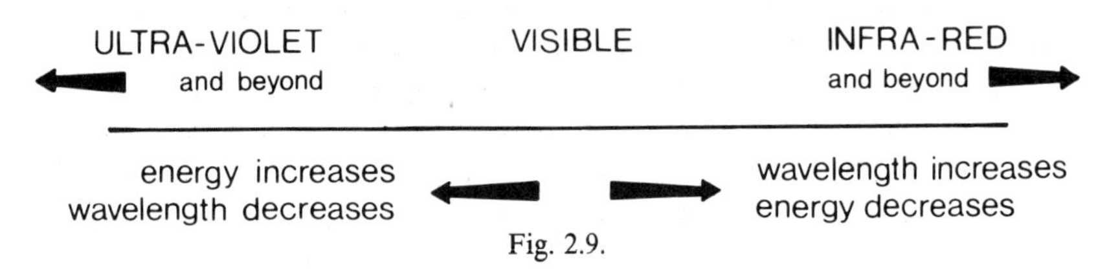

Fig. 2.9.

As a first approximation, we can subdivide the analogous spectrum of meanings which can be measured or sensed into three categories based principally on how such meanings are sensed: subjectively, objectively, and something in between which we will call participatory (where one is both subject and object). We call attention to the fact there are no sharp boundaries between any such divisions in either the electromagnetic or the meaning spectra. They are aids to thinking.

THREE APPROACHES TO REALITY

SUBJECTIVE	PARTICIPATORY	OBJECTIVE

Fig. 2.10.

So here we have our multispectral observer, with detectors for picking up meaning at many different levels or "wavelengths," which reality is radiating unobtrusively—"not parading."

"In the Beginning, was the Word"—the meaning radiated by reality. In the present, there continues this word, this meaning, detected by the senses of human beings from the various parts of reality.

A Subdivision of the Whole of Reality

We may also address the subdivision of Reality very differently. Instead of classifying by how we acquire meaning, we could divide all Reality into different areas or classes which constitute the objects whose meaning is sought. I have found it useful to divide Reality into three areas: Nature, Society, and the Person (see Fig. 2.11). Everything that exists can fit into one or another of these categories. Now, if we compare the two scales, we see that they do correspond rather well and complement each other. (Not, of course, as closely as wavelength and energy which are mathematically related properties which can both be used to describe the electromagnetic spectrum.) Moreover, their accuracy and value can be tested by checking our experience to see if our measuring scale is, indeed, comprehensive. Is there anything we would call real which is not covered under Nature, Society, or the Person (or some combination thereof)? Is there any other way of knowing outside the subjective, participatory, and objective? One does not easily think of anything. Let us expand on how human knowledge about each of the three parts of Reality has been and is being acquired.

THREE ASPECTS OF REALITY

PERSON	SOCIETY	NATURE
human	collective	animate and inanimate

Fig. 2.11.

Studies of *nature* can be done with a high degree of *objectivity.* This means that easy replicability over time and distance is assured. From charting the heavens, mapping the earth, measuring the voltage and current in a semiconductor circuit, or studying the unraveling of a double helix, all human beings extract "very nearly" the same meanings. That's why science "works" so well. From antiquity and in different places of the earth, astronomical observations of remarkable precision enabled different cultures to predict the same events such as eclipses. Today, scientific results flash instantaneously across the globe and Germans, Americans, Britons, Indians, and Japanese use the same threads of data to weave essentially identical new patterns of knowledge. The degree of objectivity and generalizability are maximum (although by no means absolute) in this part of our meaning spectrum. There remains a participatory or community aspect to the conduct of even this natural science, especially at its cutting edges, but it grossly distorts the picture to concentrate on these fuzzy edges when 99 percent of every day workaday science and engineering has the characteristics of "objectivity," reproducibility, and transferability to a fantastic extent *when compared with any other human perception.*

The middle section of this subdivision of reality is our knowledge and experience of *society.* In this domain, to detect or sense the meaning requires some involvement simultaneously as both subject and object. All our knowledge of society is subject to a personal slant. But because as objects of study any group which involves or affects the observer may be only one among hundreds or thousands studied, the observer has "less at stake," and can attain *a certain degree* of detachment. Even as *subjects,* individuals are part of a group (of some dozens or hundreds) and, hence, the unavoidable personal biases are somewhat modified, averaged, or filtered. All human beings make contact with that part of reality we call society, and do so partly in a collective mode.

Lastly, we have the category of Reality we have titled the *person.* Our knowledge of persons may also be acquired, in part, objectively. But the most important meanings which can be discovered about these parts of Reality are intensely personal and extremely subjective. This is the regime of I-Thou knowledge among humans, and between humans and their transcendent thou's.

Where is [illegible]? The Pervasive Influence of Spatial Thinking

No one in the Western world can avoid being "infected" with the God "up there." So many representations repeating the upwardness of heaven—the abode of God—have passed before our eyes and ears and have left at least a "ghost" of an impression. Of course, if any readers of this volume were asked, they would immediately abjure any loyalty to the "up there" metaphor. But it may fairly be asked, then, "where is your [illegible]?" The Bible recounts the truth of the house cleared of seven devils, standing empty, only to be filled by worse. The spatial metaphor of Michelangelo's heaven having been swept out of our psyches, we require some new, more contemporary one to replace it.

In this section we will examine the spatial models which will clearly distinguish at a common-sense level some of the gods of theology from the panentheist understanding of [illegible]. We have said that we start with the individual human.

We must then study the human being's relation to the triply segmented reality of the last section and to [illegible]. *All* human knowledge and experience must be displayable somewhere on the Reality spectrum; there is literally no *thing* outside this reality. And the first major answer, surely, that systematic contextual theology is called upon to give in our world, where reality presses in on us, is to the question: *What is the relation of [illegible] to Reality in all its observable manifestations?* Three classes of answers are possible as we have sketched. Before turning to them, it may be instructive for the reader to try to answer the question for her/himself. Sketch on a piece of paper yourself, as the participant observer, every kind of reality you know and .

In the next few sections and chapters, I will resort to the use of many diagrams and models—physical and spatial representations of the relationships of individuals vis-a-vis reality and . I do this unabashedly. Humans need and *use* visual images as condensed statements about reality. All scientists use models even while they recognize their limitations.

The first or classical model (Fig. 2.12) describes the "linear relationship which puts the individual in the middle between the 'real world' and the 'spiritual God.' " This tug-of-war *linear model* is certainly very close to the spirit of St. Paul's writings and the position of the Medieval Church: the human being is poised between the realities of the world, the flesh and the devil on the one side, and God on the other.

The second model (Fig. 2.13) I believe fairly represents the actual views of most traditionally Christian, or indeed religious, persons. I did not at an early stage in my exploration of these ideas imagine how powerful a hold the classical, nearly Deist views of this second model held over many persons in the pew or in the street. The very terms "God the Creator" and a "wholly other" puts a distance and relationship between and the reality of the universe and earth. That very language leans strongly toward the God *somewhere else.* The common expressions "God the Father," "God the Son," and "God is a Being," and the entire religious linguistic climate have so fashioned the contemporary Western religious psyche that God and the rest of reality are clearly separated.

Even modern process theologians such as Charles Hartshorne tried to (unintentionally) support this "triangular" relationship by their insistence that "God is a living person." But Schubert Ogden, a later exponent of the same school, has correctly identified the dilemma:

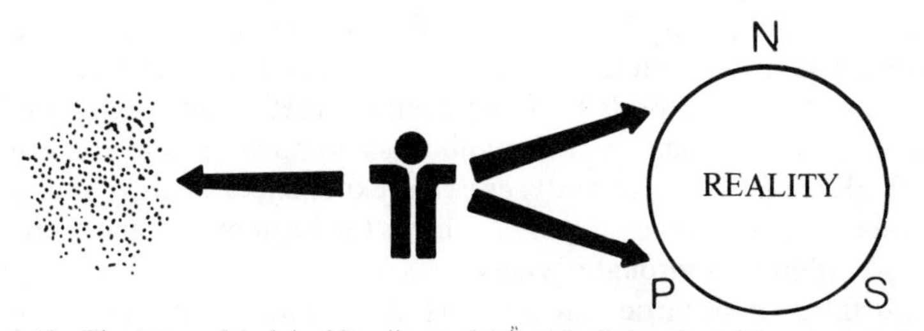

Fig. 2.12. The *Linear* Model of Reality and . "God" is a "spirit" and as such distinct from, and opposed to "flesh" and material things. (Some Biblical and Church language clearly encourages this image of a tug-of-war between God and spirit on one side, and the real world and "flesh" on the other.)

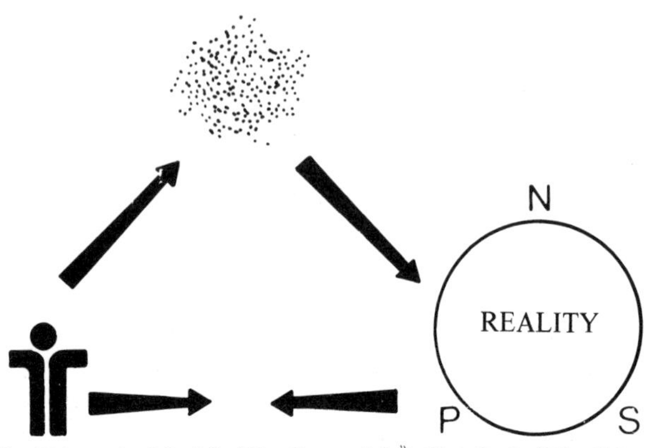

Fig 2.13. The *Triangular* Model of Reality and . The God of Tradition is a creator of and separate from ("wholly other") both reality and the observer. God may be reflected in reality but is separate from it. This is no less true if God is a personal reality *within* each individual as he/she deals with reality.

> *Either one must conceive of God with Aquinas as wholly external to the world, something merely alongside it, and so but part of a whole somehow including God and the world together* [i.e., in a triangular relationship] *or else one must say with Spinoza that it is God who includes the world, but only so as to make the world itself wholly necessary and our experience of its contingency and dependence an illusion* [more or less in the concentric model to follow].

Moreover, all these concepts are so deeply embedded that only very slowly can any change be expected. In spite of *Honest to God* by Robinson and all the writings of Tillich, neither the "depth" metaphor nor the "Ground of Being" has yet taken hold. The "God within" and "Inner Light" of the Quakers, on careful examination, still fit this triangular model; the only difference is that the separated out "God" is now *within* the person, but still distinct from Reality.

Will our concept of "essence of, or radiation from all Reality"—experience of nature, society and persons—fare any better? Possibly, for two reasons. The newer generations in the West and the secular masses of the Second and Third Worlds have not been exposed to an overdose of the *personal* and *anthropomorphic* metaphors so dominant in Judeo-Christian culture. Even more importantly, *everyone* experiences Reality; and everyone *wants* to make some sense of it. That is the beginning of the search for the within and through Reality.

This third "concentric" model, (Fig. 2.14) with the individual at the center embedded in concentric layers of Reality, soaked with , is extraordinarily rich in potential for reconciling religious and scientific perspectives while retaining a great deal of precision in describing the

Fig. 2.14. The *Concentric* Model of Reality and [symbol]. The individual is embedded within her/his own Reality. The fundamental assertion of this view is that [symbol] can *only* be approached *through* Reality. Reality is interposed between humanity and [symbol]. Ours is not a surreal but a perreal [symbol]. The arrows connecting the person to [symbol] show the distinctiveness of the third position very clearly. It is always I → R → B; an individual gets to [symbol] *only* through reality.

human condition. We are, after all, surrounded by Reality on every side. Our drawing is not to be compared with the ceiling of the Sistine chapel, but its intent is not dissimilar. We show the individual in the womb of Reality; a Reality with three faces of nature, of society, and the personal dimension. Not only cars, houses, flowers, and TV sets, but parental love and children's disobedience, the gullibility of the masses, and the beauty of the B Minor Mass are realities that surround and impinge on us. Moreover, it is our personal, repeatable, and verifiable experience that *some* of them speak clearly to us of the "Beyond." The fact that this theology of Reality has not been the basis for earlier major religions is not surprising since it is the SbT revolution which has rubbed our noses, so to speak, in the complex muck of Reality. Yet, the concept has hardly become a household cliché, for there is a hiddenness to Reality's deeper meanings. The symbol for [symbol] is, therefore, shown "beyond" or behind reality, but penetrating into the reality itself whether in the realm of nature, of society, or personal events. The sketch even attempts to represent the density of meaning that we humans can extract from the different aspects of reality. [symbol] is more accessible (more present as [symbol]) beyond the interpersonal realm than through society, and even more so than nature. We have used the expression that all Reality is radiating "meaning," but we have also repeatedly stressed that Reality only "betrays but does not parade" its meaning. Teilhard's expression (here reformatted) "the diaphaneity of Reality," also implies the veiled nature of this transaction. Our common sense experience tells us that Reality does not *proclaim* [symbol]. "The heavens declare the glory of God" is the utterance of the person who has already put on his red and green spectacles and has "fused the images" to see *hidden meaning*. It is not obvious, observable reality. How else can we explain the large fraction of the human race that sees NOTHING BUT the reality of pots and pans, and spiral nebulae, and price wars, and energy shortages? It is quite certain that all human beings agree on the existence and nature of a very large fraction of this reality—in nature, in society, and even about persons (Fig. 2.15). There are, of course, areas of disagreement on the details even about Nature, some are narrow, some wide. The best theoretical physicists quibble about boot straps and ha-

Fig. 2.15. An image of the pan-en-theist [symbol] present in and beyond all the different realities within which all humans are set. Reality is divided for convenience into the areas of Nature, Society, and Person. The different density of dots is meant to signify that some parts of Reality may be more "pregnant" with meaning than others, and that these differences vary from individual to individual.

drons, while the rare fundamentalist preacher still hangs on—against all of modern science—to a flat earth 4000 years old. But all in all, even the common, shared experience of, say, this particular Reality—of a universe some fifteen or twenty billion years old, a heliocentric solar system, a four billion year old inorganic earth giving birth to life, life evolving with steps and starts into ever more complex forms—does not directly and clearly speak of the same [symbol] to all.

Yet, having said that, I firmly believe that, for the nonbeliever and the nontraditional Christian (evolving in his or her religious thought as in all other thought and gradually replacing much of the childhood imagery and language), this approach is sure to make the best sense. For one has little basic difficulty in communicating the concept that our observations of nature, events, and things *may* have much deeper meaning, and form patterns beyond the observations themselves. Our spatial metaphor of the human individual experiencing [symbol] *through* all the surrounding realities is accurate if perhaps too unsubtle. But before one can elaborate further on the totality of meaning of [symbol] as the essence of Reality, it is necessary to move from studying the *object* of this observational process back again to its *subject:* the human being.

All humans make contact with Reality in the continuum of stances which we earlier arbitrarily divided into subjective, collective, and objective. But each one of us also functions in a few specific roles in the varied situations of our lives. Individuals let in meaning through the different filters at different times depending on these roles. "Our many selves" is a familiar theme in contact with different slices of Reality. Therefore, our total image of [symbol] is a superposition of many images, obtained by our different selves, much like the many layers in a color photograph. But, and this is the very important part, the development of the fuller, multidimensional image of [symbol] does not, in the least, need to deprive oneself of using effectively an image obtained with a particular filter which is tuned to a particular role or a particular purpose. Translating into traditional language, this means that for those who have found great meaning through, let us say, a particular form of worship and the majestic cadences of the *Book of Common Prayer,* there is no reason to abandon either that approach or the image of [symbol] perceived through that vehicle. It does mean that the new integration will permit an integration of this view of [symbol] into a richer and deeper Reality. I will return to this extremely important matter later. But first, we turn to the "distortions" humans can introduce because of the stances they start from, the different selves they bring to the task.

2.6 Our Many Selves and How They Perceive Nature and Society

Earlier we quoted notable scientists such as Bridgman and Born who affirmed the central importance of the human observer in the total system of arriving at truth. As we turn our attention now to this human self as observer, we immediately find that the self is often not described as a unity. Much of the recent literature on the different selves of a human being is concerned with the different "roles we play in life." In *Our Many Selves;* Elizabeth O'Connor writes: *"There are helpful aids in identifying the many selves. We see them in the different* roles we play *(parent, sister, worker, expert, scientist, organizer, creator)—there are myriad roles we take on ourselves. . . ."* Yet the categorization of our behavior roles in the last decade or two has focused almost exclusively on our roles in interpersonal transactions. The division into the three-fold parent, adult, and child is by now part of our cultural history. But surely that is only a partial view of the total self. Very little is written, for example, about how *these* different selves perceive reality or understand their own world (that is, how they deal with nature and society). For, after all, the interpersonal interactions are not the only functions or activities in life. While the parent, adult, child categories would be some of the major determinants in how we react to other *persons,* they do not determine how we deal with or view *nature* or *society.* What has been apparent in much of the recent focus on the self is the failure to grasp the truly "religious" nature of life, namely its wholeness. Human beings are *not only* concerned about themselves, their interactions with other persons, and their emotions. Only the tiny, soon to decrease, minority of the Western affluent middle-class has had the luxury of this narcissism. Others worry about food if not survival, how to make a living if not good work, and other basics. They do have a continuing and lively interaction with *society* and *nature.* Besides these survival needs, there is also a "dimension" to life which spurs all human beings to curiosity (thence to science), to explanation, to wonder, to awe (thence toward religion). Can we find some generalizations about our different selves in these situations?

I do not believe that it will be difficult to show that, in addition to the self which "experiences" persons and *immediate* surroundings, each and every human being plays the role of the "scientist" (exhibiting curiosity, analytic thinking, "experimenting") and the "reflector" (standing back, pondering, wondering) every day in a dozen ways. Just as we can ask ourselves whether it is the parent or adult in me that makes me react in a certain way to another person, so can I analyze whether I am reacting like a scientist or religionist to nature or society or to other humans. Remember that every time the housewife (or husband) follows a recipe carefully* s/he is playing the "scientist role." When s/he *purposely* changes the recipe from dill to cumin, s/he is experimenting like a scientist. On the other hand, sitting back and appreciating the food, the table setting, and the company is a "religious role." The student of music watching carefully the fingering of the first violinist of the New York Philharmonic orchestra is exercising her scientific role, but leaning back with eyes closed to appreciate the whole orchestra puts her back in the religious role.

Let us look in somewhat greater detail at these two unfamiliar selves, and perhaps we will all recognize hitherto hidden dimensions of *new* selves within ourselves. Millions of persons, turned off from science in high school, will discover that they are actually (though not, of course, professionally) playing the role of "scientist" for a great part of their lives. Many persons who have not been near a synagogue, church, or mosque in decades will find that they often function in "religious" roles. Here are some examples:

Your Scientific Self (represented in the figures which follow as the "O" for Observer self in Fig. 2.16):

a. "Mary, come over here and look at this flower on my cactus. Look at its funny texture and the peculiar colors. I had no idea these plants blossomed. I am curious as to how often they do this. I think I'll look it up in my plant book, so I can feed it properly." *This is the scientist in you coming out, curious about nature, trying to shape it, organized in your approach.*

b. "Joe, I can't believe that although 70 percent of the people in the United States are in favor of permitting women the choice of whether or not to bear a child, the lawmakers are still leaning so heavily against this social change. It says here that the difference between the Catholic sample and the Protestant sample is only 3 percentage points. That makes the actions of the legislators even less intelligible since it means that even in a 90 percent Catholic district they could not be significantly hurt politically by the issue." *This is the scientist in you analyzing the detailed facts, looking for patterns, comparing.*

c. "From all that I've read, the meditative state is quite different from the hallucinogen-induced states. The heartbeats, α rhythm and rapid eyeball movements were all different in the charts which I saw in TIME magazine." *This is the scientist in you breaking down reality into smaller parts, measuring them, even when it deals with the personal dimension.*

These are the reactions of ordinary persons to relatively common as-

* Recall that for many generations it has been traditional to refer to certain types of empirical research as "cookbook work" or "kitchen chemistry."

O Your OBSERVING Self	E Your EXPERIENCING Self	R Your REFLECTING self
is operating when you find yourself:	*is operating when you find yourself:*	*is operating when you find yourself:*
Limiting the field of interest Isolating the subject under study	Dealing with what's accessible to the "naked eye," the ordinary environment Dealing with the local givens, neither isolating nor aggregating	Expanding the field of view Relating the subject to its surroundings and then on to the larger surroundings and on and on.
This self deals with, or is:	*This self deals with, or is:*	*This self deals with, or is:*
The point in the picture	Small patterns within the big picture	The big picture
Attention highly concentrated	Natural	Deliberately relaxed
Reductionist of neccessity	Extracting meaning from the givens as they are	Integrative of necessity
Attempts to develop universal, transferrable language for: Measuring, Quantifying, Comparing	Attempts to find sufficient commonality of language for useful interaction	Acceptance of "personal reality": Measurement, quantification, and comparison are meaningless
Working together with others and learning from them is easy because of common language which communicates precisely	Working in a small group requires discipline and commitment but is accessible to all as the taste of the meaning of community	Learning from other cultures and ages requires great effort; it is more demanding because it requires imaginative empathy in absence of shared language and experience

Fig. 2.16 *Descriptions of our threefold self.*

pects of their lives—or reality. The reader will recognize (a), (b), and (c) as the "scientific attitude" to Nature, Society, and Persons respectively. What is important is that the self which is looking at reality in this isolating, analytical, detailed, semiquantitative way is what we will call the characteristically scientific self. In order to avoid the language barrier stereotype, we will use "Observation" as specially characteristic of this self.

Your Religious Self (represented as the "R" for Reflective Self in fig. 2.16):

a. "Mary, come and look at this flower! Just look at the play of light through the petals—and to think that it was just one among the thousands or millions of wild flowers right along the road—all different, all beautiful. When I just sit back and consider the variety and richness of Nature, I simply marvel that it can actually exist." *That is the religious self standing back, looking at the big picture.*

b. "Joe, I can't believe that even though 70 percent of the people in the United States favor 'choice' for women in the matter of having children, our political system permits the laws to enforce the opposite. But then, as I reflect on representative government, direct democracy, and all the monarchies and oligarchies that have gone before, I realize how it is *both* the system *and* the individuals involved that are related in a complex way to give us bad or good government." *That is the religious self taking stock of all the influences present in society.*

c. "From my own experience I can tell you that the experience of kneeling at the communion rail at the 8 a.m. service on Easter Sunday with the purple vestments and the lilies standing out against them, as we stand to sing "Christ the Lord is Risen Today," puts me in touch with the deepest wellspring of joy and meaning that I know—I suppose that is one of my most repeatable I-thou experiences of [illegible]." *That is the religious self,* not *measuring, only experiencing directly.*

2.7 Reality Viewed by Our Many Selves

We are now prepared to bring together the images we have been constructing of the object (reality) of our observations and the subjects (our different human selves). What can we "learn" or "experience" of reality from the perspectives of these different selves; how do such learnings differ from each other? We will return to our models and diagrams to supplement our words. For simplicity's sake, although I prefer the sketch in Fig. 2.15, which shows the human being encased in three-segmented reality, I am forced to use the other projection, [illegible], for Fig. 2.17, to keep the sketches manageable. In this sketch we show all of Reality as a sphere—

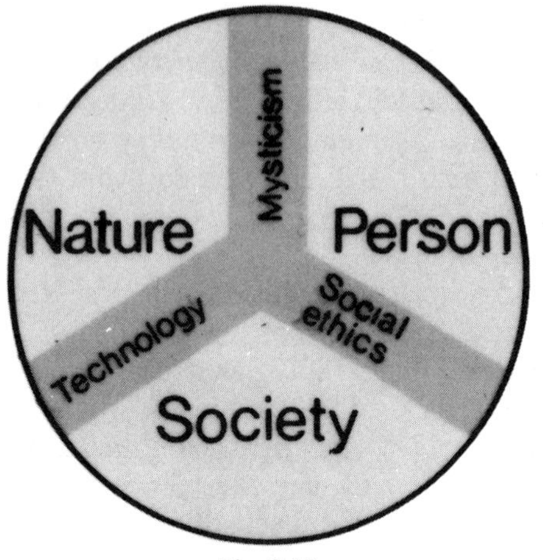

Fig. 2.17

with your imagination helping—divided into three regions of Nature, Society, and Person. This sphere of Reality is meant to encompass all possible aspects of human observation or experience. And I find that these three major subdivisions are necessary and sufficient to describe the vast majority of what most people can encompass under the term Reality. This can be understood especially as we see how well all human *technology* can be represented as the area of overlap between Nature and its organization, control, and manipulation by Society. Likewise, we show the domain of morality and ethics as the area where the domains of Society and Person come together. And mysticism is the border area between Person and Nature.

We now bring to the task of trying to know and experience this total Reality the three prototypical human selves we have described in the immediately previous section. We recognize immediately that each human being is a mixture in different proportions of these three selves. The stereotype of the scientist as a white-coated figure peering down a microscope from morning till night is an accurate description of only a very few. But even such a person has some experience of joy or pain in her or his home life with/without spouse and children. She or he will likely spend *some* time reflecting on the larger political and social issues of the day and how s/he should act in the present situation. How can we describe qualitatively the nature of the mixture of selves, and distinguish it from another person's mixture in different proportions? Let us try it by representing the extent of development of each of these selves by the size of the figures placed on a triangular diagram where each apex corre-

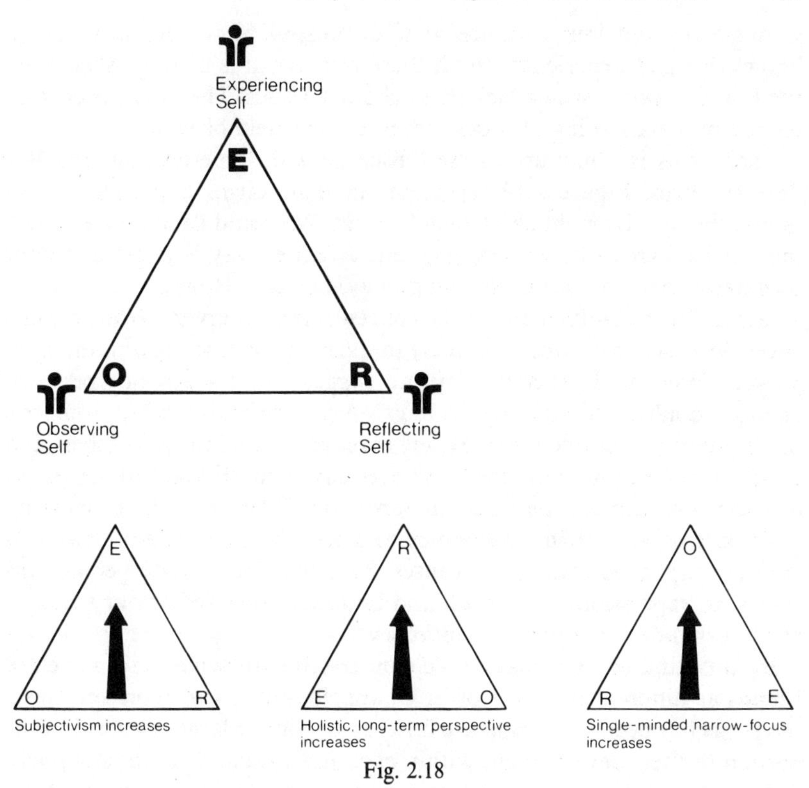

Fig. 2.18

sponds to one of the prototype selves. Our triangle in Figure 2.18 has apexes labeled *R* (the philosophical or *r*eflective self), *O* (the scientific, *o*bservational self) and *E* (the personal, *e*xperiencing self). We will return later to the very important question of the relative importance or value or usefulness of these three approaches. At present, we focus on the description of typical human beings in terms of the mix of selves present in each of us.

At the bottom of the larger triangle we show, by use of the smaller triangles, one characteristic of such representations. As you move toward any one apex (that is, develop that particular self), you can describe your behavior or yourself by certain parameters. These parameters which describe the characteristics peculiar to the self shown *at the apex* are labeled appropriately. Thus, the E–self (personal *e*xperiencing in its approach to Reality) is characterized by subjectivism and inwardness in which respect both the O and R selves are lacking. Correspondingly, the R self involves a long-term and long-distance view of Reality; it is integrative of all knowledge and experience. In all these respects, it is distinguished from the E and O selves which lack these characteristics. The O self is characterized by a narrowing of focus, limiting one's field of view.

Each of us is a mixture of the Observational, Experiencing, and Reflective selves. Figure 2.19 represents in these terms a sample of real human beings. How much of each is in us? We could decide by examining our backgrounds, our training, etc. A better way is to examine our own daily behavior, our time (and money) budgets. How long do I spend as a careful (scientific), narrowly concentrated observer? What experiences do I have in a week (or year) in quiet reading, reflection, thought, prayer? How do I react if someone suggests that I am not personal enough, don't deal with my feelings? Am I defensive when someone points out my scientific illiteracy, my avoidance of all those numbers and details, or when I am reminded that even my guru, William Blake, urged a careful concern for the "minute particulars"? Or am I the calculating analytical person, giving my money to many charities, writing letters to the newspapers, crusading for causes, but not at home with people, uneasy with expressions of warmth and intimacy, offended at our society's newly expanded interpersonal intimacy?

By this kind of examination we can describe ourselves and our close friends as different mixtures of E, O, and R selves, and represent those selves (as has been done in figure 2.19) as smaller or larger figures in proportion to their development within each individual. We are now ready to see how the many selves within each individual will react to the three major facets of Reality. The first question we will need to examine is: Do these three selves remain separate, or do they communicate with each other and try to integrate into *one* whole *personal* view?

2.8 The Dis-Integrated Views of the Selves

Let's summarize what we have here in this oversimplified model (Fig. 2.20): A trinitarian Reality of Nature, Society, Person, perceived by the three-way split personality of the scientific, experiencing, and religious selves. It is no mean task which confronts our human subject—to integrate, put together, and make sense of three different kinds and intensities of responses to signals from three different sources. Is it any wonder that contemporary humans are so thoroughly confused? We have so inundated ourselves with signals, information, perceptions, and experiences that no ordinary person can possibly organize it all for herself or himself. But what is worse is that the intellectual and spiritual and moral leaders have so far been unable to make a credible beginning on this problem.

Three average citizens

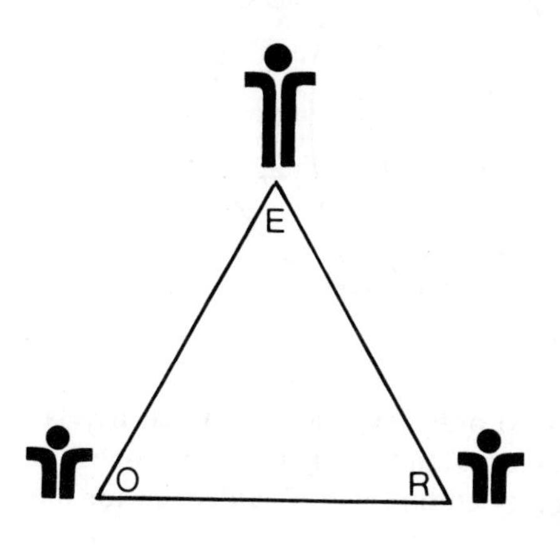

A homemaker with two or three children, active in community and church, greatly enjoying her experiences of many aspects of life. Her scientific self developed in bird watching and plant care; her reflective self through a love and study of choral music.

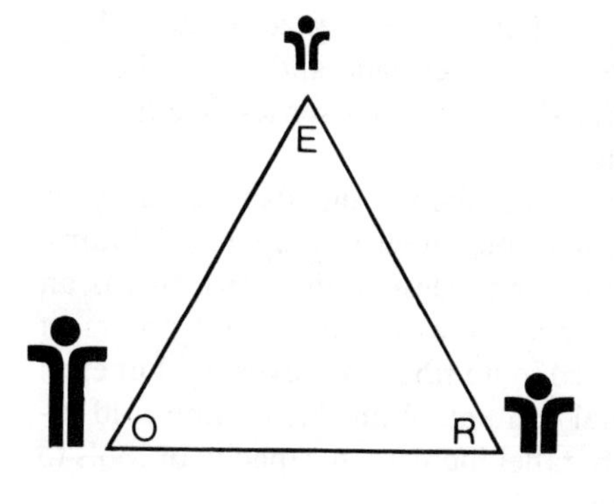

A workaholic scientist who spends nights and weekends in the laboratory trying to track down better preventive measures for influenza. He does not spend much time with nor desire much satisfaction from personal encounters with friends or family. He occasionally reflects on the meaning of his scientific work in the context of understanding nature as a whole.

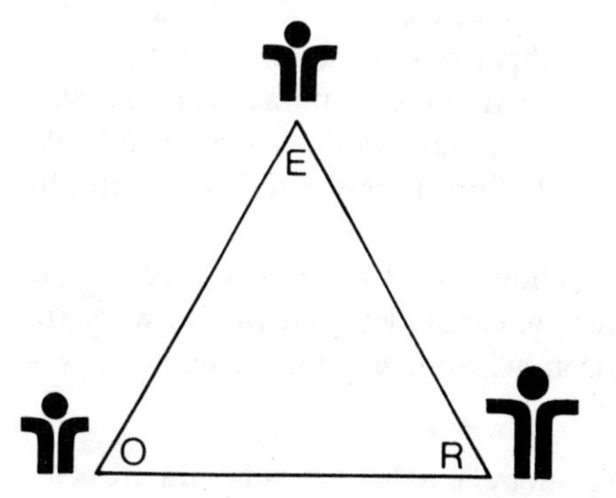

An activist clergyman relating well to parish friends and family, with a wide range of experiences; concerned about society's future, reflecting and meditating on it. Alienated from science at an early age, he is now afraid of analytic, careful thought about nature or society.

Fig. 2.19. DEVELOPMENT OF THE THREE SELVES IN *THREE AVERAGE CITIZENS*

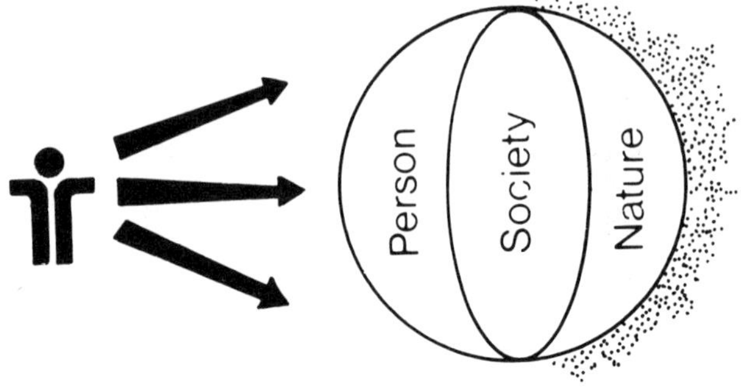

Fig. 2.20

They have no framework in which to order experiences, no clearly labeled compartments to separate oranges and orangutans. No one has provided a map of twenty-first century culture, nor a guidebook for the tourist, even of her native land.

We recognize immediately that much of the root cause of this lostness is the result of modern technology. Alvin Toffler has accurately diagnosed our condition in the terms "sensory overload" and "over-choice." We literally have far too many input signals via our senses. We literally are confronted with too many choices.

A helpful exercise is to compare the number of signals reaching your brain with the number which reached your great grandparents' brains. For all those who come out of farms or modest-sized towns, this is an eye-opener. The number of signals has increased by several orders of magnitude. The sources have increased in number and diversity, but even more so in richness of informational content. With this million-fold increase in information has come no parallel increase in capacity or tools to order or make sense of these signals.

Toffler's examples of "overchoice" are well known. Go to the "drugstore" and look at the 20 brands of toothpaste or deodorant; the 50 varieties of soap. Buying a car, even after selecting the manufacturer, means a choice among dozens of models. Our ordinary radio brings in 50–100 stations in the evening; the television set offers us between six and a dozen different channels 16–18 hours a day.

All this sensory overload and overchoice must inevitably confuse our negentropic,* or organizing or ordering, capacities. Our file drawers are full, and the new pieces of information, wisdom, experience lie in piles—

* Entropy is the measure of disorder; "negentropy" is its opposite—the measure of ordering. Increasing the information content, or the amount of order, means increase of negentropy.

unsorted on our mental desks. Pretty soon we forget that organizing knowledge is possible, that it is valuable, indeed, that it is essential. We are less and less able to usefully integrate signals and choices; indeed, we learn not to do so. We *dis-integrate.* We are simply unable to put things together, to fit sensory signals into a picture, to see connections between different parts of our lives, to bring our values to bear meaningfully on choices regarding ourselves and our society. The result is widespread anomie. The masses get into the habit of keeping the different parts of their lives in untidy piles inside separate compartments.

Indeed, the hallmark of modern culture is the divided self. Just think about your own life, or that of your friends, community, or national leaders for a minute. As I enter the laboratory building, I get caught up into a separate "system," a different world, with its language, its activities, its values. Do I bring into this building, into the entire research proposal to publication system, my concerns for social justice, for changes in income distribution, for finding transcendence in immanence? Of course, one can answer that we cannot at each and every moment be responsive to each and every bit of information or value we have absorbed over the decades. But this is the very "cop-out" which Hitler's citizens also took. Is there not much to be learned from history about the extremes to which disintegration can lead us? Has it perhaps not already led scientists and the SbT enterprise there? Some scientists in responsible positions think so. Here is Adriano Buzzati-Traverso, Italian geneticist, in a commissioned work for UNESCO, writing of the "trahison des scientifiques ("the treason of the scientists"):

> *We have accepted uncritically the trends of our time because they have made possible the rapid growth of our beloved research.... We have not had the courage to refuse to partake in endeavors and enterprises that were endangering the survival of our species and, at the very least, the very values for which we had chosen to become scientists. We have indulged in unethical practices of rivalry, competition, and keeping secret the results or methodologies to make a discovery before our colleagues... practices that we have uncritically introduced into the research system, borrowing them from industry and trade.*

Is this not caused by the inability to make sense out of the world of work with that of value? Does the politician do better? What of the treason of the lawyers who manipulate human situations of extreme need for their gain? How many physicians are concerned about the whole person rather than showing their skill? How many clergy have done the intellectual hard work to connect the values they proclaim to the real world of their parishioners?

But we do know of persons who have really "gotten their *act* together." Strangely enough and as a witness to the many deeper human capabilities genetically coded into us, only a fraction of these have gotten their *"script and* their act together." Far more *act out* creative and meaningful lives they have integrated their tri-focal selves' views into a self consistent theory or theology. So how do we start to make sense out of this wide variety of experiences, perceptions, meanings? Is it, in fact, possible? Is there more than one kind of integration?

Let us begin at the simple sensory level. Our experience is that humans receive different signals from their different senses about any given reality. How do they put them together when they may appear to conflict? We may receive signals, for instance, from the same event via two different senses? We can both *see* lightning and *hear* the accompanying thunder, and long before science explained the connection, human beings still associated one with the other. We often read about an event which immediately explains or fits in with other facts we know. Scientists are continuously putting together old and new facts, ideas, theories, and results of new experiments to weave a new pattern of knowledge. We all have had the satisfaction of dropping the last piece into the jigsaw puzzle. But equally often we get signals which are, or appear to us to be, mutually contradictory. The common expression is "I am receiving *mixed signals.*" It is quite obvious that for healthy functioning every one of us tries to construct a *self-consistent* picture of the reality we must deal with. A woman wearing perfume walks in the room and her presence is communicated by sight and smell. But if the woman who normally used Chanel #5 walks into the room from the outside, and we smell a skunk, our mind searches through plausible alternative explanations for the apparent inconsistency. These might include:

- *There is a skunk near the window and the woman's appearance at the same time was pure coincidence;*
- *The woman was outside and actually came in contact with some of the skunk's oil;*
- *My nose is acting up.*

What our minds are doing is comparing the sensory data with *patterns* stored in the memory. Only after eliminating some of these alternatives would someone consider the possibility: *Maybe I was wrong in my first association of this woman with Chanel #5; she really does have an offensive odor.* The reason by which we reject the last explanation (at least until very much more thorough examination requires its consideration) is our own memory of experiences and empirical learnings that fresh-looking women use perfume and tend to smell pleasant.

This process of integrating data from all our senses and the direct and indirect input from our fellow humans, and then using the calibration of our own past experience and knowledge is a routine practice we all utilize for ordinary tasks, such as driving a car, buying food, etc., every day. Most of this "information processing" is, of course, done quite unconsciously. Yet, as I will show in detail, this integration is almost never performed at the deepest or more general levels of human existence. The three selves write out three parts for their separate players; seldom are they woven into the same play. Life becomes an inside out "Rashomon" play. WE DO *NOT* integrate our deepest religious convictions and values with our beliefs and actions in political, societal, and technological areas. WE DO *NOT* reconcile the hundreds of statements about nature in the Bible, the Koran, or the Upanishads which are strongly in disagreement—if taken literally—with modern science and technology. WE DO *NOT* integrate the rich and powerful insights and effectiveness of SbT with the equally rich, but not immediately powerful, directions pointed by Christian or other religious values.

The empirical and absolutely certain fact is that the vast majority of humankind will experience the partial truths of scientific statements and their reliability at the workaday level of technology. Because it can be verified in simple matters, SbT will become inexorably the standard reference for truth. It behooves those of us who affirm this truth, and its power and simultaneously affirm its partialness, to make sure that this partialness and, hence, need for complementing with other truths be spread wherever SbT is broadcast. Since I will build my case on the absolute necessity for the integration of the SbT perspective with our religious concerns and values, I will begin first by developing an example of the human capacity for integration of signals. I choose an example based on contemporary science which can be experienced by virtually everyone, and which shows that, while life can go on apparently quite adequately without such integration, its absence literally causes us to forfeit a whole dimension of life.

2.9 The Human Cyclops: Integrating Similar Signals

In the foregoing model we have written of a (arbitrarily) segmented reality being perceived by a human observer (arbitrarily) divided into three selves. We now turn to discussing how the multiplicity of observations and inputs reaching the observer are dealt with.

We have started by observing that in many—perhaps most—cases such different inputs may NEVER be synthesized or correlated. They may be and very often are stored in very separate compartments, to our loss. After all, who does not know of a brilliant scientist with a Sunday School level of religious development; or of pious men of faith talking scientific nonsense or standing passively by at incredibly inhuman acts? Our thesis is that we will gain enormously by performing an integration of these signals received from different viewpoints. We start by establishing that such gains can be not only quantitative but qualitative; i.e., integration can lead us to wholly new "levels of perception."

Since I will be using optical analogs and imagery extensively, let me start by making the case for the visual sense as being a good model for the processes in the whole sensate human. First, we note the summary findings of psychologists as recounted by R. Montgomery in "Memory made easy" that 85 percent of all the information used by humans enters via the eyes (ears supply another 11 percent). Next, we recall the profound importance of specific optical processing of information upon human consciousness. This is not some recent discovery. The connection of memory with spatial orientation has been utilized for centuries. Alan Mackay makes this point:

> *However, our visual sense is undoubtedly the most powerful and other faculties can be boosted by coupling them to our spatial imagination—which must have developed from the earliest stages of evolution. Clearly man as an animal was greatly advantaged by a good visual sense and memory and this improved through natural selection long before civilisation. We have not only a memory for flat pictures but can put them together in the solid to visualize and recognise views which we have never seen before. Later other more civilised arts were harnessed to the visual sense. For example, before literacy became common, advocates and others learnt special techniques for remembering their speeches. This continued to be taught until at least the foundation of the Royal Society in the seventeenth century. Mnemotechnics teaches speakers to visualise an actual theatre of the ancient Greek pattern and to see each of their topics in a particular place represented by some visual analogy. The different items could then be read off in sequence or even recalled in any desired order. The art of memory was one of the major subjects in a professional training. In fact the word "topic" is just from the Greek "topos," the place where you put your images.*
>
> *Salvator Luria, the Russian brain expert, has shown that in the case of his patient, "the man with the wonderful memory," all feats of remembering were geared to visual representation.*

For two decades, the Hungarian scientist Bela Julesz, now Head of Sensory and Perceptual Processes Research at the Bell Telephone Laboratories, has devoted himself to the optics, computer science, and psychology of these processes. His papers and book, *Foundations of Cyclopean Perception,* are truly the foundation work in the field. They deal basically with the process of "stereopsis," the "fusing" of the two images sent by our two eyes to the brain to be "fused" as it were into a single-eyed human cyclops and convey the sense of the third dimension. We are all familiar with 3-D viewers and 3-D movies which we observe with red and green glasses. Julesz is concerned with the fundamentals of the process of depth perception. The original work has hundreds of black-and-white and red–green pairs of images which illustrate the different principles involved. It is impossible to give the reader the full experience of the phenomenon without the proper physical arrangements. However, the reader is urged to turn to figures 2.21 and 2.22 to study the stereograms, and carry out the exercises which will explain the phenomenon in a less abstract way.

The stereograms reproduced in the figures were generated by B. Julesz at the Bell Telephone Laboratories by programming a computer to produce random arrays of dots in pairs. In fact, each individual view has literally *no useful information;* it is merely a random array of dots. (The analogy to the perception of reality of events by one of our selves, as a series of uncontrollable random events, should not be missed.) Only the *difference* between the two random sets contains the information which shapes the three-dimensional images and give the stereoptic effect. And only by combining the images from two eyes (plus integrating that information with stored information) can one bring out the full three-dimensional image. The analogy that we draw in the following sections is the absolute necessity for binocular (or more generally multiocular) perspectives on reality to provide a true image thereof. Such binocular images, together with the best of human memory from its religious traditions, represent the only sure way to obtain both depth and perspective about the deeper-lying realities. When you perform the "stereoptic fusion" or watch others do it and see in succession the puzzlement, then sudden excitement and pleasure which comes over them as they experience the sensation of an added dimension, you are reminded of those who have suddenly perceived the added dimension of which lies hidden in the day-to-day realities which surround us, after years of sheer unawareness or puzzlement at the meaning of it all. The vast majority of us see exactly the same realities (in our analogies the same individual pictures as in the figure *viewed with one eye monocularly*) and can have no idea of all the information they contain,* that they "betray (to the initiated) but do not parade."

The two random-dot stereograms which appear when "fused," show a spiral ascending toward the viewer. I chose this symbol of the evolution of the universe and of human history with humanity at its arrow point as a key concept where the scientific world view and the Judeo–Christian story provide complementary insights. The actual random dot symbol I have used through this book for God, , is a fragment taken from such a stereo-pair. In a nearly literal way it represents the Meaning Beyond in the Meaningless Midst.**

---

* See the footnote referring to Elizabeth Barrett Browning on page 87.

** I wish I could also have claimed for it the property of the hologram, whereby one could have reproduced the full original from even a tiny fragment of the image.

Fig 2.21

PROOF OF THE VALUE OF INTEGRATIVE VISION

Each separate diagram above is a computer-drawn random array of dots. In a literal sense it has no information. But the pair viewed together reveal not only a message, but a message with three dimensions. That is what you can expect of a multidirectional approach to Reality and the Beyond: discovering the higher dimensions to life.

How to view the random-dot stereograms: Sit comfortably with the sheet flat on a desk or on a backing, at a comfortable reading distance (12—15 inches) and more or less perpendicular to your line of sight, (i.e., you are looking straight down if it is on a flat desk). Get comfortable as it may take many minutes. Start by looking up at some distant object—out of the window or across the room—then quickly move your eyes down to the diagrams. Your eyes will tend to cross and the two diagrams will tend to merge (but they'll drift apart, and you've got to keep *gently* trying to bring the two images to overlap completely in a single image. Don't try too hard). Rest for a few seconds, look out, try again. Focus on the overlapped image in the center. Suddenly, the single image will "lock on." You will, like Archimedes, shout "Eureka," for a three-dimensional symbol will stand out clearly from the page. Be patient. It took me three tries, days apart, to succeed. *Once you do it you will never forget how to do it again.* If you cannot, it is possible that you belong to the 15 percent of the population who can never do it. The learning from this exercise is that only two eyes can see the beyond one-eyed Reality.

Julesz' summary of the process of human vision is shown in Figure 2.23. Notice first the two steps in the mixing of the separate signals from our eyes. In a very real sense, we can say that the mere optical superposition of the two images (i.e., the binocular combination) does not give one depth perception. For that to happen there must occur an interaction of this superimposed information with memory, with information previously stored in the brain (form recognition). Then a second combination occurs in a single "cyclopean eye" (stereopsis). The most dramatic ilustration of this comes if you perform the experiment of trying to see the third dimension (with or without the special glasses supplied in Julesz'

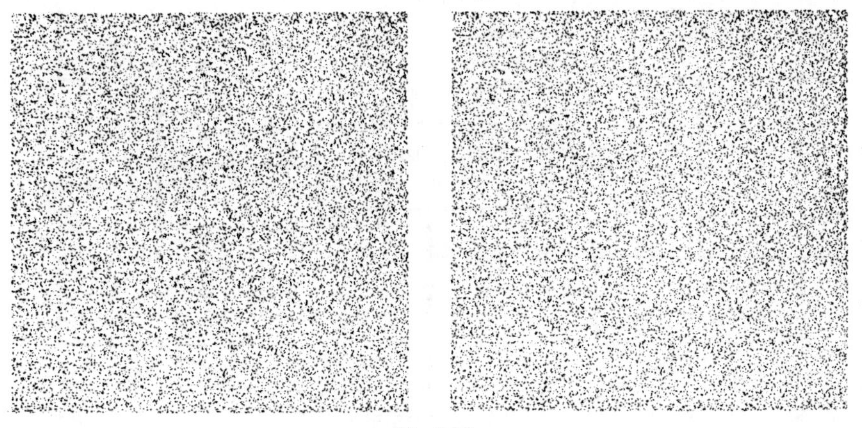

Fig 2.22

The images you can find by integrating these two pairs of meaningless dot-patterns are.*

a. *In this set* an appropriately modern symbol for [illegible], you will see a helical spiral coming out of the page, representing the evolutionary core of the universe.
b. In the set on *the facing page* a classical symbol for [illegible], a triangle set above the background.

book). It often takes several minutes till you suddenly see the pattern emerge from the two images of the truly random set of dots. Some see the image nearly instantly and some can never do so. Try it. You will break out into a "knowing smile" as soon as you succeed. Another important property that Julesz notes is that, once you have seen the image, the next time you try, days or even years later, you quickly see the pattern.

What a good analogy this process bears to our perception and experience of [illegible]. Once you have integrated many images from meditative, affective, and cognition experiences, you can immediately see the depth in the pattern again and again. A new painting in the National Gallery recalls the image. A new scientific discovery sheds new light on the same. A guitar hymn with a particularly good symbiosis of words and music makes that image shimmer anew. And even when you are confronted with bewildering (random) experiences in one plane—be it the loss of a child in an accident or confusion in the theological world—your heart can remember that when you put together and "fuse" all the images, the same reality will emerge.

To sum it up, we have shown that human knowledge-experience in the

---

* Julesz' book carries red-green overprinted versions of these stereograms and a viewer. This makes it very much easier to see the third dimension.

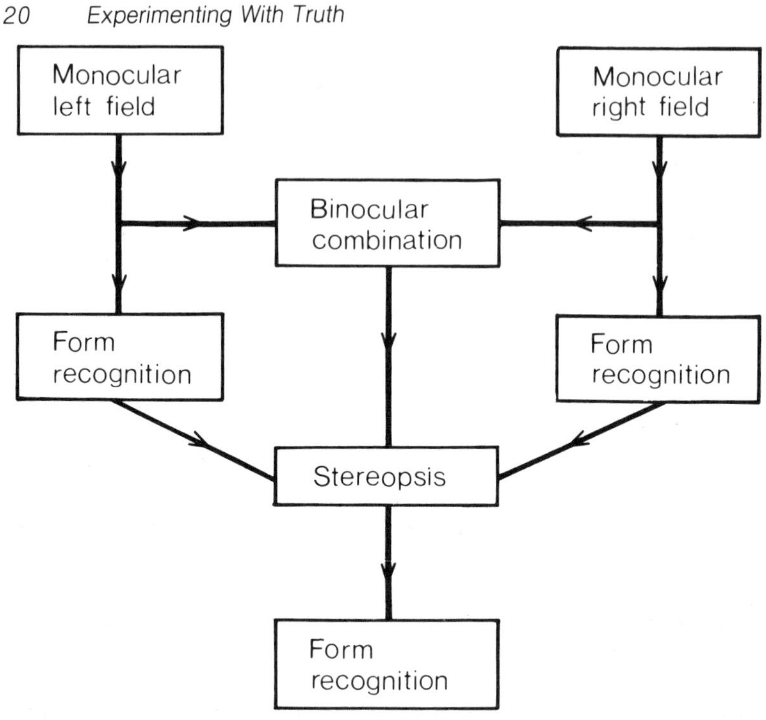

Fig. 2.23

area of visual images demands two-eyed or binocular data. We have shown that such two–channel information is fused not only optically but, after processing in the brain and comparison with known images, into images with a totally different character of depth. We will also develop the theme that a complete view of reality demands such fusion of different images formed at different distances.

2.10 The Brahma Posture: Universal Integration

If Cyclops is the appropriate mythos for integration of commensurable (that is, of the same nature or measure) signals by humans, perhaps Brahma is the analogous symbol for the most universal synthesis or integration. The traditional representation of Brahma the Creator facing in all four directions is almost literally the model we have used. But Brahma is, of course, the appropriate "symbol" because Brahma is the name for the Universal Reality used by Hinduism. It is appropriate in our specific connection here because not only does it imply a synthesis from four viewpoints, but also an integration of apparently conflicting and apparently incommensurable data. This theme of the rediscovery of Both-

And-ism is a major part of the third book in this series. Emerson has caught up this theme in his poem with the same title:

Far or forgot to me is near;
Shadow and sunlight are the same;
The vanished gods to me appear;
And one to me are shame and fame.

They reckon ill who leave me out;
When me they fly, I am the wings;
I am the doubter and the doubt,
And I the hymn the Brahmin sings.

The Brahmanic Person is the one who, in this our model, has completely integrated into one Reality the views of its segments obtained from these perspectives. Let us conclude this section by following through the same model and understanding the many kinds of integration which can occur.

Multifocal Integration

We come to one of the most important points which this little book tries to make. How do we, as individuals and as a society, relate and either separate or integrate our "observational," "experiential" and "religious" selves? We have described these selves as short, middle, and long focal-length views of Reality, and we recognize that if properly equipped one can get a sharp image of the whole just as one can get with a trifocal pair of glasses. For simplicity and brevity, we will deal in the following first with the bifocal case. If you have had the experience of switching from ordinary (monofocal) eyeglasses, to bifocal glasses, you will remember how excruciatingly awkward the latter were for weeks. You tripped going down the stairs because you forgot to move your whole head; you squirmed when you looked down at a page and up to see a visitor and so on. Bi*focal* is, of course, different from bi*nocular* (Fig. 2.24). Bifocal refers

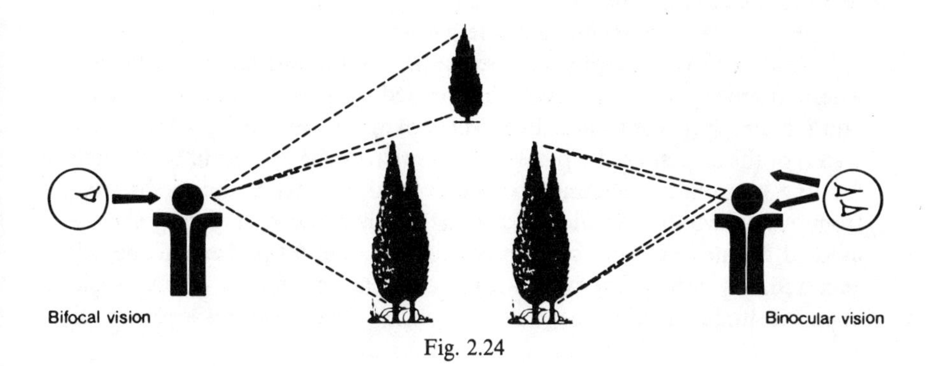

Fig. 2.24

to two focal distances—looking at objects which are close up, e.g., newspapers, and those far away, e.g., the scenery.

A high percentage of humans, in late life, need to have "reading glasses" to examine clearly anything about a foot away. Many also need glasses to see distant objects clearly. The bifocal pair of glasses used by millions of middle-aged persons has a precise analog in larger life. Not only in our human *vision,* but in our entire perspective on life do we need bifocal (really trifocal) aids. It is essential that in addition to our megascopic or naked-eye view, we have both the close-up, "microscopic" view and the long-distance, "telescopic" view, to be able to get the fullest picture (see Fig. 2.7 on p. 94). It is not difficult, therefore, to make the connection between what we have called the "scientific self" of the last section with the close-up, microscopic viewer; and of the "religious self" with the long-range, long-distance perspective.

The sequence of three photographs (Plates 1–3) can help illustrate the concept of multifocal images of the same reality. The big picture—the R (reflective) or religious perspective reveals the well-known view of Mount Rushmore in South Dakota. A middle range view shows a sculpture of the head of President Theodore Roosevelt. Taken by itself, one couldn't tell whether this was a close–up of a small bust in a small museum or the twenty-foot carving on the side of a mountain, which it is. Likewise, the close-up view of only the bridge of the spectacles on his face (or to carry it further, a photomicrograph [not shown] of the sandstone from which it was carved) has intrinsic useful information, but much of it would be nearly useless, except when the context or setting of the two lower figures is properly taken into account.

One can find three very basic correspondences between this physical metaphor and our observations of human behavior:

1. Many persons manage life without ever getting distance glasses or reading glasses. Some don't need them, but many seem to manage without them seeming not to care about really seeing the full picture clearly. Neither the scientific self nor the religious self may be very strongly developed in a large percentage of the people.

2. One can easily develop one perspective to the exclusion of the other. There are many who look through unaided eyes or telescopes at mountain streams but would not dream of looking at the teeming life in tap water, or the structure of a petal under a microscope. It should be obvious that the information obtained from one focal distance is simply different from but yet wholly complementary to the other. It can in no way ever be used to "contradict" the other meaningfully. Yet 99 percent of the science-religion debate has been a fight over the differences of our world observed under a microscope and through a telescope, respectively, as

Plate 3
Close up: the perspective of the scientific or observing (O) self.

Plate 2
Middle Range: the perspective of the experiencing (E) self.

Plate 1
The big picture: the perspective of the religious (R) self.

though there should be a direct fit between them. No one would expect the telescopic picture of a galaxy to be similar to a scanning electron microscope picture of rocks brought back from the moon, just because they are both views of extraterrestrial nature. Yet that is precisely what some have tried to do with scientific and religious insights.

3. It must be obvious that for the fullest picture one must use the trifocal perspective of microscope and telescope to aid our naked eye. Moreover, the simple but absolutely applicable analogy tells us that properly inserting the microscopic information into the megascopic or telescopic picture in a useful and enriching way is not a simple task. It can often give downright misleading results.* Indeed, much of this bifocal switching of signals has been thoroughly confusing for society in much the same way as the newly fitted bifocal spectacle wearer is confused. The proper "fusion" of information from three focal distances is difficult but absolutely necessary to "see" the fuller dimensions of existence.

Binocular "Fusion"

We have already introduced the concept of binocular fusion in a highly specific way in discussing the beautiful experiments of Julesz with the perception of stereopsis, and seeing the extra dimension. What we learn from this example in the science of vision is that using two eyes can really give a person an experience of the third dimension which *simply cannot be obtained from a monocular view.* Not only is the God of much public religion much too small, "He" is also "flat." Binocular fusion as we have seen introduces us to the process of mixing signals and comparing them against a stored memory bank of patterns. This process allows us to perceive, nay, experience, one more bank of dimensions of reality which transcends the planes of observation or experience. John Robinson, after his exploration into Eastern religions and their relation to the Judeo-Christian tradition, has written of "Two-eyed Truth." His parallel is exact. These are two views, each with the long-distance focus of religion, but they can complement each other binocularly to give the dimension of

---

* In the earliest years of my professional career, I was involved in the beginnings of the application of electron microscopy to study the shape of the very tiny crystals which make up certain kinds of mineral matter. The clays and asbestos are typical examples. The danger in such work was that we could never be sure that the intriguing or spectacular shape we had in the field of view after magnifying it 50,000 times was "representative" of our whole sample. If you had a small thimbleful of sample, a typical small shape may be only one trillionth (i.e., a millionth of a millionth) of the whole. That small part may not even have belonged to the original whole, but merely be "dirt"—misplaced matter. Much of the world viewed through the scientific self's microscope is real enough; but it just does not give a *representative* view of our reality.

depth in the combined image of . Yet these two binocular long-distance views must themselves be complemented with a microscopic or close-up perspective to give a *bifocal* enrichment to the image, of a wholly different character from that obtained by the *binocular* feature. This imagery of the combination of the binocular and the bifocal (more accurately, multiocular and multifocal) will lead to rich analogies.

Simultaneous Bifocal and Binocular Mixing

We can now summarize how the human subject as observer makes sense of its encounter with Reality. A human perspective on Reality using the full capabilities of our senses and our whole person is made up of many sets of stereopairs of bin*ocular* fusion. Then this information obtained at different focal lengths is combined to yield a sculpture of the real world around us in proportion and correct perspective.

Now all this may sound terribly complicated, but it is obviously possible since we *all* do it so naturally *all* the time with our optical information. Even as you are reading this with a close-up perspective you can glance out of the window to see the nearby landscape, and look out further to the sun shining in from 93 million miles away. What each of us has learned to do quite effortlessly is to take these signals received by our eyes and, by combining them with past experience (for the near and middle ground) or more abstract learning (for really long distances), create a truly three-dimensional sculpture of Reality. Although the optical signals received from different objects are identical, there is no doubt in our minds that the book I'm reading is only twelve inches away, the nearby woods a mile away, and the sun a hundred million times further. When I move my papers or reach for a pencil I know that that information lodges in my nearby plane; a line of cars in the valley is in the middle range; the stars at night in the far distance. This universal experience of the human capacity to process signals from various distances, to mix binocular signals with essentially monocular ones, and create a Reality-sculpture is the model and the guarantee that one can repeat the process to the multidimensional situation (Fig. 2.25).

2.11 Completing a Contemporary Sculpture of Reality

We have now come to the final stage of the assembling of our three-dimensional sculpture of Reality.

Since the dawn of human history, I believe humanity had a unified picture of Reality. Whatever it was, however "wrong" it was, there was, as it were, a place for everything and everything was in place. It was, I

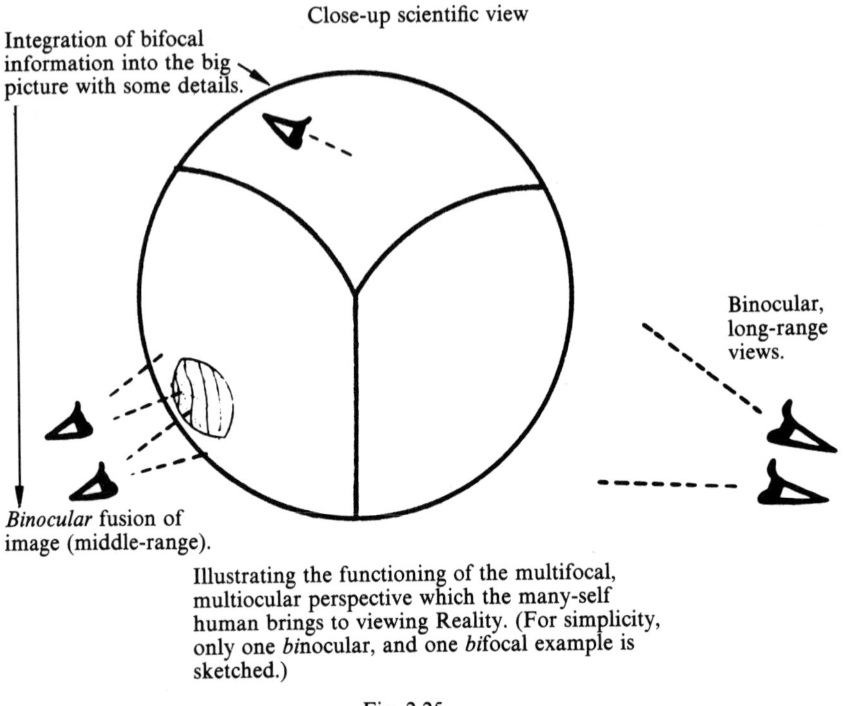

Illustrating the functioning of the multifocal, multiocular perspective which the many-self human brings to viewing Reality. (For simplicity, only one *bi*nocular, and one *bi*focal example is sketched.)

Fig. 2.25

think, only as a concomitant to the growth of science and technology that the disintegration of the unified view has taken place. The new task is to reassemble and reconfigure the views of the three selves so that what they reveal can be put together to develop a coherent sculpture of Reality.

It is quite clear from the immediately preceding section that one of the distinctive positions developed in this book is the very different relationship between scientific and religious truth from that usually pictured. They are, by definition and by experience, concerned with exactly the same Reality. Yet the pictures they present may bear absolutely no resemblance to each other because they are from completely different focal distances. We must now examine in detail the information on Reality collected by the three separate selves.

The scientific or observational self can most accurately be portrayed as the close-up, the microscopic, worm's eye view of the terrain. It starts with the decision to narrow one's focus, work with a small area, to consciously exclude most of reality in order to concentrate one's attention. In my field of thermodynamics of matter, we start by defining a "system" as "that portion of the universe isolated for study," with nothing going in or out of it. I have developed the thesis elsewhere* that *the* constitutive nature of science and the absolute limitations to its usefulness to society is this isolating out of a small, manageable element of existence. By definition, science works with parts and never with wholes. It avoids the connectedness, the relationships of things one to another, in order to focus on the part. And the justification for this strategy is all around us. The might of modern science and technology have resulted from just this discipline of NOT looking outside one's immediate field of view. By detailed attention to the placing of one's single brick into a specific place, scientists and engineers have built a most imposing edifice. Of course, scientists also stand back and develop comprehensive theories, and a Newton or an Einstein daydreams under an apple tree or in a patent office looking at the big picture. But as thousands have testified, when a scientist is performing the latter function of integration, of taking the long-range view, of looking at the grand design, she or he is functioning just like an artist or philosopher. The grand designs of nature are revealed to scientists functioning in the reflective (= R) mode, not when they are functioning as quintessential working scientist-engineers. It is not coincidence but simple existential fact that science started as natural philosophy and ended as the cooperative machine of thousands of people putting a man on the moon. And even today, the theoretical physicist or mathematician, who does not even examine in detail the data utilized in his/her theories, functions therein as a philosopher and not as a typical scientist (as defined herein and as understood by most humans). In our terminology, the same human being may function four days a week as an experimenting, working scientist-engineer *O* (isolating a small system, analyzing rocks, studying mitochondria, building this bridge), and she may switch on the fifth day to a *R* mode as she serves on an advisory committee examining the impact of certain research on the nation or community. There is, of course, a cumulation. The human person integrates these "inputs" from the individual selves, and that newly integrated person no doubt functions somewhat differently in the next event, whether as R(eflective), O(bserving) or E(xperiencing). Before developing the nature of this integration, let us look in some detail at everyday examples of our functioning in these separate modes as we examine Nature, Society and the Person.

(In the larger figure (Fig. 2.26) we show reality as a large sphere divided into its segments of Nature, Society, and Person.) We then represent each perspective (O,E,R) as a cone of viewing, with the shaded area being the area of concern which comes into focus (Fig. 2.27). Thus, we

* Proceedings of the ITEST Conference, 1977.

REALITY AS VIEWED BY THE "SCIENTIFIC SELF"

(Note the characteristic feature of the close-up or microscopic view, and hence the narrow field of view in each case)

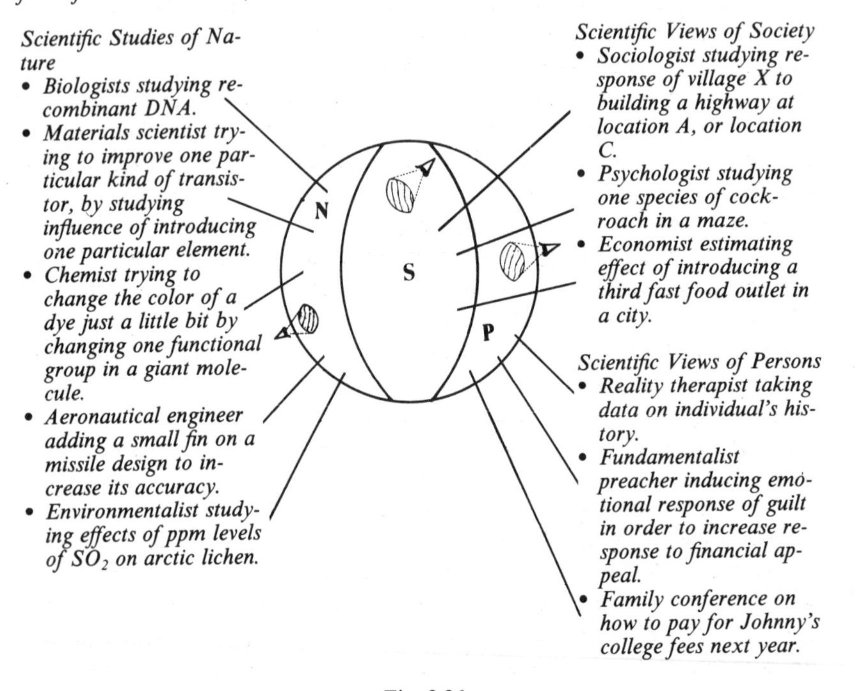

Fig. 2.26

portray the scientist selves characteristically focusing on the very small circles of interest. The characteristic tool of the scientist, the "microscope," automatically limits one to such a narrow field. The power of science comes from this intense focusing. It comes from building onto contiguous to, or on top of, the existing body of knowledge. Here and there in the edifice of Reality the scientist self spots an interesting tiny lacuna. Curiosity is aroused. It goes to work on this isolated, limited segment, and fits her results into the neighboring structure of knowledge.

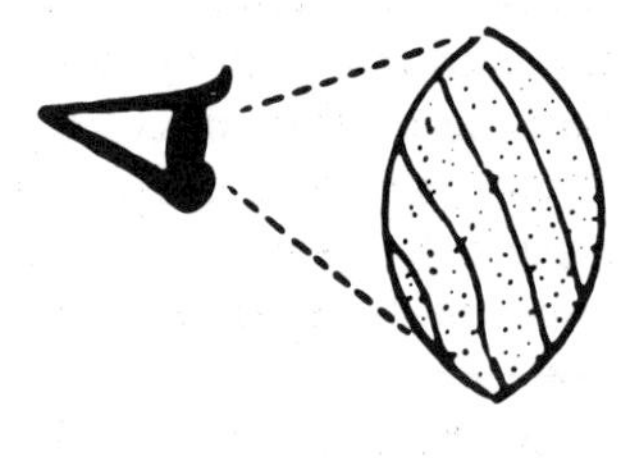

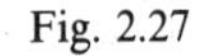

Fig. 2.27

Up to the present time, the part of Reality which has received the lion's share of the interest of the scientist selves is Nature (and its interaction with society in technology). The diagram shows this concentration on natural science and gives examples of the limited scope of scientific fields of view. However, among the examples it will be seen that the scientific self may also take as the object of its study, Society, and even the Person. Sociology, psychology, and medicine are disciplines in which the scientific self takes the reductionist, limited view of society and the person. On the one hand, while such precise and detailed knowledge of the relevant natural science has resulted in many of the "miracle cures" of science, it is now becoming much clearer that the very words *social* (societal) science may be a contradiction in terms. Can *society* be ever "known" only at the microscopic level? Is not society *essentially* a matter of connections? Likewise, when studying the *person* must we not bring in the experimental and reflective levels? In spite of the marvelous and very tangible benefits of modern medicine, we are all becoming much more convinced that the full person's healing demands more than biochemical and biomechanical monitoring and adjustment. And the track record with one of science's most spectacular successes—space technology and its so-called spin-offs—reveals that the scientific self's perspective, while it can be applied to the society and person domains of Reality, will always find its major value in revealing Nature.

The second self through which Reality is perceived is that of experience. Our diagram has characterized this self as one which makes contact with Reality unaided by instruments—working only with the "naked eye," or more generically the "naked personality." Its field of view is larger than that of the scientific self. Its observation of Nature is not made with the geologist's pick, astronomer's telescope, or biologist's electron-microscope. It functions as the whole person, unaided by instruments. This self experiences Nature as the beauty of a cherry tree in full blossom, the glory of sunsets and mountain vistas. On the reality of Society, it makes no statistical survey of poverty, but experiences the effects of poverty in the black ghetto in Washington or the sidewalks of Calcutta. It learns a great deal about the personal dimension of Reality through direct I-Thou experiences of others with colleagues at work, a small group of friends, and the beauty, pain, and complexity of the interactions of two human beings in love.

The second sketch continues the lengthening of the focal distance. It describes the perspective of the third self, that of philosophy or religion. The characteristic of the mood of reflection is taking the distant view, painting in the total picture, putting together the wholes from the parts. We have called this the reflective self (R). Our sketch shows that there are many *directions* from which one can take this long-focal view. Every direction corresponds to a different religion or philosophy for approaching the whole Reality segmented into Nature, Society and Person. Let us start with the mainstream scientific world view, which is of this genre. The view seen from this direction has in its center Nature. Only on its periphery does it deal with society and even to a lesser extent the person. Conversely, most religious world views would have the person and personal relations to society in their center of attention. Religions do not pay as much attention to Nature which appears typically on the periphery of their field of view, although obviously not all religious viewpoints are identical. The Judeo-Christian field of view would have the personal and societal (loving your neighbor as yourself) area clearly in the bullseye. Only on the fringes of its field of view would there be reference to Nature (and, for example, the creation myth*). Some eastern religions, in contradistinction, may focus further over toward the personal dimension and even encompass the relation to Nature, so to speak, on the other side of our sphere, where the Nature and Person domains of Reality meet. A political philosophy-religion such as Marxism has the domain of Society sharply in its center, and its relation to Person and Nature on its periphery. The reader is encouraged to test the accuracy of these sketches and perhaps make up one of her/his own viewpoint.

2.12 Science and Religion: A Clarified Complementarity

The approach which I have taken here toward the alleged or possible "conflict' between the contributions of the scientific self and any religious self is substantially different from the usual. Instead of stressing the part of Reality (see Fig. 2.28) which occupies most of the field of view (i.e., matter for science, and spirit for religion), this approach defines the difference as differences in focal length—close up or long distance. Correct scientific insight will, in general, provide the details which firm up or embellish any big picture of a religious world view. Conflicts can arise in two ways: first, when a religious view includes a statement or claim at the focus or detail level which is properly within the scientific perspective. Such a conflict is merely a scientific debate and will be resolved at the level of and by the rules of scientific debate. Two examples will illustrate. Fifty to a hundred years ago the Protestant churches in the United States, on the basis of what they would have had to connect to a "revelation" (by some tortuous argumentation), held that alcohol consumption (and possibly tobacco smoking) was evil because it was bad for your health (it abused the "temple of God," etc.). But a liberalized society threw off the yoke of religious hegemony and assumed that since smoking was not "sinful," it was also not harmful. For most of the century, science provided no insight on the matter. But in the last few decades, after innumerable detailed scientific studies, the incredible toll of alcohol and the

* B. Davie Napier has defined myth most helpfully, as "a truth that never was but always is."

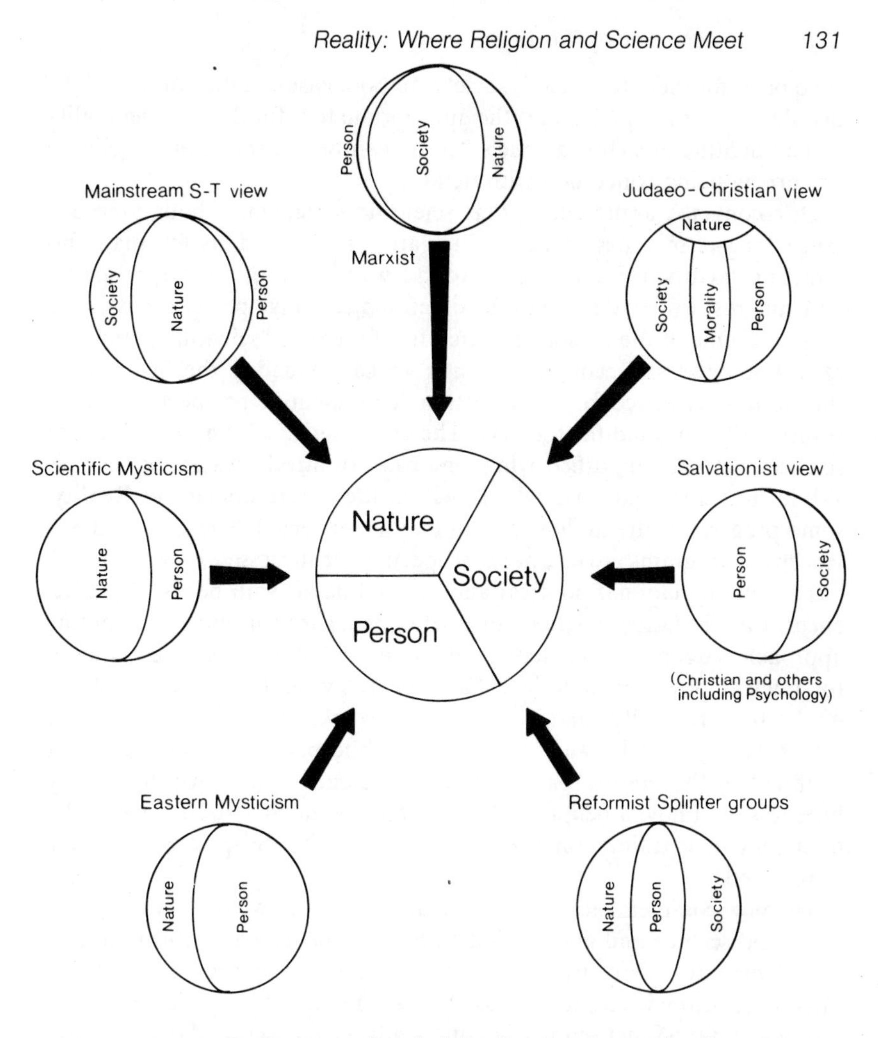

Fig. 2.28. Within the circular field of view as it appears from that direction, we represent as proportionate parts of the circle the concerns or emphases of that position.

many deleterious effects of tobacco smoke on human health have been well documented. The original long-distance view—though based on intuition—turned out to be right on a detail.

A counter example may be found in the many dietary and sexual behavior laws of the Old Testament. Such detailed orders obviously do not constitute the big picture of human existence. They are really out of place in a religious world view. And now modern science has shown that there is no basis for them for today's society. In both cases, in the domain of the detailed, "microscopic" issues the appropriate tool for discovering reality is the scientific one. Just as one's "God" can be too small, one's religion can err by being concerned with details.

Our converse argument is that scientific statements about long-distance, long-term issues or those which are complex and involve many interacting factors are likely to be found wanting and, after appropriate adjustments, will give place to the older, longer-range perspectives called religious. One of the reasons for the utter failure of "scientific planning" of technologies and economies which we catalogued in the first part of this book is evidence for this assertion. The scientific perspective is constitutionally unsuited for the task. The characteristically narrow focus of science is already modified when one tries to introduce systems science. While such a system stays wholly within the nature domain of Reality, some progress in the understanding may be expected. The U.S. and Soviet space programs are examples of spectacular successes. As soon as one has to couple national political and societal needs with personal preferences, the "isolation mythos" of science is destroyed and the scientific approach is doomed. Excellent examples are all around us. The planning for nuclear power installations has repeatedly, and in all parts of the world, been radically changed or come unstuck, not because of any real safety hazard, but because it involves public perception, i.e., it is not confined to the Nature part of Reality. Science and reason have very little to say in how a people will use or misuse the SbT itself. That is the final seal of certainty on the correctness of the perspective we have introduced.

The new complementarity which is at the heart of what I have to say is that good science and good religion are *automatically* and *always* totally complementary. Only by using both can I form an accurate and full three-dimensional sculpture of Reality. All my day-to-day existence, my contact with the functioning of nature, gadgets, devices, and organization is a means to establish the nature of this reliable responsible microstructure of Reality. My hypotheses about the relations of Nature to Society and Person, about the just society and "right" behavior—i.e., my religious views—require longer to form and test in the fire of experience. But as this, my life-tested "framework" for the big picture, takes shape, it gives much more meaning to the fragments of the findings of my scientific self, for they find their place in a pattern. And the science improves because the patterns themselves may add insight or detail to the new findings at the detailed level.

Figure 2.28 also made another important point which has been made by many others, but not as precisely as it is made here. It is claimed on all sides that, in general, the scientific method is bested suited for the Nature domain of Reality, and religion for the Person. There is truth in the statement, but we should be careful to state that much more explicitly. After all, religion has important things to say about the relation of humanity to the rest of Nature, and science can provide useful and reliable analyses of the individuals, and certainly of Society.

The scientific method is most effective when applied to Nature because Nature is not a moving target. The edifice of scientific knowledge can be built brick by brick—by narrowly focused work—because bricks don't get up and turn around or move away. The scientific method, at best, is marginally useful in studies of society. The lack of reproducibility and total lack of transferabililty across cultures of all that has passed for social science is notorious. Also highly significant is the lack of ability to predict in scientific studies of Society or the Person—all of these are a result of the interactive nature of the subject-object combine.

The religious approach is totally inappropriate for the detailed study of Nature itself. It is designed to reveal, describe, and prescribe relationships among Persons, Society, and Nature. Because it has had the benefit of long-time and long-distance averaging, it is the most reliable guide to the shape of the larger Realities. The basic religious "laws" (guidelines) for persons and society—for example, the primacy of other-centered love—are, therefore, as immutable and effective on a large scale as the laws of physics (e.g., electron behavior in a semiconductor) are in a narrow field. Religious claims cannot be translated to the microscopic level, i.e., in a literal legalistic manner to every situation, any more than Newtonian mechanics can apply in the subatomic region. Especially where totally new situations have been created (e.g., in the universal need for birth control rather than ever larger families), we need to hybridize the viewpoints of science and those of religion. One final example of the complementarity is drawn from a similar borderline area. In the realm of science policy, as soon as we attempt to bring in the question of what is good for society and persons, it should now be evident that the pseudoscientific paradigm of "technology assessment" is inadequate. One of the principal themes I develop later is that, in this long-range planning, it should be time-tested religious insight combined with some detailed studies that will be of greatest value to national governments. It would be childish for the political and technical communities to refer back to the era of Galileo as the model of what I am proposing. Nothing could be further from the truth. What I am asserting here is the proposition that it is only the insights of the R(eflective) self, which can possibly be relevant when one is trying to plan over long times and for long distances. Hence, science and technology policy *cannot be made* by rules inherent to SbT, it must turn to the "religious" perspective for help (not to another religious *establishment*).

2.13 Needed: A Set of Instructions, a Zoom Lens, and an Experimental Attitude

God is for Real, Man was the title of a popular paperback by Carl Burke, ten years ago. It was an attempt to make "God" less remote to the younger generation by using contemporary language and addressing God about everyday problems. It was a step in the direction of bringing "God" into relation with Reality. Perhaps we should now paraphrase Burke's title to *God is per Real!*

Central to our approach has been the affirmation that all of Reality is the (only) vehicle, the essential courier, the reification of [symbol]. John Robinson quotes Coventry Patmore: *"You may see the disc of Divinity quite clearly through the smoked glass of humanity, but not otherwise"*; and Robinson adds: *"Indeed its key preposition is* through." Precisely. Yes, but through *all* Reality. What I have been at pains to do is to increase the number of lenses through which [symbol] is revealed, from Patmore's single domain of "humanity," to include Nature and Society. God revealed through persons alone leads to a fragmented [symbol]. This "God" is then inevitably apposed, then opposed, to the [symbol] revealed by the less personal, but no less important or impacting, other parts of Reality. Twenty-first century humanity must look through humanity, through societal structures, and through nature to "see God," to become *fully* "aware" of [symbol].

I do not believe that this is any more or less complex than the Church's traditional attempts, for example, to codify our views of the Trinity. The task is different. But it is much more in consonance with the lives of the vast majority living in the modern technological era. It is in tune with *our* hymn of *our* universe at the center of which we stand. To accomplish this task we need: (1) a rather different set of instructions from our earlier catechisms or theological training; (2) a zoom lens. Our model calls for separating clearly the minutiae from the big picture without denying the importance of either. The zoom lens metaphor implies the ease by which we can change our "focal length" and, hence, our field of view; and in our brains and hearts integrate the information exactly as we do with the information we acquire through our eyes alone; and (3) an experimental attitude to life. Life is experimental. Biological evolution throws out a hundred different forms, new mutations, in trying to find whether some slight change may not be better adapted to the ever-changing present. Bio-psycho-social evolution is part of our Reality. Human beings living on patterns adapted to the past are doomed to stagnation and eventual extinction. Many persons not trained in the natural or social sciences tend to be afraid of, or offended by, the idea of experimenting with life. Unknown to themselves they do it every day. The only choice is whether one repeats the old experiment, or tries the new. Perhaps the stumbling block can be softened if we recall that the French word for experiment is "expe-rience." In our existentialist day, and with the younger generations' willingness to experiment—in many other areas—we can surely all accept the urging to *carefully planned* new experiences. Teilhard writes that he was *"guided by the general principle of my life that one should lose no opportunity of trying out, or finding out, things."* Mahatma Gandhi's autobiography is entitled: *My Experiments with Truth.*

There may be, of course, limits to "useful" experimentation. Such limits range from the very subtle question of whether biochemists today should proceed with DNA-manipulation work, to experimentation on oneself with hallucinogenic drugs, to experiments which impact (involuntarily) on others. The scope of this book does not permit me to follow these very important questions of ethics in this context. Suffice it to say, at this point, that there is plenty of room for experimentation involving oneself and one's attitude and relation to the beyond which is beyond reproach. In general, the criteria of no coercions of any persons, careful planning and collective oversight, reversibility, and reciprocity where others are involved provide initial guidelines to examine borderline cases.

1. New Set of Instructions

The new set of instructions includes, first, getting the instructions out and studying them; i.e., clarifying our theoretical concepts or the life-policy (= faith) we will live by. To such a set these lectures may make a small contribution. We all "believe in" something, in the sense of using something as an operational guide to behavior. We all have a "life-policy" of some sort. Sometimes this is a coherent, thought-through, synergistic set of flexible guidelines. Often, regrettably, it is just the postfacto mixture of reactions to the random events of life. Our life-policy is absolutely defined by the overall patterns present in our observable actions, not by any verbal statements alone. The first requirement is to be conscious and intentional about our life-policies.

While urging that we "read" the new set of instructions, I am fully aware that we are living in a time when "reading instructions" is at the very bottom of everyone's priority list. I personally have the irresistible urge, whenever I get a new household appliance or laboratory instrument, to try to get it to work without reading the instructions. On all such matters I find myself a victim of the "when all else fails, read the instructions" syndrome. Many of these minor experiments may, of course, be nothing more than an intellectual challenge, one more chess game. The experiment is repeatable and not much is at stake—usually an hour of time. In the larger game of life, this pattern of behavior is a blueprint for disaster. We need to study carefully the instructions. In our time, this conclusion stands four square counter to the prevailing trend. To claim that we need to study, to think, or to organize our instructions may sound absurd to a generation which claims that our culture is "too cerebral," "too verbal," "we think too much." A "head-trip" is the cardinal sin, and so on. First, I will establish that these claims about the excessive "head-tripping" are utterly false for the very persons making the claim. Second, I will show that it is a defense mechanism by those who feel that they cannot make any sense of their world with body, mind, and spirit, i.e., the instructions don't work—and the way to solve the problem is to ignore the latter two components and throw away the instructions. Third, I will lay the blame for this state of affairs on those who write the manuals or make up the instructions.

The evidence for the falsity of "excessive head-tripping," "over-intellectualization," etc. is that it is made by persons who have made and make no systematic efforts to understand anything, not even their life-instructions. The myriad study groups which dotted the churches of the land in the fifties and sixties have all disappeared. In secular life, except in one's specialty, lectures by brilliant women or men go unattended. In political life, it is not substance, but style; not concrete achievement, but charisma, that rules. Since reality is converted into a metareality by television's capacity to amplify a tiny segment in space and time to fill the attention capacity of tens of millions, the necessity to carefully study or read anything—such as "the instructions"—fades into the background. Soon it was "march first and ask questions afterwards,"* since manipulating the media was the only "game in town." The study of the *medium* totally obscured the study of the *message.* What becomes evident as one pursues the topic in some depth (with those willing to carry the conversation further) is that there are very few relevant statements of "theology" or "life–policy' available. Moreover, any such set of instructions which dealt, let us say, with the impact of science and technology is out of reach of the reader's linguistic framework *without some hard work.* Thus, in defense of an insufficient personal background, unwillingness to engage in some hard work as a student instead of an equal discussant, and inade-

* As an example, one may cite the hundreds of persons (including many of my own friends) who have participated in some antinuclear power activity, who have never read *any* purely informative material on the subject: something as neutral as understanding what pico-curies and "mrems" mean as measures of radiation. The result of not reading is further evidenced by the enormous numbers concerned about possible death or health effects from nuclear *power,* who are not aware of the thousands or millions of times greater danger of *the same effects* (death and radiation) from nuclear weapons.

quacy of the resources, many have been reduced to attacking the "head-trip." Getting our picture of Reality straight, "reading the instructions," is, of course, the analog in the sciences of reading up carefully on all existing theory before planning one's experiments. C. F. von Weizsäcker has put it very well: *"Anyone neglecting to further his theoretical understanding of our complex world as much as he can, will in the long run do more harm than good in his practical efforts. On the other hand, anyone retreating from the demands of practical work into the tower of pure contemplation will end up with philosophically sterile thoughts."*

2. Use the Zoom Lens

The zoom lens is just one more example of the wonders of modern engineering. It is, in effect, a combination of many lenses, a close-up (microscopic), regular, and telephoto. This little marvel now appears on ordinary home slide projectors and cameras. It allows one to change the focal length by twisting a knob, instead of tediously changing instruments or unscrewing and screwing lenses. It is a concrete, technological expression of our capacity to change from one perspective (not *direction*) to another with great ease.

No one creates a good photograph by starting to look immediately through the viewfinder and the tiny focusing spot. We start by "composing the (big) picture." The integrated person sets the zoom all the way back to compose the big picture, including subject, foreground, and background in good proportion, even if not precisely arranged in every detail. To do that, it is also necessary to shoot from different angles, to have more than one long-range perspective: "two-eyed, long-range vision." This means that in today's world no mature religious person can ignore a serious look through other "religious" telescopes (including that of a scientist-philosopher) than the one of her/his own culture. The integration that can be performed here requires one to view the three segments of reality from different directions with different parts in the center and sort out any *apparent* conflicts in those areas where two or more fields of view include areas of overlap. In the twenty-first century, universalism of the kind that requires a serious look from the direction where Society is at the center (Marxism-social gospel) and one where the Person is at the center (traditional religion) and one where Nature is at the center (scientific philosophy or natural theology) is mandatory. Moreover, we will find that the integration or fusion of such "binocular" information will make our flat painting of reality reveal itself to be a 3-D sculpture.

But before we get mesmerized by a single view, *keeping the field of view fixed,* we change our zoom lens down to come closer. We focus on where we spend much of our lives, in the domain of personal and interpersonal relations. Not functioning now as the experiencing, but the reflective self. This change of focus allows one to test experientially (experimentally) the general lay of the land hinted at in the distant view. We can walk over the ground, test the hints from our tentative long-range view, and correct or embellish it. Most importantly at this middle experiential level we participate in human community. Bridgman's "We can never transcend the human reference point" can be modified to state that *humanity's most reliable reference point is a small group of humans* where information, knowledge, past history, and direct new experience is uniquely synthesized, calibrated across the handful of individuals, and used to direct the future. Examples of the enormous power of a small dedicated group abound. From the dozen disciples of Jesus, to the tightly disciplined orders of monks—Hindu, Buddhist or Christian—to serious communal experiments such as the Oneida Community and, in our day, the Bruderhof, the Ecumenical Institute, the Taize Community in France, and the Church of the Saviour in Washington, D.C. In science, also, the importance of a small group has been emphasized repeatedly. Lee DuBridge, former President of the California Institute of Technology and once Science Advisor to the U.S. President, has written that, wherever you find scientific excellence, look for the cause in "an individual or small group" of persons. Lewis Thomas, Director of the Sloan-Kettering Institute, writes of the special creativity of a "bunch of people." But even as we are "synthesizing" new experiences into our memory, we are, in fact, zooming back again to the long-range focus. And the symbol of the zoom lens is used to signify the ease, even the effortlessness of going back from one perspective to another.

And, of course, we will also zoom down to the "close-up"—the scientific view. We will have selected, from the big picture of Mount Rushmore, perhaps one part of the President's face for the painstaking perfectly detailed shot, getting the angle just right, catching the sun, so that it reveals the maximum detail. But, as we go easily from close-up to middle range to long view—back and forth, putting together the beautiful and the true—we note that we never confuse the actual image of the big picture with that of the bridge on the nose. We do not expect them to be the same kind of information because the camera is pointed in the same direction.

We have learned to integrate *multifocally* the optical images to obtain a detailed sculpture of Reality. It is this model which this set of instructions offers for integrating the experiences of our curious, detailed, scientific selves, our personal and interpersonal talking and touching and hearing selves, and our reflective, meditating, praying selves.

3. An Experiential Attitude to Life

For the last 30 years, as a physical scientist with a strong bias toward the experimental, I have had the attitude epitomized in the "bumper sticker" used by experimentalists: "One *good* experiment is worth a thousand expert opinions." I carried that attitude over into my concerns with society and politics and religion. We needed to experiment with ethics, values, lifestyle—or so I went around preaching in the churches. It received a very cool reception generally. It simply didn't do to mix *experimentation* with the *fixed* eternal verities. This is illustrative of one of the gross errors in all theologies—the idea of fixed verities—the misunderstanding of the "unchangeability" of truths. Max Born writes: *"I am convinced that ideas such as absolute certainty, absolute precision, final truth, etc. are phantoms which should be excluded from science. . . . This loosening of the rules of thinking seems to me to be the greatest blessing which modern science has given us."* The era of SbT has given us a wholly new attitude—a loosening of the rules—toward the results of experiments which could *expand,* not abolish, older verities. The pioneers of the faith—like missionaries to new lands—have done for centuries what Teilhard advocates, participating in *"the anxieties and joys of trying all and discovering all. . . ."* You can also imagine my surprise and pleasure when I found that the last chapter of Sir Alister Hardy's *Biology of God* is entitled "An Experiment with Faith." I refer you to it for a most enriching personal witness. I have already quoted Teilhard's "general principle of life" of "trying out every thing."

Experimentation is the centerpiece of modern science-technology. It is on experiments with nature that all the new theories have been built; otherwise, Aristotle would have beaten Galileo and Newton to it. And experiments are not at all alien to the rest of life. For millenia, humankind has experimented: in agriculture to find new edible plants, the ideas of crop rotation, of pesticide by interplanting different species, and so on; in exploration, as frail craft crossed oceans thousands of years ago, humanity experimented. Conscious experimentation with our lives is Instruction #3.

But instruction #3 comes after instruction #1—you must get your theory straight first. My life-long advocacy of "experimentation" in life has been invariably hyphenated as "carefully-planned-and-executed experimentation." No scientist worth her/his salt starts an experiment without having a clear view of the question which it might answer—i.e., having her/his theory and concepts straight. No scientist works with new apparatus without instructions, tutoring, apprenticeship in its use, or without knowing what to do with, or at least how to start interpreting, the data.

Lastly, no integrated human being who is a scientist is unaware of the difference in experimenting in a laboratory and "experimenting" in life. Indeed, it is only the witness to the value of experimentation that the scientist can offer. Dumitriu places the witness from scientific models in the context of complex social problems in the following: *"The man who thinks he has mastered Nature and then finds social nature, or simply human nature, confronting him like an unpredictable, ironical and dangerous face of God—he at least knows enough to discover the eternal Thou."*

In our optical imagery, it means that one must be willing to zoom in and out, move all around the scene, viewing from all angles and all depths. In life, it means that having *tentatively, for the present,* understood ourselves, our environment, our place in society and nature, we carefully plan forays into the unknown. *Only* in this manner will our sculpture of Reality stay up to date, enriched in detail, exciting, and interesting to pursue. It is impossible to start with a full 3-D sculpture, detailed in every part. We all start with a very partial view at best. But as John Platt attributes to Jesus, the crucial last point of the Christian instructional set is: *"Start here!" where you are, now,* with your given limitations and potential.

Reality-Theology: A Common Starting Point

The rather tedious process we have followed in this section was a studied attempt to bridge a gap. Through it I have attempted to lead all citizens of the contemporary developed world, whose working and relaxing lives are deeply and thoroughly influenced by the idea-structure, the products and the inevitable consequences of science and technology, to examining the possibility of being able to affirm the existence of a "Beyond" in the midst. All through this process, I have insisted that we start with whatever is most real to us: the physical environment in which we live out our daily lives; the complex society which so constrains/supports us; the plethora of personal events and encounters which most affect our persons. All these are shared by all humans. Our "life policy" (= faith) is shaped by the sum of what is most real to us. By that test, it is modern SbT that functions today as the most widespread and potent "religion" of our times, since it shapes more life-policies than any other. But, unknown to most of the devotees of this religion, it is increasingly recognized by scientists that the insights of modern science point insistently and consistently to deeper realities beyond the immediate sense-perceived ones. And by peeling layer after layer through increasingly abstract scientific studies we are led from depth to wonder to mystery. Harold Schilling has a moving pasage on this topic:

The science community does have interests beyond those of a more narrowly conceived science, and it does achieve insights that transcend by far any that are derivable by formal experimentation and theorizing only. From this point of view I now suggest that for an increasing number of scientists the awareness of the reality and significance of mystery in nature is one of those transcending understandings.

If the "worldly" citizen, scientist, or person would focus only on the Essence, this Meaning, this Beyond or Reality, they would open the door to a fruitful dialogue with religious traditions.

The person reared in a traditional religious language framework can obviously affirm exactly the same Ground of Being, the Essence of all Reality. But such a person has to be challenged to abandon too small, too flat, too monocultural a conception of "God." A "God" who, although by religion's own definition is infinite, omniscient, omnipotent, often is grossly distorted as being contained within a human being. The Judeo-Christian tradition must be challenged to avoid the pervasive danger of overpersonalizing, of hominizing the Almighty and the Infinite. Because of its unique strength in stressing the personal and interpersonal dimension and the unique relation to Jesus, the Christ, to [illegible], it often falls prey to the human idol heresy. As a significant gesture to the attempt to enter into the dialogue with other religious viewpoints, including modern science and technology, followers of all religions need to use a new word for the Essence beyond Reality. A neutral symbol, [illegible], has been introduced.

Thus equipped with a new linguistic unity, some scientists, Jews, Christians, Buddhists, Hindus, Muslims and others may now start to relate this [illegible] to their experiences, and their own previous descriptions of "God." Here again, I have insisted on working through the given realities—the realms of Nature, Society and the Person, as THE ROUTE by which human beings can reach [illegible]. This is a fully panentheist position: [illegible] known and experienced *through,* per, all of reality. Every*thing* (can) speak to us to [illegible]. It is an attitude at once consonant with the positions of Teilhard and of Einstein.

Why, then, have religion and science and the new experiential emphasis of the last decade appeared to be in a three-cornered fight? Because they have never been clear about their interrelationships, insofar as their inputs are utilized by, and affect, ordinary human beings. One of the novel approaches in this book is to disclose the nature of this complementarity. It is depicted as a matter of perspective or focus. "Science" (here taken as a world view) and religion deal with the same total Reality, although from slightly different perspectives. Where the same part of Reality is in the field of view of both, it is purely and simply a matter of focus, of scale, which distinguishes them. Of the views through the microscope and through the telescope of the same object, it would be absurd to choose one as being right and the other wrong. Yet, this is the history of the science-religion debate. Likewise, the reality of personal transactions is not of some other genre or plane, but at an intermediate level of focal distance.

It is in creating a three-dimensional Reality, informed by a multidirectional, multifocus approach by the separate human selves within the self, that we find the unity among religions and between all religions and science-technology. In affirming the [illegible], the meaning of which is "betrayed but not paraded" by all of Reality, we reach a unity among a new grouping of seekers. This is a very secure commonality upon which to build a "life-policy" (= faith) for the twenty-first century. In the concluding segment of this book we develop the transitions from Reality to [illegible] through the experience of persons of varying backgrounds.

Postscript: Difficulties and Unanswered Questions

It will be evident to the perceptive reader that throughout this chapter I did not "define" Reality, meaning, radiating—terms which were very important to my argument. That was a conscious decision. It is no more possible to define Reality than to name [illegible]. What I have attempted is much more modest. I have attempted to erect a sign post pointing to a different road to [illegible]. This road lies through what everyone knows as Reality, even though very few have thought about the many deeper meanings of the term. It is very important that we *start* with the commonsense understanding of Reality—the world that *any* individual can touch, feel, see, and the experiences of pleasure or pain caused in direct human experience. Born has called this "Naive Realism: Reality to a simple unlearned person is what he feels and perceives." Reality, I have said, has many onion-skin layers. But well might we ask: Where does the onion end? If you speak of the Beyond in the Midst, the Beyond hidden by the screen of Reality, is not the second or third layer already the Beyond? Or is it still Reality? There is no sharp or clearcut answer to this. There is, as it were, a continuum between Reality and the Beyond. The deeper layers of Reality are already partly Beyond and *not* "pure" Reality any longer. This is the nature of the [illegible] we have tried to address, infused into Reality yet "in its pure form" separable from any specific reification. Our spatial metaphor (fig. 2.28) showed this in the differing densities of [illegible] penetrating into the segments of Reality.

The terms "meaning" and "radiating" of meaning by Reality have similarly been incompletely defined. I have used the expression "Reality radiates meaning" but always qualified the nature of the "radiation" by the expression "betrays but does not parade." Yet the analog to the electromagnetic radiation from a body cannot be pressed too far. If Reality radiated meaning like a hot body sends out infrared waves, that would be parading its meaning. Whatever the "meaning" and the process of its transfer, it is clear that the difference from the physical model is in the role of the observer. We have highlighted the crucial role of the subject, the observer. The detector of radiation, the extractor of meaning is the observer. Only when the detector is in resonance with the radiation will the [illegible] behind the Reality be perceived. Only when there are already cognate images existing within the observer will stereopsis occur and the higher dimensions of meaning be perceived.

I am not clear in my own mind as to whether it will be fruitful to pursue further precision in definition of the terms Reality, meaning, radiation, and their interrelationships. In these matters, I believe we may also one day see that we have a Heisenberg-like indeterminacy: where the product of the precision in meaning and number of observers who share it may be constant. For human progress, I believe with Conant that what we need *"in order to assimilate science into the (religious) cultures of our . . . society, we must regard scientific theories as guides to human action and thus an extension of common sense."* I have tried to make a beginning in that direction with these ideas on "Reality–Theology."

Bibliography

Fritjof Capra, *The Tao of Physics,* Bantam Edition, New York, 1977.
Gary Zukav, *The Dancing Wu-Li Masters,* W. Morrow, New York, 1979.
James B. Conant, *Modern Science and Modern Man,* Doubleday, New York, 1953.
Percy W. Bridgman, *Reflections of a Physicist,* Philosophical Library, New York, 1955.
———"Philosophical Implications of Physics," in American Academy of Arts and Sciences, *Bulletin* 3, no. 5 (Feb. 1950).
Max Born, *Natural Philosophy of Cause and Chance,* Dover, New York, 1964.
Petru Dumitriu, *Incognito,* Collins, London, 1964.
Dag Hammarskjöld, *Markings,* Knopf, New York, 1964.
B. Julesz, *Foundations of Cyclopean Perception,* Chicago University Press, Chicago, 1971.
Ben Shahn, *The Shape of Content,* Harvard U. Press, Cambridge, 1957.
George Leonard, *The Silent Pulse,* Dutton, New York, 1978, pp. 165–66.
Paulos Gregorios, *The Human Presence,* WCC, Geneva, 1978.
P. Teilhard de Chardin, *An Album,* edited by J. Mortier and M. Alboux, Harper and Row, New York, 1966.
Michael Polanyi, in *Christians in a Technological Era,* H. White, editor, Seaburg, New York, 1964.
John Platt, *The Step to Man,* Wiley, New York, 1966.
Alister Hardy, *The Biology of God,* London, Jonathan Cape, 1975.
Harold K. Schilling, *Science and Religion,* Scribners, New York, 1962.
Rustum Roy, "Science, Technology, and Society," in Conference Proceedings *Limitations of Science and the Solution of Social Issues,* ITEST, St. Louis, Mo, March 1977.
Alan Mackay, *Models of the World,* Zaheer Science Foundation, New Delhi, 1977.
Susan Sontag, *On Photography,* Farrar Straus and Giroux, New York, 1977.

3 Experimenting With Truth: Doing Theology

3.0 Through Reality to [illegible]

In the final chapter of this book we must push beyond our efforts at determining the most accurate, multidimensional picture or sculpture of Reality. Theology is the study of [illegible], not of Reality. The panentheist holds that [illegible] will be found, known, loved, "worshipped" or otherwise related to by apprehending *in some way,* the content, the essence, present "beyond" this Reality. We are, therefore, confronted with two tasks. First, we must describe in some detail the relations between [illegible] and Reality. Second, we must deal with the issue of what "knowing" or "relating to" [illegible] means. Is the "knowing" of [illegible] of the same category as knowing the Pythagorean theorem or Latin grammar? Or is knowing closer to Biblical use of a man "knowing" his wife? In the second chapter I made the point that the world's greatest scientists, from theoreticians such as Max Born to experimentalists such as Percy Bridgman, agree that all "knowledge" is strictly limited by the person involved. In Michael Polanyi's happy title, it is all "Personal Knowledge." We will, therefore, try to show that meaningfully relating to [illegible] can only occur in a continuing interactional mode. But we will go on to amplify the nature of these interactions, to show that knowing or loving [illegible] in an absolute sense requires *acting* upon the knowledge we have. And adopting the concrete steps outlined in the last chapter, it follows that to discover the logos about theos requires the scientific panentheist, who claims that [illegible] is only found through Reality, to experiment carefully with Reality, with Truth. Let us start with a brief recapitulation of the argument so far.

A Summary Up to This Point and a Synopsis

The sequence of ideas which we have tried to present in this book has followed this pattern:

In the first section "Situational Theology," we started with a review of the human prospect as we enter the decade of the 1980s.

- The world's situation has been changed dramatically in the last two or three centuries by one human activity: science and technology.

- This change has impacted all aspects of human existence in a major way.
- The changes now appear to be out of human control at any level; SbT has become an autonomous juggernaut.
- The changes have not been assimilated, as yet, into any coherent world view, philosophy, or religion.
- Modern theology is a disaster area. Most theologians are unable to define "God" in sufficiently inclusive terms to deal with these advances in human understanding over the last 200 years.
- Contrary to conventional wisdom, I assert that due to human, terrestrial, and natural finitudes, science and technology will be dramatically slowed down in the decades immediately ahead. There is already convincing evidence for such a slowing down in the rate of change brought about by science and technology. There will be less and less *additional* impact (on advanced societies) starting almost immediately and leading to a much more steady-state society in, say, fifty years.
- It is imperative for human survival to reconstruct a total view of Reality which incorporates the enormous changes introduced by SbT into a religious world view which alone can provide values and direction for this new plateau of human achievements and capacities.

In our attempt to construct a new "theology" for this new situation, we started with "Reality" and our perception of it.

- Reality exists independent of our views of it.
- Different human views (such as traditional religion and modern science) of Reality must be mutually reinforcing (except where they are wrong).
- Hence, it must be possible to construct a science-reinforced theology much stronger than either of these single-visioned truths.
- The linguistic problem in constructing such a joint statement is acute. The term "God" is too strongly *and too differently* weighted a word to be useful any longer, except in an individual's direct relation to God. A symbol, [symbol], is used instead.
- The present panentheist position is based on secular philosophies held by leading scientists and religious views long held by some Christian thinkers.
- Reality theology affirms that [symbol] is knowable through, and only through, our personal knowledge, understanding, perception, and experience of any or all of Reality. Reality is a screen between [symbol] and humanity.
- The continuum of Reality can be divided into the trinity of Nature, Society and Person.

- The human being in dealing with Reality functions in a continuum of selves, also arbitrarily divisible into three groups: the scientific self, the experiencing self, the reflective self.
- Our three-dimensional sculpture of Reality is formed by combining the information obtained by each of the selves about all of Reality and the domains in which each specializes.
- Integration of information is essential for optimal functioning and if performed properly—such as in binocular stereopsis—can reveal totally new dimensions of Reality, especially the [illegible] beyond.

In this short section I deal with the question of how human beings experience or establish the most meaningful contact with [illegible], that which is beyond Reality. The sequence proceeds as follows:

- Establishing the widespread acknowledgement of such a Beyond.
- Accepting and working with the severe limitations imposed by our finitude as human beings.
- And, within that, playing through our strengths, i.e., using the window of personal experience, of I-Thou relations as the clearest channel to [illegible].
- Yet retaining as absolutely essential the holistic integration of all of Reality viewed by the integrated selves.
- The final synthesis of a life-policy is achieved in practice, in doing theology, by experimenting with truth. (Some of my brief prospective glimpses of what this may mean in different directions are provided.)

It is necessary at this point to deal with what will have been detected by students of philosophy as the inconsistency in my position regarding Reality. The "first article" listed above—"Reality exists independent of our views of it"—states a classical "essentialist" position espoused by Newton and Einstein. How can this be compatible with the emphasis I give here and elsewhere to the Heisenberg-Born school of quantum mechanics and the subject-object interaction? I do not believe that the views are in any way contradictory. They are complementary in the same sense that quantum mechanics simplifies to classical mechanics for "large" bodies. Thus, at the sensory and common-sense levels, both science and our simplest experiences agree on the "objective reality." Just as Bohr has explained wave particle complementarity as the way light functions when large numbers and small numbers of photons are involved, so the realm of the interactive object-subject takes over when *small* numbers of individuals (in the limit, one) are involved. A single individual may and does experience essentially a unique Reality—what I term "differentiated" reality. Insofar as she/he has no reason or cause to share this Reality, the unique personal "picture" of reality is reality. But as soon as large numbers of persons must share a Reality, then we come under the classical "essentialist" regime—which I term "integrated" reality. A result of this is the fact that the relevance of quantum physics to human society is in the realm where only one or two persons are involved; hence, the validity of situation ethics, the validity of personal "prayer." Moreover, we recognize that our personal picture of Reality is influenced by the collective picture held by groups of which we are a part. Just so, any "differentiated" reality is linked to the "integrated" reality of classical science.

The principal question which now faces us is: Given that we have acquired the facility to construct a reasonably accurate (as checked against and verified by the small community of dedicated fellow seekers) multidimensional sculpture of Reality, what does this tell us about its essence, [illegible] or the classical God? What is the *content* behind *this shape?*

A Christian panentheist—in the line of Teilhard—will affirm that [illegible] is the essence of meaning behind, or infused or hidden, in Reality. She would say that [illegible] bears the same relation to Reality that sweetness bears to any sweet food. Reality is the ultimate form, [illegible] is the ultimate content. This meaning or essence of Reality, this [illegible], is not obvious, nor proclaimed by Reality; Reality only *betrays* [illegible], it does not *parade* it.

Indeed, in our experience we might even say that there is a continuum between the reality and its meaning or the [illegible] beyond. There are many stages, many layers of onionskin, between the most opaque reality and the [illegible] we meet through it, just as there are many stages in the refinement of sugar cane. At each step, the evidence of sweetness becomes stronger; we get closer to the essence, which in its pure abstract form will always remain exclusively in the domain of personal knowledge. We must continually bear this in mind as we search for the [illegible] beyond Reality. The [illegible] beyond the midst will become clearer *in stages,* but remain eternally beyond our comprehension.

3.1 Transcending Reality: Who Says There Is a Beyond?

This section is addressed to those readers principally from the science community who, although they have no traditional religious allegiances, have followed the argument so far, permitting me my loose connection between the Reality whose existence they affirm, and *anything* beyond. It will, I believe, be easy for such persons to agree with the argument for the need for each person to have a coherent, self-consistent "picture" of the whole of Reality. Philosophically trained scientists will recognize that the use of the term "picture" itself is a trap, since it suggests a possible objectification separate from the observer. Today both the quantum mechanicians and theologians such as Martin Buber have made us aware that any individual's picture of Reality is formed, partly, in an interactive I-thou mode with the observer in the picture, so to speak. There is sure to be support among scientists and engineers for the importance of the trifocal and trinocular synthesis of integration, even though most of the scientific community is unwilling, personally, to be distracted from monofocal, monocular propensities. But we need now to bring forward not only the reasons why many have found it necessary to postulate a "Beyond," beyond this integrated Reality, but first of all to ask: To whom shall we turn to learn about anything beyond reality? to scientists (because they know most about operational Reality), to theologians (specialists in the Beyond), or to those who probe the subtleties of the human condition as a whole?

The efforts of research scientists who have thought through and written about such matters certainly do not constitute a significant corpus of work. What little there is, while it does not provide us with any systematic view on this issue, is remarkably homogeneous. My explanation for this is rather straightforward and I believe very generally applicable to analyzing the relations of scientists and many other intellectuals to all discussions about transcendence or "God" in any form. I attribute half the problem to the linguistic chaos in which we persist around this most central question of human existence. The other half is attributable to a curious narrow and closed-mindedness on the part of most Western intellectuals brought up in nominally Jewish or Christian homes. The linguistic confusion whenever anyone writes or talks about "God" is so severe that one wonders whether there is any hope of ever communicating between large groups of persons drawn from diverse backgrounds. Certainly, there is little hope if undefined terms and undisciplined use of language continue to dominate the dialogue.

It is at this nexus of human civilization that we have gone astray. The creative geniuses who have the most to offer each other have been divided by tissue thin walls of terminological confusion. The good has been separated out from the true by theoretical laxity. While scientists all over the world prattle somewhat naively about beauty in science, hinting in a vague way that the true and the beautiful must be consistent,* most have

* Max Born has commented in this connection: "For I have on occasion made the sad discovery that a theory which seemed to me very lovely, nevertheless did not work." I must agree. In thirty years of active research I have found hundreds of cases where an idea, hypothesis (or theory) which is esthetically pleasing or satisfying in bringing symmetry or rounding off to a larger work is simply disproved by the experiments. Nevertheless, a strange personal bias persists toward those solutions which are both true and beautiful. Beauty may be necessary for truth, but it is far from sufficient.

not spent a tenth as much intellectual energy on what is surely at least an equally important premise and vastly more significant to the human condition, namely, that the true and the good must be closely interwoven. The roots of this omission are to be found in the history of the science-religion sociopolitical relationships. The vast majority of twentieth century scientists were not very educated in philosophy or religion. The distinguished exceptions which prove the rule are, of course, the source for many of my ideas. The science community had learned instinctively and instantaneously to reject any physical phenomenon that appeared to violate the second law of thermodynamics. However, the community did not also learn to question the simplistic assertions made by their colleagues about well–established "theories" in another's field (e.g., religion) made by nonexperts, violating their own canons by never having isolated the system under study, never having defined the terms, and almost never having read the literature in the field!

The human causes of the human tragedy are all too well-known: territoriality and jealousy. For, as the rising power called "science" turned any attention toward matters beyond "its own field," the resistance from the guardians of the Beyond increased. The philosophers and theologians, who by then held shakily onto influence over the mental and spiritual domains, could not possibly have shared gracefully part of this last vestige of power. The parent culture of Christendom did not recognize its own child, science and technology, as a family member and legitimate heir of its own heritage.

For 400 years, the gap between the well-established referant of truth, theology, and its new branch, science, has been widening. A few brave individuals have, indeed, made the effort to jump the widening gap. Newton himself devoted at least as much effort to theology as to science. But in the post quantum mechanics era, perhaps only a very few persons would qualify as a personal bridge with distinction in both theology and science.

The reason for lack of greater interaction may, indeed, be that the chasm between theology and science is now too wide. And since, in a sense, they represent the ends of a spectrum, it may be easier to find interpreters from disciplines and communities which are located closer to the middle of human existence. If we start very broadly with the field of the arts, we find among the visual artists almost as great a separation from both science and religion as exists between the latter two. But "verbal artists," poets, dramatists and writers, seem to be very suitable. Another reason for starting with this group as witnesses to the religious "beyond" of the scientific "midst" lies in the fact that, because of the power bestowed on it by the technology of printing, its members have become teachers and interpreters of the best (and worst) of human achievement and understanding to the masses.

Literature as the Starting Point for a Witness to the Beyond

Is not theo-logy, the word about "God," the province of specialists called theologians? Yes! But are the theologians the only or even the most effective interpreters of the [illegible] beyond Reality for contemporary society? I do not believe so, because they neither understand the Reality too well, nor do they any longer have access to the mass mind as other communities do. In order to make this point, I shall start with illustrations from literature, for all great writers inevitably hint about the Beyond of their characters, story line, and the human condition.

Does T.S. Eliot not speak of the "Beyond in the Midst," in the *Four Quartets?* Is not the idea of [illegible], the Beyond, much more "efficiently" conveyed to Eliot's audience by his writing than by three quarters of the Bible and nine-tenths of all early theology? Is the "Hound of Heaven" less profound theology than two-thirds of the Psalms or the Koran or the Gita? Can one really believe that in his day George Bernard Shaw would be labeled an atheist instead of one of the most effective witnesses to that beyond Reality? Shaw, the author of "Saint Joan," the definer of "miracle" as "that which creates faith," the creator of "Major Barbara," labeled an atheist? I do not include either author's own explicit confession of faith, but merely claim that, seen with cyclopean vision, Elliot's and Shaw's writings are some of the most readable, intelligible, profound yet direct witnesses to the [illegible] betrayed by the Reality in which many of us live.

Let us continue with examples of writers who affirm that Reality has a being and a meaning beyond what we can perceive by our senses. Will the ordinary person in the street not learn "theology" from Barth, Moltmann, and Robinson but more easily and as well, if less precisely, from Graham Greene, Nikos Kazantzakis and Petru Dumitriu, to select three of the most effective among many. To my scientific colleagues, many of whom would call themselves and be called atheists or agnostics, were they to enquire seriously about the nature of my faith or "life-policy," I would say the following: "The [illegible] I know, and the life-policy I have chosen can be understood best, definitely not by starting with the Bible or even a contemporary theologian, but by reading Graham Greene's *The Power and the Glory,* or Kazantzakis' *Report to Greco, The Last Temptation,* or *Saint Francis,* and from Dumitriu's *Incognito,* from which I quote so liberally in this book."

I think that there is special significance in the fact that the writers coming out of the situations of struggle and suffering—in the Third

World or Eastern Europe, Pablo Neruda, or the long line of Russian protesting writers from Pasternak to Solzhenitsyn—come closer to dealing directly with "theological" issues than most in the affluent West. Yet, even in the West, the works of many of the best from Auden to Updike are effective windows into the beyond of the ordinary life situations of our day. What these books testify to with lesser or greater degrees of explicitness is the presence, nay the dominance, of some beyond in the midst of all the glorious complexity of contemporary human existence. The "witness" of this enormous body of some of the best of literature is to some form of transcendence of our ordinary facts and figures, our daily beings and doings. There is more than a hint, perhaps even a sketching out of a shadowy presence, of a Beyond in the intricately and often beautifully woven pattern of human and societal realities which the authors describe. I would and I do start with such literature to make my personal affirmation of the third article of the Revised Westminster Confession: *"Reality is the manifest form of the hidden ultimate content, the unnameable* [illegible]."

The Views of Reality-Experts: The Scientists

But what of the scientists, those specialists in the nature aspect of Reality? Does their Reality also betray the presence of meaning beyond itself? It is not fruitful to rehearse again the well-known attitudes of scientists during the early or middle stages of science. These were either shaped by the religious world view of their times or they reflected the triumphalism, indeed often militancy, of science and technology in the ascendance. If we consider only the leading scientists writing after World War II, we find a most curious phenomenon. The typical scientist simply ignores (but does not deny) the presence or absence of anything behind the screen of reality. (In fairness, it must be pointed out that their specialization often forces most scientists to ignore even the neighboring fields of science.) Only handfuls have been concerned even about science policy in spite of its terrible relevance to all of society. But not only have they thus narrowed their monocular focus to a sharp point, they have also focused in only one plane, so that the question of what is beyond reality is doubly "meaningless." So, just as it would have been to the great writers referred to above, it is literally absurd to formulate a question such as was asked of Einstein a thousand times: "Do you believe in God?" The absurdity lies in the questioner assuming that her/his meaning of God would have any correspondence to Einstein's associations with that word. Several possibilities arise. The questioner has in view a naive picture of a loving Father personified, sitting in Heaven, answering prayers, intervening on Earth on the side of justice, love and mercy, while the person questioned may think of God as the Ground of Being, the Essence of Reality. S/he may, therefore, say "Yes, I do believe in God." Now error is compounded, because at the next occasion the questioner having now described her/his own narrower view of "God," will go on to say or imply "and Dr. . . . also believes in (this) God." It is this kind of error which is perpetrated by the mindless sociology of Gallup polls on "the percentage of (Britons or) Americans who believe in God." (At the time of this writing, this is alleged to be 94 percent).

The converse type of misunderstanding is the one which exists for many mature scientists today. Many theologians, lay colleagues, and their own scientist peers have a much more subtle picture of [illegible]. They are deeply interested in what the great minds of science think about the "Ground of Being," the " 'Cry' of Evolution" pervading the Universe, the first law of active, sacrificial love. Yet they may not use the word "God" as a shorthand for all this. Thus, in responding to the "Do you believe in God" question, they identify God with what they *last* learned to associate with the word God. In most cases, this last was an adolescent learning from a classically trained Sunday School teacher or parent. It may well have included a God who has alleged to have made the world in seven days. A God who kept daily track of several billion individuals' personal activities, and one who seemed to be inordinately interested in keeping one from interesting experimentations with life—smoking, drinking, swearing, sex. A God who was, in some paradoxical way, contained within one human being, Jesus, or belonged in a very special way to one tribe, the Jews. They, therefore, answer "No."

I believe that one could show statistically that this latter is the picture conjured up by the word "God" in the minds of a large majority of the workaday leaders of science. Do they believe in *this* God? Of course not. But do they believe in the "God" which their questioner, their fellow committee person, Jewish or Christian peer noted above, asked about? We shall never know. But we do have excellent empirical evidence of the likely answer. We have this from the responses of those leaders of science who have thought about it.

The same Einstein who very properly would never say he believed in God, could never outgrow his own Jewish upbringing which was based rigorously in order and justice. For half a lifetime, Einstein protested against even a physics which revealed a statistical instead of a determinist (and determined by God?!) "law" at the very core of nature. Of course, Einstein believed in, as a matter of pure faith or intuition and acted out in life-policy, the absoluteness of Reality.* He affirmed categorically the

---

* Born comments on how often even in his physics, Einstein uses the expression "ich glaube," "I believe."

mystery beyond Reality. He proclaimed and demonstrated his caring about one's fellow human in order to be committed to peace and justice. I challenge someone to write down in two columns what Einstein "believed in," and what Teilhard de Chardin "believed in." They were scientists. They were contemporaries. They were co-explorers of the mystery of the universe, working albeit in different regions of Reality. It is not recorded that they ever met. They died within eight days and eighty miles of each other—each having traveled over every corner of this earth in body and all over the infinities of space and time in their minds. What a fascinating conversation those two explorers would have had. What if Oppenheimer—he who at Alamogordo remarked that physicists "had known sin"—had invited Teilhard, as he had T.S. Eliot, to join the Institute for Advanced Study at Princeton, when the Jesuit order banished Teilhard to the United States. Think of the possible fruitfulness of five years of collaborative work by Einstein and Teilhard, of the disciplining of Teilhard's vague scientific generalizations, of the tutoring of Einstein into a contemporary, mature theology. Imagine papers and monographs coauthored by Albert Einstein and P. Teilhard de Chardin. But it was not to be. We were still in the disciplinary specialization era. We know Einstein's scientific contributions were not very significant in his last decade. What if he had spent that mature phase defocusing from his specialization into the unified field theory, indeed, from any detailed, purely scientific research, into enlarging his vision, making it bifocal and binocular? Perhaps a new unified REALITY theory might have been born.

Of one thing I believe we can be rather sure: they would soon have learned to speak each other's language. To Teilhard's question: "Do you believe that we live in the Divine Milieu as I have defined it?" I believe Einstein would have shouted "Of course, I do."

What of the others who were "present at the Creation" of modern physics—Planck, Bohr, Franck, Born, Heisenberg, Schrödinger, Pauli, von Weizsäcker? For many of them, their interest in and study of contemporary religion was exactly as described above. The world's specialization model had led to the anomalous condition that these intellectual giants who were reshaping the world had left their knowledge of the rest of Reality (other than nature) frozen at the high school level. Bohr, Heisenberg, and von Weizsäcker stood out as having both background and interest in philosophical issues. In Heisenberg's later years his interest in the "Beyond" issues is evident in his three books *Physics and Philosophy, Physics and Beyond* and, suggestively, *Across the Frontiers.* In the last chapter of the last named book, he wrote:

> *Although I am now convinced that scientific truth is unassailable in its own field, I have never found it possible to dismiss the content of religious thinking as simply part*

> *of an outmoded phase in the consciousness of mankind, a part we shall have to give up from now on. Thus in the course of my life I have repeatedly been compelled to ponder on the relationship of these two regions of thought* for I have never been able to doubt the reality of that to which they point. (emphasis added)

Heisenberg specifically, though very briefly, addressed the question of the relations between scientific and religious truths. The germ of the ideas which formed the framework for the last section of this book are present as in the following:

> *But it is not my business to talk about society, for we were supposed to be discussing the relationship of scientific and religious truth. In the past hundred years, science has made very great advances. The wider regions of life, of which we speak in the language of our religion, may thereby have been neglected. We do not know whether we shall succeed in once more expressing the spiritual form of our future communities in the old religious language. A rationalistic play with words and concepts is of little assistance here; the most important preconditions are honesty and directness. . . . we must bend all our efforts to reuniting ourselves, along with the younger generation, in a common human outlook. I am convinced that we can succeed in this if again we find the right balance between the two kinds of truth.*

What is of significance, I believe, is the fact that, among the handful of prominent scientists who have taken on the task of binocular inquiry, a goodly majority arrive—each in their own time and circumstance—at a position affirming the Beyond in the midst of equations, galaxies, or conducting electrons, or new organic syntheses of DNA helixes. A representative sampling would include A. N. Whitehead, mathematician and philosopher; Sir James Jeans, the British astronomer; Michael Polanyi, Hungarian physical chemist turned philosopher, tutor of two Nobelists; James Conant, chemist President of Harvard University; Charles Coulson, mathematical chemist at Oxford; my colleague, Harold Schilling, physicist and Graduate Dean; Charles Townes, Physics Nobelist; and Charles Birch and Alister Hardy, contemporary biologists.

All these persons have taken the trouble to inquire explicitly into other perspectives on Reality and report on them. Their positions span a wide spectrum and, though hardly any one of them would be regarded by the Pope or fundamentalist Baptists as orthodox Christians, they bear one and all a direct and powerful witness to the transcendent Reality beyond.

Who is left among the scientists who have done serious thinking in the field? The names of P. W. Bridgman, Julian Huxley, J. D. Bernal, Fred Hoyle, J. Bronowski, Denis Gabor, and P. B. Medawar come to mind. Here, one finds a group that may be regarded as much more critical of traditional religious formulations. But, even in this most critical group, I believe that most readers would conclude that they do not deny the mystery beyond the scientific realities. Bernal, for instance, demonstrated in his life and work his profound concern for the impact of science on society and his socialist formulations thereof. An interesting example of the ambivalence in attitudes is that displayed by Raymond Cattell, the distinguished psychologist. His book, *Beyondism, a Morality from Science,* already betrays in its title that he would subscribe to our thesis, while abjuring God-language. In this book, which contains a devastating critique of all the naive criticisms of religion by psychologists, Cattell attempts to find the morality beyond the findings of social science. In a telling passage at the end of the book he notes:

> The incompatibility of Beyondism with revealed religions (*which latter many modern intellectuals and Humanists consider obsolete*) turns out, *as regards conclusions* (*rather than ways of reaching them*) to be less uncompromising than with a mass of modern writing which some "intellectuals" embrace *in "Humanism," "Existentialism," and some ill thought out varieties of "liberalism." Humanism now has the quality of a social value movement* (*no longer restricted to the academic meaning of Humanistic studies*) *which, like other secular religions, claims to contrast itself as "free thinking" and "rational" with the "dogmatic" basis of revealed religions. Actually, however, it is not one iota less intuitive and a priori in the source of its values. Indeed many of the values in Humanism and Existentialism are a digest of fragments eclectically and uncritically absorbed from various religions over two thousand* (*and particularly the last four hundred*) *years of Humanist thought. In some cases their emotional inheritance from dogmatic religions has favored more the comfortable illusions than the austere truths.*
>
> *Lacking any doctrinal precision and dogma these "secular" religions are open to steady attrition of values.* (emphasis added)

To end the survey of scientists and their views on the Beyond of reality must be added the name of Carl Friedrich von Weizsäcker, for he is without peer in representing a model of the twenty-first century holistic approach to reality and Beyond. The point I am trying to make in choosing to describe his case is simple: Those scientists who have taken the trouble to study seriously other aspects of reality all affirm (the more emphatically so, the more they have studied the other viewpoints) the multidimensional Reality perceivable from many angles. Moreover, they all affirm, to the same increasing degree, the Beyond, the Essence, the Meaning of Reality. C. F. von Weizsäcker, a close, younger associate of Heisenberg, was one of those responsible for explaining the nature of the nuclear fusion processes in the sun and similar stars. After World War II, throughout which he had remained in Germany working on nuclear physics but non-bomb research, von Weizsäcker became interested in other approaches to reality. He was centrally involved in the German physicists' declaration against a German nuclear weapons capability. Concern for lessening the East-West tension involved him in the Pugwash Conferences. It is notable that his political activities were neither naive nor of the "activist" or "protest" genre. He became seriously and deeply involved in the muck of technopolitics. Finally, being a theoretician, he decided to explore seriously the long-focus picture of Reality. He became a serious philosopher and held the chair of philosophy at the University of Hamburg. Later, he set up a new Max Planck Institute where an interdisciplinary group of scholars could seriously study "Living Conditions in a Scientific–Technical World." Here could be combined holistically the insights from two aspects of Reality: Nature and Society, in order to understand and act in the world. It is the only such institution in the world. But his holism does not end there. Von Weizsäcker is deeply interested in and sympathetic to the aspects of Reality most clearly revealed via the domain of the Person. Indeed, he has sought not only to learn from the East in a binocular approach to religion, but has explored sympathetically the mystical domain between nature and person and the possibility of stepping into the penumbra where direct contact with the beyond beckons. Writing a major introduction to the book, *The Biological Basis for Science and Religion,* von Weizsäcker introduced its author Gopi Krishna and his interpretation of Kundalini Yoga to the West.

Do nontheologians affirm the Beyond in the Midst? The answer is that many if not most of those that have taken the question seriously certainly do. Whether from the world of the humanities or from the sciences, we have found the same response. And the most significant fact is that, the more seriously they take the question, the more deeply do they affirm this Meaning beyond Reality. But this is not the end of humanity's relation to the Beyond. We are still left to answer: For those that *affirm* any [illegible], how do they *approach* [illegible]? And what relation do they (or should they) develop to it? We turn now to address these two final questions of a Reality-Theology.

3.2 Approaching [illegible], Limitations Imposed by Our Humanity

One of our theses has been that it is our capacity as human observers that ultimately limits our knowledge and understanding of Reality. Though with Einstein and the science community, we can postulate or hypothesize that Reality exists at an "integrated" level independent of us mortals. Though we can affirm with great writers, scientists, and the religious community that [illegible], the essence of Reality, is. Nevertheless, we must often remind ourselves that all these constructs are the products, concepts, and projections of human minds and hearts. Scientific experiments and religious humility agree on the limitations of the human capacities. It is absurd to take an absolutist position on the truth or accuracy of what we "know" or "believe" about [illegible]. With our distorting communication system between two humans, across time, across cultures, it is quite certain that most of what we as individuals "know" is only "personal knowledge." But there may be even more significant limitations on human capabilities to discover the meaning beyond Reality. Viktor Frankl gives us an analogy which illuminates the nature of this second level of limitations. It illustrates the thesis that, as Bridgman asserted, we cannot transcend the human reference plane. Common sense and scientific rigor agree that in our search for [illegible] beyond Reality, it is not unreasonable to assume that there are levels of meaning which are totally inaccessible to us, as to these apes in Viktor Frankl's story:

> *"Imagine an ape that is punctured, again and again, in order to manufacture an antipoliomyelitis serum. Is it possible that this ape could ever understand the purpose of its pain?..." The group of simple women responded by saying that this was sheer impossibility—because the purpose of inflicting this pain was located in a higher dimension, in the world of man, and an ape is not capable of reaching out into the dimension. Then I asked: "What about the human world? Are you absolutely sure that it is the last dimension, a terminal in the cosmos as it were, that there is no dimension beyond the human world, a dimension in which the ultimate meaning of our human sufferings would be understandable? But then we too have no access to this higher dimension...." There was general agreement.*

It would be very rash indeed to pretend that, at any stage in our life or study, we would have penetrated to some ultimate level of meaning. How strange, therefore, that it has always been in religion where unchangeable and absolutist dogma had its major sanctuary. In the very area where the evolutionary attitude could play its role most decisively, rigid, brittle, dogmatic attitudes have thwarted the needed continuous, gentle change. Nevertheless, I believe that there remains, on a much more pragmatic level, a very strong agreement between the Judeo-Christian values and Western scientific tradition that a self-critical evolving approach to any human understanding or perception is the most effective.

A final human limitation is on how humans can communicate to each other whatever meaning they have extracted from Reality. Words, certainly, are not the only vehicle we use. The [illegible] that we experience with all our combined faculties shapes our life-policy (= religious faith).

Analogous to U.S. foreign policy, this is not only the verbal statements in the State of the Union message by the President of the United States, but the sum total of U.S. actions. The viewpoint that "beliefs" (or theories) are static opinions or verbal entities is absurd. James Conant, a chemist and long-time President of Harvard, described verbal formulations even in the world of science thus: *"A scientific theory is not even the first approximation to a map; it is not a creed; it is a policy*—an economical and fruitful guide to action *by scientific investigators."* Humans communicate both via their verbal statements and the actions which constitute their life-policies (Fig. 3.1). The term "life-policy" is much preferable to

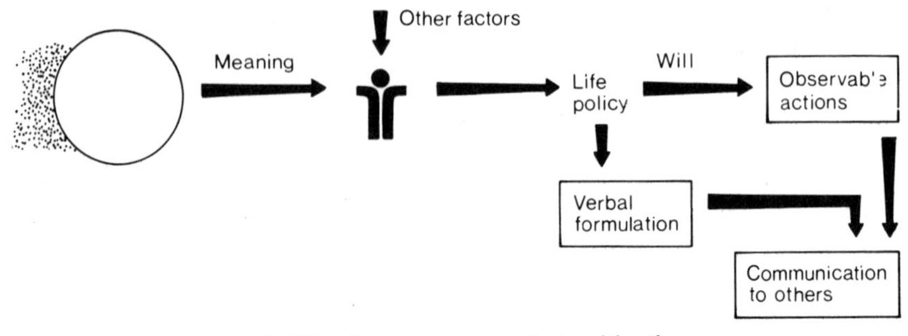

Fig. 3.1 How humans communicate with others.

such totally meaningless terms as "Christian faith"* or "belief," because the latter have come to have so many meanings.

Moreover, our "life-policy" is automatically made explicit via verbal formulations, and inevitably through our intentions and observable actions. For just as [symbol] is reified in some aspect of Reality, so also is our individual faith or life-policy reified in our actions. Again, we note the complexity of human communication, since simple physical, uninterpreted observation may be totally misleading. An individual speeding away at 90 miles an hour may be on a desperate errand of mercy or escaping after robbing a bank. Hence, our life-policies can best be known and interpreted by our closest friends—our community of significant others. It is human will that connects our life-policy to observable actions—and will is, at best, a weak reed in most of us. Hence, we recognize that the signals another person receives regarding our life-policy based on the meaning beyond Reality that we have apprehended will be rather mixed at best.

We approach [symbol], the Beyond in our Midst, with an appropriately humble attitude, recognizing these limitations of the instruments of communication, and the possibly inaccessible levels of reality. All this leads to a permanent openness to correction and refinement.

[symbol], the Meaning From Our Combined Picture of Reality

The theological position of panentheism is that [symbol] is the essence beyond and revealed by experience through *all of Reality taken together.* [symbol] is not restricted to nature; animism is too limited. Nor is [symbol] limited to so-

* Of course, many theologians, Paul Tillich for example, have defined the term faith carefully. But I do not believe that it can help anymore since, at the level of ordinary usage, his definition is unknown. The only hope is to abandon the use of this term also, just as we have indicated we need to do with "God."

ciety, Marxism is far too narrow. Nor is [illegible] contained within a person, Jesusism is untenable heresy. On the other hand, [illegible] is not equal to all of Reality. Pantheism confuses the casket for the jewel, the berry for sweetness, the gift for the love. A human being may come to know, feel, appreciate, and love the Ground of Being or, as we use it here, the Essence of all Reality through her/his seeing through any part of Reality. If we do run into a serious temptation or danger, it is to equate not only that *part* of Reality which we can most easily perceive or experiene to the *whole* Reality, but the meaning of *part* of Reality with [illegible].

Panentheist Reality-theology affirms that every bit of matter from smallest atom to giant star, DNA strand or silicon chip, every growing living thing, every mountain, every tree, chipmunk and cheetah, pride of lions, gaggle of geese, emits its meaning, whispers about [illegible]. It also affirms that Kazantzakis' "Cry" implanted in the cell, manifested in the struggle of evolution of all life forms, that especially human history, and here and there the story of a particular tribe or people, of a redeemer king acting like a suffering servant forms a trail of clues to [illegible].

But panentheism is very clear that [illegible] is the meaning of the *whole* Reality. Any part of Reality may give us a less or more clear *entry point* for experiencing [illegible], but confusing the part for the whole must be avoided strenuously. To get an accurate total picture demands multiplicity and inclusiveness in all aspects of our search for [illegible].

A Note About "Evil"

As soon as one relates [illegible] to all of Reality inclusively, the panentheist is faced with the charge of heresy, of including evil within the nature of "God." The issue is framed in *Incognito* in the following passage:

> *"God is cruel and harsh because He challenges us to undergo the trial. But He is good and wise and loving because he gives us the chance."*
>
> *"And God is a demented monster?" said Erasmus, speaking for the first time with a kind of satisfied serenity.*
>
> *"God is everything. He is also composed of volcanoes, cancerous growths and tapeworms. But if you think that justifies you in jumping into the crater of an active volcano, or wallowing in despair and crime and death, or inoculating yourself with a virus—well, go ahead. You're like a fish that asks, 'Do you mean to say God isn't only water, He's dry land as well?' To which the answer, is 'Yes, my dear fish, He's dry land as well, but if you go climbing on to dry land you'll be sorry.' "*

Far from being a difficulty, inclusiveness is one of the strongest aspects of this theology. We will not develop it here, since Robinson, following Dumitriu, has done it more than adequately. For thousands of years theologians have struggled with the relation of misfortune and evil to their ideas of the loving God. In a single stroke, panentheism removes all the clutter by including good and evil under Reality, through which [illegible] may be experienced or known. Every single human being is surrounded by [illegible], but screened from it by a dense thicket of objects, feelings, and events—both good and evil. Not all the [illegible]-revealing objects or events or parts of Reality are "good," healthful, beneficent, creative, or uplifting. I will not add to Dumitriu's treatment of the relationship to his ideas about God of all the evils—volcanoes, cancer, hatred—which traditionally are excluded from and indeed seen as the opposite of "God." Reality surely includes all these "negatives," and [illegible] must, therefore, include the *meaning of all* of them. I can see no difficulty whatsoever in including the meaning of all the evil which is an inexorable part of our Reality under [illegible]. Being thankful for the waving fields of grain is easy enough, for that is the human, almost biological, response of warm feelings toward the [illegible] which we perceive behind *that* reality. But what of the locusts? The Mennonite test is more pointed: "You only pray aright when you learn to give thanks not only for a good harvest but for the locusts which deprive you of any harvest." The [illegible] behind this attitude is the essence and meaning of a total Reality—good and evil. On the face of it, this statement is contradictory to the kind of literal statement exemplified by "God is a loving Father who desires only the best for his children" (sic). This contradiction should be seen for what it is: a direct challenge to an overly anthropomorphic view. Our situation-theology does require changes in traditional theology every bit as demanding as situation ethics requires changes in traditional ethics, or as post-modern science has required of modern science. There have been dramatic changes in, for example, the institutional Church's position on sex-ethics, in regard to homosexuality and premarital sex. Even more basic changes in our understanding of [illegible] are needed for humanity living on the plateau of its own SbT advances in knowledge and control of the reality around it. We can affirm that, at the personal level, to love the world as it is—to love our friends, sexual partners, spouses, children, our colleagues, political leaders and enemies—provides us the route for the most direct knowledge of [illegible]. But this does not commit us to the traditional "God the Father"–"God is Love" syndrome misinterpreted widely as [illegible] is "only" love. Even "evil" in all its everyday manifestations and its meaning is part of Reality, and its meaning is part of [illegible].

But just as our humanity imposes many limitations on our approaches to [illegible], it also provides certain special avenues which are more effective than others. It is natural that we will exploit these more productive avenues to [illegible], but yet try to avoid being overly biased in our combined view of Reality.

3.3 Finding [symbol], Translucency of the Personal Dimension

The empirical facts clearly establish that the veil of Reality is thinnest for most of humanity where the personal ingredient is most deeply involved. Even from the viewpoint of the nonreligious scientist, Julian Huxley can write: *"The primacy of human personality has been a postulate both of Christianity and of liberal democracy; but it is a* fact *of evolution."* Most humans are more aware of the meaning behind the Reality in their dealings with persons. And, even among these personal events, Judeo-Christian traditions hold that it is at the point of other-centered loving action we come closest to edging out of the full shadow into the penumbra. The joy of a mother at childbirth, the compassion of the brother at the deathbed of a young man, the debonair unselfishness at the end of *A Tale of Two Cities,* these personal experiences can glow with [symbol]. It is, of course, only natural that to human *persons,* it would be through the *personal* dimensions that [symbol] would be most effectively reached.

In *Exploration into God,* John Robinson devotes a chapter to "The Divine Field," his terminology for what I (coming at it so to speak from the other end, the empirical, scientific end of starting from Reality) have labeled the "Meaning" or "Essence" of Reality. Much of what I have said so far is but a paraphrase of this outstanding summary of the panentheist position. However, at this point regarding the special nature of the personal dimension, I propose a slightly different interpretation from his. Robinson introduces a paraphrase of the beginning of the Gospel According to John which is surely one of the masterpieces of revivifying of scripture by rendering it accurately into contemporary, meaningful idiom. The first paragraph runs:

> *The clue to the universe as personal was present from the beginning. It was to be found at the level of reality which we call God. Indeed, it was no other than God nor God than it. At the depth of reality the element of the personal was there from the start. Everything was drawn into existence through it, and there is nothing in the process that has come into being without it. Life owes its emergence to it, and life lights the path to man. It is that light which illumines the darkness of the subpersonal creation, and the darkness never succeeded in quenching it.*
>
> *That light was the clue to reality—the light which comes to clarity in man. Even before that it was making its way in the universe. It was already in the universe, and the whole process depended upon it, although it was not conscious of it. It came to its own in the evolution of the personal; yet persons failed to grasp it. But, to those who did, who believed in what it represented, it gave the potential of a fully personal relationship to God. For these the meaning of life was seen to rest, not simply on its biological basis, not on the impulses of nature or the drives of history, but on the reality of God. And this divine personal principle found embodiment in a man and took habitation in our midst. We saw its full glory, in all its utterly gracious reality—the wonderful sight of a person living in uniquely normal relationship to God, as son to father.*

But in using the whole passage which draws us from theology to issues of Christology, I believe that, in addition to stressing the centrality of one aspect of [illegible], the meaning of personal Reality, he has allowed in through the backdoor the total *personification* of [illegible].

A universal panentheist position, which will include Christian as well as other positions, gets around this difficulty by using, instead, our image of the different degrees of opacity of the veil of Reality and allowing a special but not unique vehicle in the personal dimension. Following our earlier constructs, I would rephrase the opening sentence as follows: *"The personal window in the screen of Reality was present from the beginning. Through the personal dimension the meaning of all of Reality, which we name God, shines most clearly. . . ."*

There is further danger to this overstressing of the "person" aspect, in making too much of *human* history, as in Teilhard's "hominization." When trying to apprehend the *whole* of the [illegible], behind *all* Reality, Christians must be very careful to be sure that their Christology does not warp their theology. It is a most natural tendency because of our human reference point. While I yield to none in assigning significance to the personal dimension of experience, and to the transparency of the personal window in our Reality screen, I believe we must retain our consistency in seeing [illegible] as the meaning of *all* Reality, not only the *personal.*

In my metaphor, the claim is that the veil of Reality is thinned down nearly to a clear window when we bring a personal (experiential) approach to the sphere of the person. With J. H. Oldham we can say: "ALL REAL life is meeting." Our companionate journeys of hope or pain on the road to Emmaus bring us very close to the "Light." Our deepest interpersonal experiences give the fullest and clearest exposure to the [illegible] beyond the I-Thou encounter. Yet, the experience of the transcendent Thou through this window puts us in touch with a fuller Reality than a person. It puts us in touch with all of [illegible] *through* part of it. In other words, it is not only the person, Jesus, that we see through the window in the person area. We may see the personal dimension of [illegible] in the center of our "image" but we see all of [illegible]. Indeed, incarnation makes Jesus part of the Reality through which we see [illegible]. A more accurate symbol for the person of Jesus in this language is a fisheye lens inset into the translucent window in the personal area. It is *through* Jesus that humans get the clearest, widest angle of [illegible]. Meaning, like light, not only shines clearly through this lens, it is concentrated by it. Many of Jesus' "particularity" or "exclusivist" statements make good sense in this metaphor. "I am the way," "I am the door," "No man cometh unto the Father except through me." These say that except through the lens of the Incarnation, through the avatar, the fullness of [illegible] cannot be apprehended or experienced by human beings. The key point at issue here is the special diaphaneity of the veil of Reality in the region of the personal concentrating, the Christian would claim, into a lens in the person of Jesus.

We must continually make the case against equating the meaning or essence of any one of these aspects or experiences, even in the personal dimension, with [symbol]. The personal is not the only aspect of [symbol]. The *only* possible human description of [symbol] is that [symbol] is at one and the same time the meaning and the essence being radiated by *all of Reality* simultaneously. Any other [symbol] is much too partial. A life-policy based on a partial view of [symbol] would be mistaken and dangerous to self and others.

Perhaps another example of relating to different aspects of [symbol], of the perspectives, will serve better for some. Any public official functions in several rather different roles: as spouse or parent at home, as "boss" to a small coterie of close associates in the office, and as a maker of laws or dispenser of justice in the public eye. Examine now the relation of, say, a son or daughter who worked in the office to his/her parent. Although at home the child would have a different personal, comfortable relationship with the parent, such a relationship would inevitably be influenced by the child's reaction to the parent's behavior in the office, and the public or political stances taken. Likewise, the son-citizen's relating to the public figure would be colored by the fact of the family tie. Our relationship to [symbol] has this same interwovenness of response, even while only one color may show prominently in a particular light. For a person to relate to a parent only as a child in the home—in the personal dimension—ignoring all the other known attributes of the parent would be unsatisfactory and irresponsible.

Seeing Around Reality: Edging Into the Penumbra

Yet, even as we attempt to speak so carefully about our contact with [symbol], many deeply religious persons from different traditions will be baffled. For much of their tradition may have placed great emphasis on Direct contact with [symbol]. Indeed, many religions bear witness to specially clear visions of "Ultimate Reality" and its meaning other than through the "personal" emphasis of Christianity. The mystical tradition within each religion does not see the avatar as the special point of most direct contact. It is not the development of the "E" self, but of the "R" self, and concentration not in the center of the Person region, but at the juncture of Nature and Person that is most fruitful in the view of the mystic. Indeed, their claims are for a direct contact and absorption into [symbol] by this route rather than through any reality. We can understand this in our terms if we modify slightly our image, and remove the essence or [symbol] some distance from its screen of Reality. We arrive, then, in more familiar linguistic territory for this arrangement of viewer, screen, and source of light

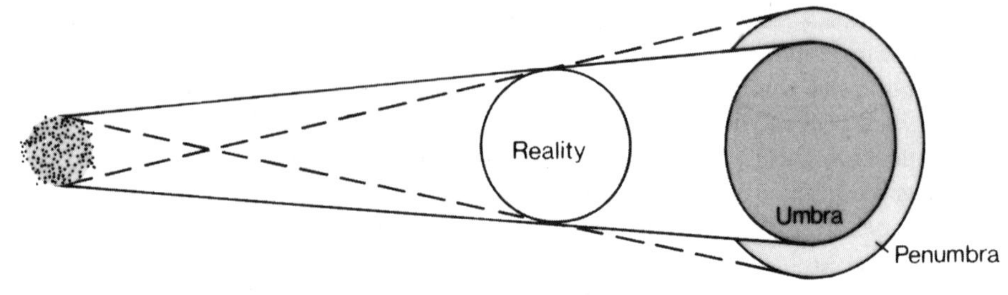

Fig. 3.2

is the same as that of the solar eclipse, and recalls the pictures in our astronomy schoolbooks.

Such an arrangement of source, screen, and observer for an eclipse is sketched in Fig. 3.2. Martin Buber has made us all familiar with the term "Eclipse of God." Using Buber's image, specific events (the Holocaust, the technological invasion, etc.) interpose a dense screen and cast their shadow between God and humanity. *Our* image has been that *all* objects, *all* events are absolutely and *always* interposed between and humanity. But these parts or realities are not conceived of as impenetrable opaque screens, but rather as a mixture of dense screen, translucent film, and lattice work, occasionally, as in the previous interpretation of Jesus, as a lens concentrating for efficient communication to humans.

The image of the eclipse, however, allows us to refine this position slightly and introduce a new concept. In an eclipse there is the region where no *direct* light at all reaches the observer—the so-called umbra (see Fig. 3.2). But around the edges of the umbra there is another region—the penumbra. In the penumbra, as the term implies, there is a partial eclipse and a partial shadow. The observer standing in the penumbra can glimpse a thin crescent of around the edge of the Reality screen. Here, the observer may have a kind of direct contact with the , the light behind the screen. Yet, in the penumbra—not to push the image too far—the observer can be in direct touch only with a small part of . The image seems to be a fairly faithful one of the potentialities and dangers of some of the revived interest in the mystical.

From the story of Moses' realization at Mt. Sinai that the Israelites could not stand the direct sight of God, the concept of the necessity for a screen between and human beings has been a commonplace.* The Beyond has always had to be located in and diluted or diffused, so to

* In medieval church architecture, the *rood screen* separates the congregation in the nave from the chancel where the altar, representing the focal point of the presence of God, is located.

speak, by the Midst. At the same time, the desire for some kind of *direct* contact with in all its breadth and depth is very widely and deeply encoded into all human beings. In our image, it corresponds to humanity's desire to move out of the umbra in the shadow of the screen, even with its more or less transparent areas, toward the penumbra where the experience of even a partial is direct. Much of religion's concentration on the mystical corresponds to an effort of trying to see around Reality (so to speak) instead of through it. Very few, if any, live in the direct light of the "knowledge" or "experience" of . All of us live most of the time behind the shadow of the screen of Reality. A few venture out in forays into the penumbra. This may take the form of a Pauline conversion, or the discipline of St. John of the Cross. It may require the remarkable integration in the I-Ching of chance into a way of life, or the detailed sexual disciplines of Kundalini Yoga, as vehicles of entering the penumbra. Yet, because of its *partialness,* these attempts to peek around Reality and see into its meaning directly carry in their very effort a slight tinge of partialness, a whiff of subterfuge, a hint of cheap grace. If the clouds were necessary on Mt. Sinai, then Reality is a necessary and proper vehicle for . Such is, I believe, the basic Christian position. In any case, the optical arrangement itself faithfully models what happens in practice: the view from the penumbra is only a slim crescent instead of a full sphere. To know , to see the fullness of God, there is only one reliable route—*through Reality.* Forays into the penumbra suffer from the same defect as the over-personalized approaches to , they may tend to replace the whole with a part.

Whether we approach through Reality; whether we balance out our use of the window of the personal with long-focus views of Nature; whether we seek to add a penumbric view through some special route, we are next confronted with a very different kind of question. How do we *relate* to ? How do we *respond* to ? Do I regard as some superfundamental propositional truth? Some fundamental equation? Should I relate to as I do to $e = mc^2$ or $AgNO_3 + HCl = AgCl_s + HNO_3$? Or do I adopt the personal, even the chummy style of a Malcolm Boyd or Michel Quoist? Or do I, in a more Hindu-Buddhist sense, strive for a kind of "absorption" into ? As we near the end of this volume we address this question of how to relate to .

3.4 Holism as the Precondition to Relating to

What if one has, over the years, maintained a growing and balanced picture of Reality, has assiduously sought its meaning by scientific thought, experiencing concern and reflection on the meaning of the whole? How does that affect one's relation to ?

The spectrum of potential readers of this volume (from secular scientists in Cambridge, Massachusetts, and Cambridge, England, or Novosibirsk in the USSR, to the liberal, emancipated Western intelligentsia with roots in Christendom, to the traditionally religious from the Bible Belt, Vatican, Benares or Kyoto shrines) *deal* with or relate to the meaning of Reality in very different ways. It is the modest hope of the author that the approach suggested herein will indicate the existence of a commonality of response. It is this commonality which has not been sufficiently emphasized. Conversely, it is not to be expected nor, perhaps, even desired that the detailed practices of different groups, religions, or otherwise be similar in relating to [illegible]. What one may expect, however, is that, since the objective Reality which surrounds and dwells in all of us is exactly the same, then through whatever balance of perspectives we *view* it, our behavioral responses to [illegible] will share some common features.

What is first required by the times in our relation to [illegible] is a radical break with a single-visioned approach. What is demanded for survival into, and in, the twenty-first century will be an absolute commitment to a new holism. No fuzzy-brained eclecticism will do. Only the precision of modern physics, the rigor of a monastic order, and the warmth of two people in love all thoroughly interwoven within the person will allow us to relate as a worthy interdisciplinary, integrated wholeness. Note that the previous sentence does not in any way suggest that each person must be a practicing physicist, contemplative monk, and in love! It is also essential to my thesis that the usual naive counterstatement on the need for specialization either to be employable in our culture or to make a contribution to human advancement cannot any longer be taken as a sufficient rebuttal to this demand for a total redistricting of the artificial territorial bounds of so-called "higher" education. It simply begs the question to assert that depth, discipline, and detailed concentration are essential for creativity. The difference in the reductionist and holistic approach is sharp and clear. The reductionist looks at a problem from one viewpoint alone, concentrates her/his study of something in *one* discipline (see Fig. 2.4). S/he explicitly ignores, nay abjures, the serious study of the same topic from other viewpoints and assumes no responsibility for the validity of the solution in other perspectives. The holiest, while not denying the necessity for depth and specialization, explicitly asserts that true depth of study requires a multidirectional analysis, and explicitly works out of more than one of these E, O, R roles.

Let me illustrate, with two examples, what the future holism will entail; one in medicine and one in teaching. Viktor Frankl responds to a discussion by S. Kety of Harvard of his paper from which I quoted earlier, explicitly on this point of the need for specialization, by stressing the retention of the multiangled perspective, in the following words:

I explicitly said that it is not only the privilege, but even the responsibility of the scientist to embark on reductions, i.e., projections; but he must remain aware of what he is doing. For some years I have given three lectures a day, 4 p.m. to 7 p.m., the first on neurology, the second on psychiatry, the third on psychotherapy. In the first lecture I sometimes discussed a patient in a reductionist manner: if it was a case of brain tumour, I had to check and examine the reflexes, I treated him as if he were a closed system of reactions and responses. In the second lecture I discussed psychogenic neuroses; and in the third lecture the first patient was discussed again, but as a human being a person whose human dimension I had to shut out while examining him neurologically.

The second example is drawn from the growing literature on "interdisciplinarity" in education. For 100 years the single discipline called the "natural sciences" in the Western system, in which a bachelor's (master's, or Ph.D.) candidate could specialize, has been subdividing, until now it has fissioned into more than 50 narrow specialties.

The Western university world has perpetrated upon the whole of humankind the crime of validating the unexamined proposition that virtually infinite specialization is the route to truth, to knowledge and wisdom. In another connection, I have discussed in detail why the finitude of the human subject forces upon every educator a critical choice.

As Figure 3.3 illustrates, either we educate persons who have a specialty but who are exposed to neighboring disciplines and understand the nature of interfaces and how the whole is made up of parts, or we continue to train one-legged, one-eyed, monodisciplinary specialists who can never construct or manage the wholeness of life. Today, while virtually everyone acknowledges that new, antispecialization devices are necessary in the university world, the entire momentum of the system is still against the holistic approach. But the grassroots trend is now unmistakable. The only field in American academe which is growing by leaps and bounds will have a familiar ring to the readers who have followed the earlier chapter in this volume. It goes under the rubric of "Science, Technology and Society." In approximately five years, nearly a thousand colleges and universities have established some sort of courses, curriculum, or degree programs where a multidirectional approach is taken to the problems of society. These programs explicitly seek to balance the scientific, observational (O), view with both the E and R views.

Holistic Religious Development

Just as small parts of the academic world are beginning to recognize the need for this multipronged approach to general education, so must our individual and institutional religious lives also change from single vision to trifocal vision. The response of human beings to [illegible] cannot only be at the point of reflection, meditation, and prayer. I have every bit as much

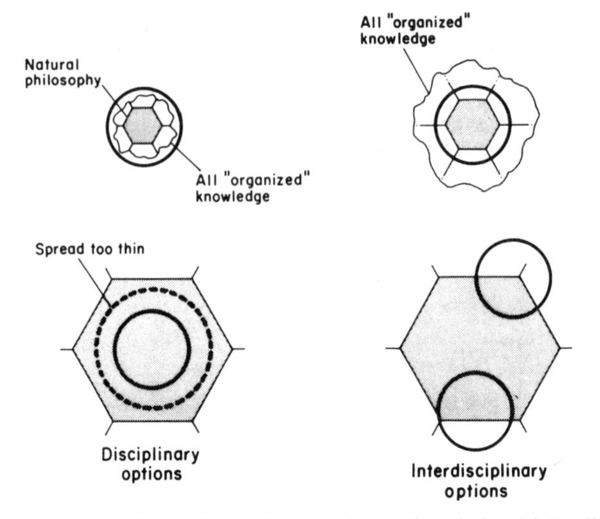

Fig. 3.3 It is no mean trick to balance the attention to the whole with "sufficient" attention to the detailed particulars. One of the reasons is that in so doing the choice of the key particulars is much more critical. Epistemologies for such iterations from wholes to significant parts have yet to be worked out. Michael Polanyi alludes to the difficulty while affirming the need for holism. . . . *we cannot always identify the particulars on which we rely in our attending on the thing.*

This fact can be generalized widely. There are vast domains of knowledge—of which I shall speak in a moment—that exemplify in various manners that we are in general unable to tell what particulars we are aware of when attending to a whole which they constitute. So we can declare that there are two kinds of knowing which invariably enter jointly into any act of knowing a comprehensive entity. There is (1) a knowing by attending to something, as we attend to the entity in question, and (2) a knowing by relying on our awareness of certain things in the way we rely on our awareness of the many particulars of the entity in the act of attending to it.

We can go further. Evidently, any attempt to identify the particulars of an entity would involve a shift of attention from the entity to the particulars. We would have to relax the attention given to the whole for the sake of discovering its particulars, which we had noticed until now only by being aware of them as parts of the whole. So that once we have succeeded in fully identifying these particulars, and are in fact attending to them now directly in themselves, we clearly shall not be relying any more on our awareness of them as particulars of a whole, and therefore will inevitably have lost sight of the whole altogether.

potential for seeing the meaning radiating from my research in materials science if I develop my ability to find that meaning in and through that Reality. This is far from easy. Some Reality is pretty dense. [illegible] does not shine through all of Reality evenly. Plodding through hundreds of X-ray patterns, or tediously cleaning up the vacuum system is essential to some scientific observations. I do not know of anyone who equates—in its diaphaneity toward the divine—an hour of that activity with an hour where a small group of committed believers are sharing their deepest convictions, or praying with a dying friend, or plotting their antinuclear armaments strategy. Having said that about the workaday world of science, I hasten to add nor does the E or R perspective have a monopoly on the most transparent parts of the Reality screen. Weeks of "11 a.m. on Sunday" attendance at a church with an irrelevant format, formula preaching from a dead text, and little evidence of life or love in the congregation cannot be compared with the excitement of discovery of a new, more efficient, photovoltaic material, and what that can reveal to the scientist of [illegible] as it relates to the service of the Third World or use of renewable resources. Neither do ritualized hugging, nor free love in encounter groups, nor two-hour meditation sessions sitting naked in the sun guarantee an authentic sculpture of Reality and a lively appreciation of its meaning.

No one, I suspect, will quarrel with the simple proposition that all humans need to use this trifocal vision to get a balanced view of Reality, but it is only the first payment of the price for this balanced relationship to [illegible]. It is in the working out of a new balance in our relations to [illegible] that the full price appears. For instance, from the secular scientist it requires a conscious development of the personal, experiential side of her/his life. It may mean studying sociopolitical issues and working on causes—prison reform or hunger in Africa. It could require, in addition, a development of the introspective life, whether it be reading T. S. Eliot with Bach in the background, or following the formulas of Transcendental Meditation, or simply learning to pray in a more traditional way. I recall vividly the passage in Alister Hardy's *Biology of God* where the author makes a telling case not only for this direct I-Thou communication, but for much of the traditional attendant physical postures such as bowing or kneeling, arguing the case from animal biology. My own operational bias suggests that we have no choice but to start with whatever we have learned as children as the effective approach to [illegible]. In many cases, regrettably, this may be a great handicap. In others, as in mine, a flying start. From this base, as we discard "childish things," it is only after some careful experimentation that one can find what works for oneself. There is the further danger of stopping at the first level where something appears to be "working." Our understanding and relating to [illegible] must evolve in precise proportion to the widening of our experience, the increase of our knowledge and understanding of all spheres of reality. It is utterly preposterous to think that any mature human being would use the same constructs, thought-forms, stories or myths to describe [illegible] as they did when they finished confirmation classes. On Thomas Jefferson's memorial is carved his own words:

I am not an advocate for frequent changes in laws and constitutions, but laws and institutions must go hand in hand with the progress of the human mind. As that be-

comes more developed, more enlightened, as new discoveries are made, new truths discovered and manners and opinions change, with the change of circumstances, institutions must advance also to keep pace with the times. We might as well require a man to wear still the coat which fitted him when a boy as civilized society to remain ever under the regimen of their barbarous ancestors.

The life-policy demanded by any meaningful relation to [illegible] includes an experimental attitude for a lifetime. With Teilhard, we must continue to "try things" continually for the rest of our lives.

3.5 Doing the Truth: Humanity Relates to [illegible]

The Emerging Unities

There is a strong temptation to start this section by saying that, after all, it is not our knowledge or understanding of [illegible] that matters, but how we relate to [illegible], and how we finally act out our relation to [illegible]. But that separation of action from knowledge I deny in the depths of my being. I believe that part of our culture's sickness is caused by simple ignorance of and confusion about the fundamentals. Five-year-olds can get the square root of 75293 in one second by pressing a calculator key but do not know the meaning of "square root," nor the value of the square root of 9. We turn on lights, heat in microwave ovens, watch TV sets, drive cars, and use tranquilizers without any attention or concern as to what is behind it all. So, as we approach life, we miss the most important learning from our own scientific era—the lock-step interdependence between good theory and fruitful experiment. Even though many good experiments have been done by chance or are based on wrong theories, the world of SbT has achieved what it has by demanding *this* integration and iteration: Past knowledge → new experiments → new knowledge → new experiments → new knowledge → . . . . and on and on.

Learning from the past is hardly confined to SbT. It is the story of humanity, it is the distinctive character of human beings, the only species continually learning from its own history. The most important learning from the past is the collective map or filing system for experience and data. We have learned to know up from down, left from right, east from west, fruitful from frustrating, right from wrong. Of course, all such knowledge is provisional, tentative, at best penultimate. Yet, each new learning can be fitted into some tentative niche. On any scale of human endeavor, no field or person can progress if there is no agreement on the construction of the map, the points of the compass, or the filing system. The lives of individuals, communities, and nations can be made right and be meaningful only where there is a collective consensus on what is "right."

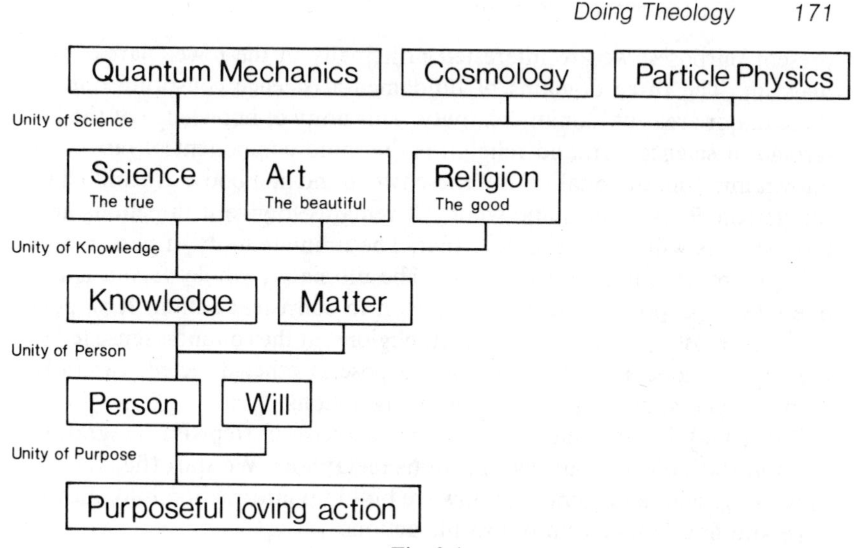

Fig. 3.4.

I have tried to develop an approach to understanding and relating to Reality and [illegible]. I believe that pantheists of both Christian and other religious persuasions will not have much difficulty with it. Indeed, many may find it so obvious as to be boring. I also believe that some persons with a scientific training may be drawn toward considering such a panentheist position by the sheer plausibility of the approach and its strongly empirical leanings. But, as I have mooted in one or two places in the foregoing, I know from long practice and experience that our *understanding* is improved and enriched, indeed drastically changed, by corresponding and consistent actions. My life–policy is not an abstract creed or statement, it is the pattern visible, to close friends, in the sum total of my actions.

If there is a Holy Grail which our culture's savants should be pursuing, it is surely integration, wholeness, and unity. We have become fragmented human beings bombarded by myriad signals of propaganda, education, and incessant advertising. Before we can address the matter of the possible coherence and synergism between action and knowledge, let us glance at the increasing "unity" which can now be perceived if we only look below the clutter. The diagram in Fig. 3.4, which is slightly modified after the ideas of C. F. von Weizsäcker,* traces the emerging unities from the level of cognitive science all the way down to loving actions. For our

* These ideas were presented at the seminar entitled "The Meaning and Function of Science in Contemporary Society" at The Pennsylvania State University, September 1971.

present purposes, we are interested principally in the lower part of the diagram. The three domains of fundamental science constitute one of these major areas of human creativity. This unity of knowledge of the interplay of science, art, and religion is the mind component of our well-known mind-matter duality. But these two, mind and body, are unified in the person. This is the static whole. It remains to give it directions and motion. It is will which provides that. The ultimate unity of person and will (or spirit) is manifest in *action.* The ultimately whole person is the one whose purpose motivates the person to consistent action. It is, perhaps, the most significant unity in all religions, at the common sense level, the highest good that the unifying purpose is other-directed, carefully planned, and sacrificially executed loving actions.

But it may be of value to repeat this exercise in stepwise integration and unification using our own previous metaphors. We start (fig. 3.4) by illustrating with an example of how we build up information into knowledge and finally turn it into possible actions.

Putting the Alphabet Into Action

We have emphasized again and again that all human knowledge is "receiver limited," that is, limited by the capacities not of a machine which produces knowledge but by the person who receives it. Our five senses receive a variety of signals, of data "bits"—as they are called in computer technological parlance. Our left and right brains process these data. The one linearly, sequentially; the other relationally as in a picture. The integrated, processed information drives and steers the human system physically, emotionally, and spiritually. Nevertheless, the data themselves do not give us meaning or constitute knowledge or even information. For example, the woman at the hairdresser is told in the newspaper that the radioactive iodine released from a nuclear power plant accident was "1150 pico curies" at noon on a certain date; she would have some data but no information. She wouldn't know if this was dangerous or not, a high level or low, etc.

The pioneers of information theory defined information as the "resolution of uncertainty." I like to use the analogy of a *letter* placed in a meaningful *word.* Many of us play the game "Scrabble" or "Word-making and Word-taking." Data correspond to the letters given to us by lot; data become information (i.e., more useful or valuable) when they are fitted into words. Indeed, the analogy is quite close because the same datum can fit into many different words and often, as in Scrabble, into two words simultaneously.

Or take another example. The radio announcer will frequently say "the barometer stands at 29.8 inches." This is data. When the forecaster adds: "and falling rapidly" we have more data. Only if—and as soon as—the receiver, on the basis of previous knowledge, realizes that this means it is likely to rain or storm does this become *information.* Just as the letter X often is unusable in "Scrabble," the data may also be unusable in a particular context. That is, the receiver of the broadcast message may not be able to make any use at all of the barometric pressure data point. Or the data can be incorrectly used. If, for example, the person thought that dropping pressure meant impending sunshine, or if one thought that 29.8 inches measured temperature on the Celsius scale they had heard so much about recently, this would constitute misinformation. In our analogy such use of the "letters" would be to make up an "impossible" word (i.e., a word which isn't in the dictionary) which is not merely an arbitrary convention but a real criterion of its effectiveness in communicating with others. The sequence "ogd" is simply not slightly different from "God," it is totally ineffective, hence, a gross error in communicating something presumably about the deity. Just as letters can be articulated into words, so words can be articulated into sentences. If information corresponds to a word, then knowledge could be said to correspond to a sentence. Just as we make use of words to construct sentences

Letter = Data bit
Word = Information
Sentence = Knowledge

so we can make "meaningful" sentences with words. What this requires is an existing vocabulary of other words, a willingness to play by the mechanical rules of syntax, and an articulation of words into the larger framework of a sentence. Knowledge is the arrangement (on the basis of knowledge and experience gained from the past and appropriate to the present context) of data so as to gain meaning.

To continue with our meteorological analogy, combining the information that it is likely to rain, with the prior context that my clothes are out on the line, or that the petunias had needed watering, establishes a new level of aggregation we call knowledge, which can form the basis for decision and *action.* Hearing the weather forecast may, therefore, form the basis, as its data are integrated successively into information and then into knowledge, for bringing in the clothes or postponing the watering of the petunia bed.

Into what more complex levels can we articulate such knowledge and meaning? Into truth and wisdom. The word "wisdom" carries a connotation of testing against the experience of the ages. And it is, I believe, very appropriate to define wisdom as the articulation of knowledge over time and space. When we integrate new or present knowledge with what has been known from the past, and/or with the knowledge from other cultures or very different viewpoints, then we are attaining wisdom. Is wisdom, then, the end of human Brahmanic integration? No, of course not, because this sequence of articulation is a sterile one in the neutral, inorganic world of information. The first step toward that is to put knowledge and wisdom into the context of life. All complete human beings must, and do in fact, become involved in integrative interaction of their three-dimensional sculptures of Reality with their own responses *in action and practice.*

Indeed, so far, the integration at each step has been with prior information. But we may also have integration not with information alone but with circumstance. Every sentence carries a significance, a meaning which is defined almost entirely by interwoven circumstances and related fact—by reality—quite independent of the sentence itself. Thus, the sentence: "The boy was killed in the flood caused by the rain," when it occurs in a TV play or newspaper report, carries an entirely different meaning from hearing those same words from the policeman reporting on the flood in which your son was trapped. Here, the sentence has been set into a preexisting and independent context of reality. Only when knowledge or wisdom is thus set into the context of real life can we extract from it, its *fullest* meaning. Only then are we ready to move to integrate it with action (see Fig. 3.5).

To follow the steps by which knowledge and meaning are integrated with action into full personhood, let us examine the relationships between knowledge and action as we progress through the steps of increasingly complex articulation of information.

Into the hierarchical connection on the left of data—information, knowledge and meaning—to wisdom, we now interdigitate this enriching and complicating factor: Action. The receiver-limitation of all human perception constrains us to remember that human beings are not merely computer memories. We do not only store digitized data bits, even after processing into knowledge. We act continually. We act by commission and by omission. And we learn from our actions. And this learning profoundly affects our image of Reality. This is what this section has been leading up to: the connection of our perception of [illegible] through Reality to action in human life.

What is the relation between knowing [illegible] and our actions? In many ways, of course, human action is more certain and universal than human knowledge. Well over three billion persons get up every morning and carry out hundreds of millions of "actions." What guides or informs such actions? Do not the actions themselves or their meanings constitute a

← Increasing "articulation" of data, information, etc, into content.

← Increasing content of "meaning"

Constraints or guidance provided by tradition or history →

Letter	Data-bit	Barometer 29.8 and dropping rapidly	Single direction, single focus input from Reality
Meaningful word (*dictionary*) Word incorporated into sentences with meaning (*grammar)*	Information	Likely to rain or storm	Multifocal or multidirectional view of reality
Sentences incorporated into paragraphs which tie in with past and future. (*English composition*)	Contextual knowledge and meaning	Total precipitation this month is very high. It will be good for the pentunias. Must be caused by increase number of satellites. Better bring in the clothes on the line. The picnic this afternoon will be cancelled.	Multifocal and multidirectional view of reality Finding the [illegible], essence of meaning through reality
Paragraphs or chapters which tell a coherent story.	Wisdom (basis for future action)	Another few storms like this and there will be floods in . . . We should stop space research.	Relating to [illegible]
A story which demands response in action or compels participation.	Love (direction and drive for action)	I get together a group to help with cleanup. Work with legislature for getting appropriate flood control measures in area. Educate people to cooperate with nature, i.e., don't build homes in flood plane.	Adsorption into [illegible]

Fig. 3.5. The information-knowledge-action ladder

powerful form of knowledge? Is not the relation of knowledge and action in ordinary human life the same as between theory and experiment in science? Not quite! Our first diagram (Fig. 3.4) in continuing its example downward as the information was articulated with increasing complexity gave examples of possible actions at some of the stages. Figure 3.6 shows that our actions also should form a parallel hierarchy in degree of complexity. The narrower or more local the origin or consequences of any action, the less articulated need the data be to achieve a reasonable coherence.

The diagram shows that while mere knowledge is *necessary* for all, it is *sufficient* and proper only for those actions which have no long-range (in time or space) consequences. A continued use of our barometric pressure analogy helps explain why. A full articulation of knowledge with contextual reality (the clothes are on the line) would lead one to bring in the clothes before it rains. A less contextual articulation tells us only that this month's precipitation has been rather high, leading to no action. Furthermore, all kinds of misleading articulation with other data-bits also obtained from the radio is possible. For instance, "Farmer Jones today blamed the rainy weather on space activities," and "the Russians announce the orbiting of three satellites in a week" are new data bits which combined with the weather forecast can lead to "knowledge" of the kind which attributes the storm to the presence of satellites in orbit. Note how such "knowledge" undisciplined by the knowledge of others, uncalibrated by the wisdom of the ages (here only ten years old and, hence, possibly less reliable) could lead to possibly inappropriate action such as "Stop Space Research."

How does one choose between one course of wisdom-in-action or the other? It is never easy. In the last analysis, it requires integration (com-

	Data	x	Insufficient basis for any →	Action
Integrate (other data	Information	x	Only appropriate for small, inconsequential →	Action
Integrate (other information on context or situation)	Knowledge & Meaning	x	Inappropriate for most → Appropriate for short range (immediate impact knowable) → Longer ranges in time or space pose problems →	Action
Integrate (knowledge and meaning from trusted reference group)	Truth & Wisdom	x	Appropriate in most cases for → Directions often not clear in longest-range case →	Action
Integrate (with certain actions)	Love	x	Necessary guidance for direction of any or all levels of →	Actions

Fig. 3.6. *RELATION of Succeeding Steps in Data-Articulation to ACTIONS*

parison) with the knowledge and meaning from the reference group of humans which one had learned to trust. Yet, one must always test their reliability against other reference groups. This, very few of us do. Most of us do not question the knowledge–meaning base of our family, our closest friends, our "significant others." That is the fruitful and creative moment: of speaking the truth in love, of questioning the very basis from which we started.

It is a commonplace in science. The experiment done on the basis of today's theory may destroy that theory. But it is the only place to start. Integrating past and present knowledge with immediate context or situation carries within it the proper guidelines for action. This may be as simple as arranging to have the site of the picnic tomorrow moved indoors since the ground will be too wet in any case; or it may extend far into time and space by realizing that if this storm were to be repeated soon, there could be very serious floods and some contingency evacuation plan should be made in certain parts of the country.

These two parallel ladders of articulation of data into wisdom and the smallest acts into a coherent pattern of actions culminate in "Love" or loving acts. Love, we claim, is at once the highest level of integration along the human "information" chain, as well as the single necessary and sufficient principle which can guide or direct all human actions. We shall return to it after considering further the nature of human action.

"Action": Experimenting with Truth

In the first two sections of this book we described reality and discussed it using the metaphor of "seeing," and the "image" perceived. There is no doubt that the sense of sight is the most information-laden of our senses. But, of course, our five senses are not the only input to our perception (observe how our language itself emphasizes sight!) or learning about Reality. There is a "passive" nature to the construction and examination of an "image," even a multidirectional, multifocal image as proposed earlier. This in itself is a danger but, when seeing it applied to apprehending [illegible] through Reality, it is obviously and totally inadequate to express the fullness of the relation of humanity to [illegible].

No one has spoken more trenchantly of the debilitating effect of too many images upon contemporary human consciousness than the critic Susan Sontag. In her recent book, *On Photography,* she criticizes the destructive potential of photography (and, by implication, all electronic recording of images). She shows how it undermines art and warps all man-nature and interpersonal relations. *"Taking photographs has set up a chronic voyeuristic relation to the world which levels the meaning of all events."* This may be translated into our terminology as a confusion of focal lengths. Since photographs do not carry any indication of the "focus" in question, they tend to confuse the views unless the latter are very carefully labeled. We are often literally lost with respect to the depth dimension in most of our images of Reality, as we jump back and forth from microscopic views of atoms to pictures of galaxies. *"Photographs,"* Sontag writes, *"are a means of appropriating reality and making it obsolete."* The idea of appropriating part of that which is imaged is well known in ancient cultures. The idea of "appropriating" the "presence" of a leader or distinguished person is inherent in the Indian term *"taking* a darshan of" (idiomatically rendered in English as "making a visit to"). But the very commonality and near infinite oversupply of images literally depletes the reality imaged, and ultimately renders it obsolete. Who needs the real thing, when 100 million have seen the image (often doctored slightly to serve the purpose). *"The attempts by photographers to bolster a depleted sense of reality contribute to that depletion."*

We clearly cannot stop our relating to [illegible] at the point of merely perfecting and seeing *through* the *images* of reality which we have created. Our relation to [illegible] and to Reality is incomplete without response in action. The role of action is twofold. First there is action which tests or verifies our images, our theories. This is exactly analogous to the laboratory experiments in the physical sciences. We analyze the rock, or measure the physical properties for ourselves to verify or validate the claims of others. But action also has the second property of confirming the true unity of the person (as in our fig. 3.1 and also 3.7). What do we mean by true unity? Let us imagine a truly committed Christian socialist in the West for whom all of knowledge clearly points to the demands on her as a person to live by a certain conservation ethic, in order that developing countries may have a fairer access to resources. That individual's personhood is unified and strengthened further whenever she acts out her convictions in her life. If she acts contrary to her own knowledge or lacks the will to act, this inconsistency destroys the unity of the person and must ultimately lead to a loss of unity at even higher levels. It can even ultimately corrode the very processes of knowledge, even scientific knowledge. When her actions are in tune with her images of Reality (when in classical terminology she is obedient to God's will) she is enabled to see an even more complete reality, and new actions are demanded of her.

I recognize that these steps by which I have tied scientific knowledge to persons, will, purpose, and love have often been held to be beyond the scope of science. This view is passé. Our world is much too interlinked to allow the SbT enterprise to continue behind a watertight compartment of unconcern for the greater purposes and the realities of humanity's existence. The great minds have always recognized this, but it has been explicitly and implicitly denied by the entire SbT establishment up to now. We are coming to the end of that era, along with the end of the hegemony of SbT. The following quotation sounds like the work of a Soviet bureaucrat:

> *It is not enough that you should understand about applied science in order that your work may increase man's blessings. Concern for man himself and his fate must always form the chief interest of all technical endeavors, concern for the great unsolved problems of the organization of labor and the distribution of goods—in order that the creations of our minds shall be a blessing and not a curse to mankind. Never forget this in the midst of your diagrams and equations.*

It is, in fact, Albert Einstein speaking at the California Institute of Technology in 1931.

A more thoughtful analysis along the lines of our own appears at the end of C. F. von Weizsäcker's book, *The History of Nature.*

> *The scientific and technical world of modern man is the result of his daring enterprise, knowledge without love. Such knowledge is in itself neither good nor bad. Its worth depends on what power it serves. Its ideal has been to remain free of any power. Thus it has freed man step by step of all his bonds of instinct and tradition, but has not led him into the new bond of love.*

Von Weizsäcker then shows how the disconnection between "knowledge" and "love" has led to despair and nihilism and, I would add, to ignoring the social and political context of SbT. In effect, SbT has become, thereby, the unconscious agent of the forces of reaction. Von Weizsäcker is, perhaps, most perceptive in his Garden of Eden analogy:

> *But when knowledge without love becomes the hireling of the resistance against love, then it assumes the role which in the Christian mythical imagery is the role of the devil. The serpent in paradise urges on man knowledge without love. Anti-Christ is the power in history that leads loveless knowledge into the battle of destruction against love. But it is at the same time also the power that destroys itself in its triumph. The battle is still raging. We are in the midst of it, at a post not of our choosing where we must prove ourselves.*

This interplay of knowledge and action so ably stressed by von Weizsäcker and the crucial role of meaning and purpose in mediating between them is neglected on all sides, even by many who have concerned themselves with the so-called science and religion interface. We have referred to Capra's *The Tao of Physics.* I will quote from the end of the book to illustrate how little attention this book paid to the action beyond the knowledge. The very last paragraph reads:

> *To acquire mystical knowledge means to undergo a transformation; one could even say that the knowledge is the transformation. Scientific knowledge, on the other hand, can often stay abstract and theoretical. Thus most of today's physicists do not*

seem to realize the philosophical, cultural, and spiritual implications of their theories. Many of them actively support a society which is still based on the mechanistic, fragmented world view, without seeing that science points beyond such a view, toward a oneness of the universe which includes not only our natural environment but also our fellow human beings. I believe that the world view implied by modern physics is inconsistent with our present society, which does not reflect the harmonious interrelatedness we observe in nature. To achieve such a state of dynamic balance, a radically different social and economic structure will be needed: a cultural revolution in the true sense of the word.

Coming as it does in the very last paragraph of a book which does not mention a single social problem, nor speak of the need for responsible action, it would perhaps not be difficult for readers of the book from within the science community to respond: "Physician heal thyself."

Yes, the "physicists" (does someone really think that this end of the spectrum of "physics" is still synonymous with science-based technology?) do not realize the "cultural implications of their theories," and it was rather generous to throw in "our fellow human beings" as an afterthought to the environment. Is not the very balance of "knowledge" and "love" in the book itself an illustration that *such* physics and *such* mysticism is the problem and not the solution? From the position we have taken in this book it would be only natural that:

. . . the mystic and the physicist arrive at the same conclusion; one starting from the inner realm, the other from the outer world. The harmony between their views confirms the ancient Indian wisdom that Brahman, the ultimate reality without, is identical to Atman, the reality within.

The harmony of which Capra speaks is, however, much too narrowly conceived:

The modern physicist experiences the world through an extreme specialization of the rational mind; the mystic through an extreme specialization of the intuitive mind.

Science does not need mysticism and mysticism does not need science, but man needs both. Mystical experience is necessary to understand the deepest nature of things, and science is essential for modern life.

The danger lies precisely in modern physicists (or mystics) who "experience the world" from such a narrow single-direction, single-focus stance. This kind of "science," far from being "essential for modern life," is totally irrelevant to it. If man needs *this science,* why is it we have no Congressional hearings, no policy debate in Parliament, no movies, or parades, or gadgets putting subnuclear structure to use. No! What humanity needs is a much firmer connection of the "knowledge" of both mysticism and particle physics to "action" in our daily lives. This connection is made *on the level of the person.* The balance between accurate image and loving response–action has been dangerously tipped by the

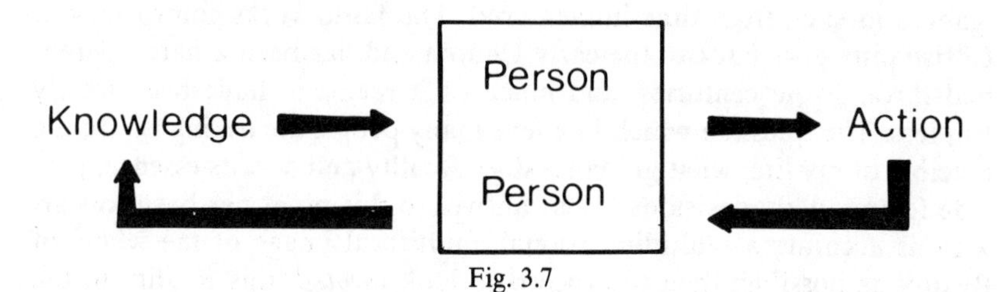

Fig. 3.7

nature of SbT itself. Like photography, science-based-technology can deplete reality while making it possible to bolster it.

In contrast with Capra, both in tone and substance, is James B. Conant. It is interesting to note how Conant, the down-to-earth chemist working much closer to the real world both in his science and his daily life as an administrator (President of Harvard University), relates the "faith in God" to faith in reality, but then goes on to question *any* "faith" which does not result in some consequent action:

> *Therefore, I am not inclined to quarrel with those who say that a faith in the reality of the God of Calvin, or the God of Catholicism, or the Jehovah of Orthodox Judaism is the same sort of faith as faith in a real external world. But I would question the correctness of considering a belief in God which carries no consequences for the believer as parallel to a belief in the reality of other people which clearly carries some meaning for everyone, except perhaps the sole inhabitant of a desert isle.*

The person who acts on her/his knowledge becomes more whole. True knowledge is that which has been validated in personal experience. True action at any time is based on the true knowledge of the person at that time. The evaluation, translation, and integration in both circuits takes place within the person (see Fig. 3.7). These statements are equally and absolutely valid in the world of SbT and in the world of religion. They will be especially meaningful to those who have maintained a balance between the O (observational), E (experiential), and R (reflective) selves.* But when the self is immersed in the real E world of hunger, crime, and politics, the role of "action-consistent-with knowledge" or "faith-which-issues-in-works" becomes central. It was the soon to be martyred Deitrich Bonhoeffer who wrote: *"Only he who obeys can believe,/Only he who believes can obey."* It was a profoundly reflective Dag Hammarskjold who also said: *"In our era the road to holiness necessarily passes through the world of action."*

These are obvious truths which have become truisms and have been

---

* Capra was, of course, writing principally from the viewpoint of the R self, and in his own E self may well combine the actions we refer to here.

ignored as such from time immemorial. The faith/works controversy in Christianity goes back to the early Church and has been a hardy perennial through the centuries, and much of it seems to have been totally fruitless. The question which I believe many people are asking is: "In the crucible of my life, what guidance does Reality and [illegible], its essence, provide for my daily decisions?" Our answer to this point has been to start with as accurate a multidimensional, multifocal image of the whole of Reality as possible; then to proceed to look *through* this Reality to the meaning and the essence beyond; and finally, to act in "obedience to [illegible]," i.e., in consonance with this essence of Reality, in tune with the hymn of the universe. You cannot *know* the truth wholly without *doing* the truth. One of the most striking learnings is that the acted-out truth is frequently much more uniform than the propositional truths about [illegible] or Reality. For example, the unity of great religions is nowhere more evident than if one compares the *total* message emitted by the human beings. Illustrated in Fig. 3.1 is the fact that human *actions* are a much more integrated, hence accurate, message from one human to another. The *pattern* of our actions reveals most accurately one's life-policy or religious faith. Our words, in contrast, are abstractions of that policy doubly filtered: once by the emitter and once by the receiver. Let me cite as definitive proof of this superiority of "actions" to "words" as the basis of measuring the comparison of "religions," the following: If one compares the literal formulation of Hindu thought with its innumerable deities or manifestations of the deity, with the atheistic Buddhist thought, with the Judeo-Christian statements about "God" and Jesus, one finds great confusion and contradiction. Without a long, convoluted interpretation, no reconciliation appears possible. But examine instead the actions in the lives of committed Hindus, Buddhists, Jews, and Christians, and you find that similarities jump out and predominate. Compare, if you wish, the *life* of Gautama and the *life* of Jesus. What did they do? Observe their teachings: inward-outward simultaneity, the concern for others. Was Mahatma Gandhi a Christian? Was Martin Luther King a Christian? If the words they used to affirm their faith were somewhat different, what about their actions? Here they were identical on all large issues: concern for justice and social change, use of nonviolence as an expression of love, even to the point of martyrdom.

Can one ever use words alone to convey something as whole as our life-policies? Of course not. Nor can one relate to [illegible] except through a total commitment to responding in loving action based on an integrated 3-D image of Reality.

To the much sought after harmony between beauty and truth in science, it must be said that while beauty and truth *abide,* only love (the good) can *guide*. Love is the active verb, and it can be applied accurately and precisely to the whole of life in consonance with the beauty-truth of science or religion. It was Mahatma Gandhi who wrote: *"Just as a scientist will work wonders out of various applications of the laws of nature, even so a man who applies the law of love with scientific precision can work greater wonders."*

3.6 Reality Theology: Retrospect and Prospect

We started this book with a look at the world's situation with respect to both the physical-biological-social milieu so strongly changed by science and technology and the social-political-religious climate dramatically transformed by the same changes. But it has become abundantly clear that these latter changes do not mean that "religion" is disappearing. The empirical evidence for the opposite is unambiguous. The context that human beings create for themselves always includes the religious, the numinous, the mysterious, the concern for the beyond. The official active attempt to "stamp out religion" in the Soviet Union, China, and other countries for a generation or more seems to have been unsuccessful. It is my observation based on several visits that, in many ways, Soviet society—except in its official language—is behaviorally a more "religious," even more classically Christian society at the personal level of actions, than any country in the West. At the other end of the spectrum, the worst excesses of Western licentiousness seem also to have been unable to dislodge the innate religious tendencies of humanity. This in spite of the swamping out of fundamental truths by the propagation of any salable half-truth or even utter nonsense, from astrology to the chariots of the Gods, by the all-powerful machinery of the all-too-free press.

The "Age of Aquarius," the student revolts, and the political turmoil which gripped the West in the sixties can now be seen in perspective. Journalistic excess proclaiming the "death of God" was premature. The historical evidence is that what died in the sixties was not God and certainly not religion. What died was the hegemony of religion over the details of the present life (what to eat or drink, whom to marry, when and with whom to relate sexually, etc.), and most especially over the future. It was Heaven and Hell that in a "practical" sense disappeared from human consciousness in this period. Religion has reappeared in myriad forms, but *all* of them emphasize the "feedback" in this life.

There is little doubt that not only the dozen major Eastern cults, but the Yoga salons, the acupuncture healers, not to speak of the recent Western recourse to running and jogging and printing the "personalized" daily advice to the zodiacal tribes in tens of millions of newspapers, are clear manifestations of humanity's hunger for some kind of religion. "To whom shall we go?" The world's confused masses seem to echo the disciple's response to Jesus. If not to these ersatz solutions, where do we turn for a true response to [illegible] in our day when we are faced with:

- the domination of the worldwide intellectual climate by science and technology,
- the active repression of religion in the Soviet bloc and China,
- the weakening of the political power of the countries steeped in traditional religion,
- the loss of meaning, purpose, and long-range direction under any guiding world view in the West.

The whole world—East and West, North and South—finds itself in need of a reexamination and rearticulation of the fundamentals of new holistic, syncretic, religious formulation. This book has been devoted to the first step in that task, the attempt to redefine, in terms acceptable to a wider community selected on parameters other than affiliation with a particular religious group, the concept of [illegible].

The book has presented a way to approach and understand [illegible] in the light of modern scientific thought. This is a way open to those reared in religious traditions for it can clarify and thereby strengthen their faith. It will have special appeal to such among them as have difficulties with much of the traditional religious formalism, and to the many who cannot connect their affirmations about [illegible] with their everyday lives in everyday language.

The way sketchily outlined in this book is also open to members of the scientific and engineering communities, many with the deepest sense of the mysteries of the universe, others firmly committed to the cocreation on earth in concern for all humankind.

The fundamental axiom on which this way is based is simply that both scientists and people of religious faith pursue passionately all that is real—that includes the true, the beautiful, and the good. Hence, the learnings of science and of religion about Reality can only—in an absolute sense—be complementary. What has been very unclear in the past has been the nature of this complementarity. By using the thesis that religion and science are related as general knowledge to specialized knowledge, as telescopic and microscopic views, as integrative to differentiating approaches, we have shown the utter interdependence of the two approaches in constructing an accurate and precise image of reality.

Part of the truth revealed by religion, by science, and by human experience is that Reality is but the reification of a Beyond, an essence, which some call God, others leave unnamed, and for which we devised the neutral symbol . The final section dealt with how humans relate to . It made the case for the centrality of the whole Person in an authentic relation to the Beyond in the Midst. This wholeness demanded not only that one's knowledge of reality be constructed from the integration of the experiential with the religious and scientific viewpoints, but also that knowledge and action, being and doing, be continuously interwoven as warp and woof of human relationships to .

Before proceeding to our final paragraphs on what such an approach to means to many different communities with respect to guidelines for living, I have tried to formulate in a series of parallel statements in two different languages the key points (docrines!?) of such a new reality-theology. In one column, suitable for all secular readers and "religionless Christians," I have used no "God-language" whatever. In the second, I have used traditional but universal religious language. (Later in this series I present a third column restating these truths using Judeo-Christian categories.)

REALITY-THEOLOGY LANGUAGE	*UNIVERSAL RELIGIOUS LANGUAGE*
1. *Reality exists.* It is everything that is directly or indirectly experienced or deduced by human senses unaided and aided by human artifice and artifacts. Reality may be experienced either integrated or highly differentiated. Integrated reality is that experienced over large numbers or distances in time and space which can be shared by the collective human body. Differentiated reality is manifest in the region of the very small, very short, and/or very few, and is subject to observer-interactions.	1. God is.
2. *Reality is comprehensible,* self–consistent, in all its vastness and minutest detail. It forms patterns and makes sense.	2. God reveals her/himself.
3. *Reality "betrays" meaning* in a continuous spectrum (which for convenience we can divide into Nature, Society, and the Person). The meaning of the wholeness of reality is more than (and essentially different from) its parts.	3. God may be perceived in nature and history, in society and in personal transactions; but the I-Thou relation to God is more than (and essentially different from) these perceptions.
4. *Reality is the reification of an essence or meaning we call* . This meaning or is more real or fundamental than the manifest realities. (The term is substituted to call attention to the totally unconditional nature of "God.")	4. God's creation—the universe, the world, nature, evolving and culminating at present in human beings—is a manifestation of God which can lead us to the deeper reality, God.

5. Reality serves as the screen and the vehicle between humanity and experience of [illegible]. All parts—nature, society, and person—are channels to allow us to see beyond; but, of those, the personal area is the most transparent.
6. Human beings function as many selves in distilling meaning from reality taken as a whole. For convenience we divide these into three arbitrarily different selves: The Observational (O), the Experiencing (E), and the Reflective (R).
7. *Living* in "tune" with [illegible], the essence of Reality at all levels requires that one's *actions* be consistent with one's understanding.
8. Each human being is constrained by the forces of bio-socio-spiritual evolution to utilize an appropriate balance of her/his O, E, and R selves to bring her/his understanding and action into resonance (tune) with the meaning or essence of reality.
9. The empirical evidence is that living in tune with the universe means "loving (accepting) the world as it is," and using other-centered love as one's cardinal life-policy in one's relation to other persons and society.

5. Human beings can know God best, most easily and accurately through such natural manifestations (but most effectively through personal witness [action] and personal encounter).
6. It is every human being's duty and glory to use mind, body, and spirit to discern the presence and action of God in the world in history and God's will for her/his life.
7. Living in consonance with this will is our true calling and goal.
8. Every human being is under the obligation to seek to "know God" and to grow and change in that knowledge as we grow and change as individuals and a species, and to complete and validate that knowledge through continuous action.
9. Based on a true and felt acceptance of self by God and neighbor, humans are called upon to live with agapeic, unselfish love as their guidance for the essential acting out of their response.

Epilogue: Projecting Ahead a Program of Experimentation With Truth

The clarification of what I believe is common to the views of both deeply religious, and thoughtful, scientific persons about the nature of transcendent reality, [illegible], "God," is but the first step in the construction of a life-policy (= faith). I assert that to be viable in today's society, such a faith will need to be a strong composite of science and the best of many religious traditions. Although written from the viewpoint of a Christian, this approach clearly has room for "other roads to Everest and beyond." This epilogue can only outline other steps which are needed to make a useful, working life-policy of value to scientists and religionists alike. Such steps are treated in detail in the companion volumes to this work, but sketched out in the following.

In effect, what is presented in the following are mutually reinforcing *Guidelines for Twenty-first-Century Living* based on the integrated insights of both religion and science. They may be grouped into four areas with some overlap among them.

Both/And . . . The New Integrative Approach to Life

From the central theme of this book regarding the all-inclusive nature of reality, and hence of , it follows that everything—literally, every thing, person, idea—is reflected in . The classical attributes of God—omniscience, omnipotence, omnipresence, etc—have simply never been taken seriously. Reality is *all*-inclusive. It holds together the great (billions of light years) and the small (the 10^{-20} m of the subnuclear regions), the true and false, even the good and evil. The dynamic creative tension of this synthesis affirms the fundamental Both/And nature of reality and . It is *never* either/or with , even where the paradox is irresolvable by humans. Science provided us with a classical example in the struggle between the wave-nature and the particle–nature of light. The resolution is in the synthesis: light may appear as *both* a wave *and* a particle. (This does not mean we can be careless in describing its properties under specific circumstances.) Religion has had its titanic struggle in the relation of to good and evil. Reality includes both, and includes the *meaning* of both. (This does not mean that confusion between good and evil is possible or permissible. As Dumitriu put it: *"Yes, God is also dry land dear fish, but if you try to climb out on dry land you will soon learn that. . . ."*)

We have come to the bitter end of the fissiparous trend in Western education and living. Specialization must be turned around toward integrative learning at every level of theory and practice. All the false dichotomies must go, replaced by imperative integration. As in each of the following, our society must learn to put together in Both + And instead of separating into Either/Or.

Nature + Nurture	not	Nature/Nurture
Science + Art	not	Science/Art
Science + Religion	not	Science/Religion
Left Brain + Right Brain	not	Left Brain/Right Brain
Body + Spirit	not	Body/Spirit
Worldly + Holy	not	Worldly/Holy
Nation + World	not	Nation/World
Male + Female	not	Male/Female
East + West	not	East/West
Individual + Community	not	Individual/Community

The effects of such a change of consciousness will penetrate into every crevice of society. It will transform the practice of education and health. Christian religious consciousness will evolve from the exclusive proclamation of a single, narrowly-defined path to affirm the Christ-image within many paths.

The Dice-Playing God: Accepting the Mysterious Role of Chance in Life

One of the issues over which both science and religion have struggled, albeit on very different parts of the battlefield, is the matter of "Order in the Universe," and the role of chance in it. Just as the scientist's resolution of the wave-particle duality helps our religious insights on Both/And, just so, the scientific findings and resolution on the statistical nature of certainty will help religion deal with determinism and free will.

That very prototype of modern scientists, Albert Einstein, for thirty years protested against the "Dice-Playing God" he saw revealed by the statistical nature of quantum mechanics at the very foundation of reality. Even so, modern science has learned that Nature, one manifestation of Reality, betrays at every level a curious but absolutely irradicable both/and of chance and causality, or order and disorder, of submission to "fate" and acts of free will. We affirm that, at its very core, Reality has a character of "indeterminacy" for the smallest units—whether electron energies, or the height, intelligence, or longevity of individual humans. Reality displays daily in our common everyday experience its dice-playing aspect. A substantial portion of our lives is totally out of our control. Our circumstances of birth—in which country, in what time, to which parents, etc.—our genetic endowments, and the infinite number of chance events which pepper our lives are givens. Yet human talent, learning, enterprise, and will are sufficient to play a major role in enabling us to control much of our destiny. Because the dominance of this controlled area has been extended by modern science and technology over some of the most impacting areas of life—food, shelter, clothing, transportation—humanity has been given a false sense of ultimate "control" during these last few decades. In an era when humanity's increase in control of its circumstances is meeting both outer and inner limits to growth, the integrative imperative is that we now learn to accept the new realities that chance has dealt out to this generation.

A deep understanding of the role of chance will save untold anguish in the relations of the religious towards [illegible] in times of tragedy. The planning of society at community and national levels must be shaped differently to keep in resonance with the bell-shaped curve of the "normal" distribution under which we all live. One profound political consequence may be the replacement of the 300–year dominance and now nearly total degradation of the so-called "election" process in Western political life. Elections as now conducted in the Western democracies are based on the pernicious philosophy that, by some mysterious process, the evil of self-praise, self-aggrandizement, and self–selling can result in the "best man" winning. The foreseeable result has been realized. From self-selling we now have reached the packaged merchandising of half-truths; the buying, selling, and exchanging of power; and, perhaps worst of all, the corruption of the spirit of the "winners" into believing their own rhetoric. Biblical tradition and the ancient Greeks, indeed most cultures, used an alternate method—with profound connections to the Dice-playing Reality we live in—of selection by "lot" (chance) from a group of qualified persons. Here, our acceptance of the inborn statistical nature of reality would provide a theoretical base for a changeover to new systems which are also being rediscovered by empirical (scientific) approaches. The abolition of election processes and the introduction of selection from a qualified set by random processes is a proper reflection of the acceptance of the Dice-playing God.

Otherward Is God-ward. Self-Fulfillment Only by Self-Transcendence

The cardinal both/and principle is also the base on which one can build a reconciliation between much of the highest-minded altruism of the major religions and the intense preoccupation with individual and personal satisfaction brought on by the scientific-technological advance and its impact on contemporary Western culture. The overriding motif of personal fulfillment forms the core of an alternative religion—in every sense of the term—which has grown up around certain parts of, and figures in social studies. One must be extremely careful here not to set up an artificial barrier and tension between the social and natural sciences. This is as much a division within the social sciences as between it and other disciplines. The personage of Freud and the views developed from what he wrote, as interpreted and propounded by two generations of disciples, has dominated this new religion focused on the self. This focus on self and the riding on the coattails of the ascendance of science (by Freudians appropriating casually the titles of "science" wherever possible) meant that this new philosophical-religious world view was a guaranteed winner in an increasingly affluent West in the postwar decades. Whatever the cause, the cat, so to speak, is now out of the bag; self-fulfillment will have become a permanent part of the expectation not only of the very top leadership but of the human masses. The new question born of this situation and yet hardly addressed is: How is this focus on self (this potential narcissism) to be tempered by concern for the other levels of society (community, nation, world) of which the same self is part?

Today, at the threshold of the eighties, the same natural sciences and historical circumstances have displaced the Freudian focus with little fanfare. Through science's pharmacological invasion of the mental processes, and the humanities' reassertion of the wisdom of history and, most of all, through the empirical failure of the Freudian conception and practice to yield anything remotely resembling reproducible results, the picture has changed greatly. Psychology has bifurcated into a branch linked more closely to the natural sciences and another developing into what has been called, perhaps prematurely, a "humanistic psychology." But central to this latter style psychology, and to much of the everyday "counseling" in the West, is a historically new treatment of self.

In an earlier chapter we were at some pains to point out the importance of the human reference point as receiver and, hence, limiter of knowledge and understanding. There is a sense in which the self is the starting point for knowledge, understanding, and action. The earlier treatment supports the importance of the person both in this role and as the personal window on Reality. How, then, does all this square with at least the Christian, if not universal, religious tradition of self-denial, self-negation, at least of the postponement of gratification in the focus on concern for *others*? Upon the answer to this hangs not only many structures of society, but all of personal morality.

It is instructive to refer back to the quotation from Professor R. B. Cattell, one of the distinguished research psychologists of our time, representing that wing closer to the classical sciences. In his massive study, *Beyondism, a Morality from Science,* Cattell compares traditional religious positions with what may loosely be called the humanistic psychological positions, and with what he (Cattell) regards as a truly (social) scientific position. He shows clearly that much of modern "humanism" is just as much an a priori affair as the religion it frequently attacks. He goes on to describe a subtle difference between a classical Christian position and the "beyondist" position in dealing with "unworthy" others:

> *Although the individual needs to move from self love to love of mankind, the latter has to be intelligently interpreted in a Beyondist framework, else it is mere neutral narcism and subject to many hedonistic perversions. . . . Yet more refined research is needed to find what the Beyondist position should be on extending love and succorance (as Christianity feels it should) to the deliberate planful parasite and criminal.* (*sic*)

If there is one thing to be learned about desirable (i.e., effective) human behavior, it is certain that, while it may start with a healthy concern for the self, it cannot end there. Our images of the relation of the person to Reality and the Beyond suggest the necessary reaching outward through this contact with the nature, society, and person domains of Reality. If our analysis that it is in the personal area that Reality is more transparent is followed, then the way to [illegible] is through other persons. The answer to the question: Where is [symbol]?, is not "out there," or "in there." It can be given in a more absolute way. Reality is everywhere. Each one starting from the center of self must struggle *toward* [symbol] *through* the surround of Reality. We know only in which direction to look. The God-ward direction is outward and otherward from the self. Looking *toward* nature, toward society, toward persons is the direction toward [symbol]. Concern for the needs of all others—e.g., closest family, friends, the helpless and destitute, the heroic souls, all of society, our natural environment—provides an unerring set of blazes on the [symbol]-ward trail. The end of the trail is undefinable; the direction is well marked. In this kind of setting the proper rationale for self-development and self-fulfillment is to provide a firm center as base, from which to find and serve the other. This journey outward, in turn, develops the center-at-self further. Self-love can be both a systemic poison and a systemic elixir. If self-love is the end or goal, our image in Figure 3.8 shows that such a person would be cut off, literally, from Reality and [symbol]. If self-love is the secure base from which knowledge, understanding, and love are directed outward to the world, society, and persons, it becomes the mandated first step of living in tune with the other-centered universe. For such a life-style, the term ex-selfish may be more appropriate than un-selfish.

Beginnings and Endings: Experimentating, Innovating, Working, Loving, Completing

"I am Alpha and Omega, the Beginning and the End. . . ." says the Book of Revelation. In Reality, there is a beginning and an end. Modern cosmology tells us with fair confidence of a beginning of our universe: A "Big Bang" some 15 or 20 billion years ago. Of the end we are much less sure, but the heat death of our sun about as many years hence is predicted. But the realities of beginning and ending I think have much closer connections to our daily lives.

The world of modern science has prospered by limiting its scope of study and carrying out endless experiments to get at the truth. Our life should follow the model of this human science. It isolates in time and space a tiny segment of the universe to be studied, pores over it, even loves it, and spins a cocoon around it. The human condition demands this boundedness of a problem for its E (experiencing) self. Coping with today's world requires that we function as all three selves: observing scientifically (O), experiencing with the total person (E), and reflecting (R). I said that knowledge began with the experiencing, experimenting, person, and as I close I try to describe the basic "nutritional" requirements of this experiencing self:

Fig. 3.8.

- *Beginning* or starting something (new).
- *Working,* expressing spirit-mind-body wholeness in action.
- *Loving* (and being loved) directing my work and life toward , i.e., otherward.
- *Completing.*

BEGINNING

"Behold, I am doing a new thing." Deeply implanted in our genetic plasm is the desire to do something NEW. The creature's curiosity and exploration and innovation reflect the fundamental nature of the creator. Newness is (much more so than cleanliness) next to Godliness! Each of us will live in resonance with the universe if we "try new things" as Teilhard put it, *all the time,* continuously, carefully.

WORKING

The role of work as the expression of our being has been greatly underplayed in our suddenly machine-intensive society. The face is that each of us has a physical, psychological, spiritual make-up and capacity. We process food and information through our bodies and minds. It is biologically certain that we were meant to complete the circuit by using our bodies and minds to express ourselves shaped by our inputs. Modern culture has not come to terms with a societal structure which *must* accept the many bell-shaped curves of our talents, and provide a work-structure of society to match this "God-given" reality. The necessity for such "talent-matched *work*" needs reaffirmation as a pillar of worldwide policy for human beings. This is in sharp contrast to recent absurdities of planning as though the human potential was that each individual could attain the maximum that any one human had attained. The bell-shaped curve is both an absolute limitation and the absolute template for good societal planning, for "appropriate work" for each.

LOVING

On every side, evidence piles up that work and love make for healthy persons. If a human being has talent-matched work, she needs nothing more than to be accepted and loved by a handful of others at the same time as the person reaches out, [illegible]-ward, to love others in word and deed.

To feel loved, and to express love in today's Western culture, requires, among many other things, as radical a rethinking of human sexuality as any needed change in our society. Great confusion surrounds the use of the word "love"—perhaps like "God" we need to impose a moratorium on its use and use a symbol. Here, my wife and I, in our book *Honest Sex,* have been firm advocates of the consistent use of C. S. Lewis' terminology developed in his book, *The Four Loves.* When a specific "sublove," such as philia, eros, or agape, is involved, they are quite suitable. We may yet get a new symbol for the more generic term. On the one side, we have the forces of hedonism and commercial exploitation which tend to equate love with self-centered personal sexual pleasure; on the other, we have the established Church—represented in its totally rigid form in the Roman hierarchy—unable to provide leadership on interjecting into contemporary culture a meaningful and balanced definition of love. Why? Because the church—unlike the world of science and technology—has failed to fully accept the fact that "time makes ancient good uncouth." Time, in this case, has brought on us the population explosion, a change which demands that, contrary to our biological drives and millenia of social custom, couples for the first time in history must strongly limit their number of children. Our times have brought the equality of men and women into a reality never before achieved in the masses. Our times have provided opportunities for contact, friendship, warmth, and "love" to an extent almost inconceivable 100 years ago, and added to it the physical catalysts of contraception, privacy, and constant stimulus via print and picture.

If loving and being loved is the primary source of human meaning and satisfaction, we will have to come to terms with, accept and indeed encourage, a vastly different and more pluralistic understanding of the role of sex as a major, but only one aspect of "love."

THE SIXTH DAY OF CREATION: COMPLETING

The story of creation in the book of Genesis phrases it thus: *"Thus heaven and earth were completed with all their mighty throng. On the sixth day God completed all the work he had been doing. . . . and God saw all that he had made, and it was good. Evening came and morning came a sixth day."* Just as human beings need a sense of *starting* something, they get an enormous satisfation out of *completing* or finishing something. This unique reaction of standing back with a sigh and satisfaction from something completed, every person knows well—the pie baked to perfection, the table set with candles lit, the painting finished, the mile run, the manuscript for the book put in the mail. Yet no one has made much of the psychological and spiritual necessity for this sense of completing. It is, of course, the root cause of the malaise of assembly-line work, and the modifications in Sweden of some assembly lines do, indeed, move precisely to give this satisfaction. She/he *never* finishes something and never sees it complete and whole. Compare that to the farmer or the artisan throughout human history. Seed time is followed by harvest. Honest labor results in the finished pot, the piece of furniture, the completed dwelling. This book has explored the areas where the insights of science and religion may feed each other for the benefit of humanity. One of the most neglected, surely, is the necessity to affirm the need for completing the circuits of our lives so that the current of satisfaction may flow, and that each one is able to stand back and find "that it was very good," if only in the microcosmic world given to each of us.

Bibliography

Werner Heisenberg, *Across the Frontier.* Harper and Row, New York, 1974.
———, *Physics and Beyond.* Harper and Row, New York, 1971.
R. B. Cattell, *A New Morality from Science: Beyondism.* Pergamon Press, New York, 1972.
C. F. von Weizsäcker, *The Relevance of Science.* The Gifford Lectures, Collins, London, 1964.
———, *The Unity of Nature.* Farrar, Straus and Giroux, Inc. New York, 1980.

Viktor E. Frankl, Chapter in *Beyond Reductionism, New Perspectives in the Life Sciences,* edited by A. Koestler. Macmillan, New York, 1968.
J. B. Conant, Chapter 2 in *Modern Science and Modern Man.* Doubleday, New York, 1953.
Petru Dumitriu, Chapter 2 in *Incognito.* Collins, London, 1964.
J. A. T. Robinson, *Exploration into God.* Stanford University Press, 1967.
Rustum Roy and Della M. Roy, *Honest Sex.* New American Library, New York, 1968.
Susan Sontag, *On Photography.* Farrar Straus and Giroux, New York, 1977.
Edward Robinson, *Living the Questions.* Religious Experience Research Unit, Oxford, 1978.
Alister Hardy, *The Biology of God.* London, Jonathan Cape, 1975.

Index

Acknowledgments

Every human being is like a pond or reservoir wholly dependent for its being, its life, and its "output" on sources outside itself: rain, springs, and streams. Whatever beauty in falling water, or food that it grows, or utility via the turbine–turning channels its water generates originates outside itself. The pool creates a new mixture, it filters, it reforms its givens, but it owes it all to its sources. Many of the streams which feed our hearts and minds have their headwaters far away in time or space in writings which shape us. These are acknowledged implicitly in the references at the end of each chapter. But each one of us is also shaped and sustained by a community, a small group of significant others. Using the imagery of the individual held within the nutrient-supplying womb of reality, the record of my indebtedness to my community is imaged below.

Leslie J. Goddard   *Narendra Kumar Roy*   *Donald W. Carruthers*
John Freda   *John Levering*   *Della Roy*   *Elisabeth O'Connor*   *Jane Nelson*
Phoebe Link   *Gordon Cosby*   *Ernest Hawk*   *Rita Yeasted*
Harold Schilling   *Mary Garbar*   *Kathleen Mourant*   *John Robinson*
Bruce Knox   *Gerhard Barsch*   *Cal Garber*   *C.F. von Weizsäcker*
Jacques Ellul   *Jack Nelson*   *Jane Leiper*   *Hal Leiper*   *Roger Shinn*
W.H. Auden   *Petru Dumitriu*   *Dag Hammarskjöld*   *Deitrich Bonheoffer*

To Ernest Hawk and Gerhard Barsch, who have been working with me at the same difficult rock-face of bringing science and Christian life-together at the workaday level for fifteen years, I owe a very special debt. And to Kathleen Mourant, for producing the typed document under unusual difficulties, while contributing more than usual help, I record my special thanks.